Regulation Strategies and Economic Policies

Regulation Strategies and Economic Policies

Essays in Honour of Bernard Corry and Maurice Peston, Volume Three

Edited by

Sami Daniel

Associate Dean, Faculty of Human Sciences, Kingston University, UK

Philip Arestis

Professor of Economics, University of East London, UK

John Grahl

Professor of Global Business Management, University of North London, UK

Edward Elgar

Cheltenham, UK • Northampton, MA, USA

Published by
Edward Elgar Publishing Limited
Glensanda House
Montpellier Parade
Cheltenham
Glos GL50 1UA
UK

Edward Elgar Publishing, Inc.
136 West Street
Suite 202
Northampton
Massachusetts 01060
USA

A catalogue record for this book is available from the British Library

Library of Congress Cataloguing in Publication Data
Regulation strategies and economic policies / [edited by] Sami Daniel, Philip Arestis, John Grahl.
(Essays in honour of Bernard Corry and Maurice Peston : v. 3)
Includes bibliographical references (p.).
1. Trade regulation. 2. Economic policy. 3. Corry, Bernard. 4. Peston, Maurice Harry. I. Daniel, Sami, 1939– . II. Arestis, Philip, 1941– . III. Grahl, John. IV. Corry, Bernard. V. Peston, Maurice Harry. VI. Series.
HD3612.R435 1999
338.9—dc21 98–53419
CIP

ISBN 1 85898 580 3

Printed and bound in Great Britain by Bookcraft (Bath) Ltd.

Contents

Figures

Tables

Notes on contributors

Patricia Apps obtained her PhD at the University of Cambridge in 1972 and also studied economics at Yale University. She is Professor of Economics and associate Dean at the Faculty of Law, University of Sydney, where she has taught since 1975. She has also been a Visiting Fellow in the Research School of Social Sciences at the Australian National University since 1986. She was elected Fellow of the Academy of Social Sciences in Australia in 1994. Her publications include *A Theory of Inequality and Taxation* (CUP, 1981) and a large number of papers in the area of tax policy, labour supply and models of the household.

Philip Arestis is Professor of Economics at the University of East London. He has also taught at the universities of Surrey and Cambridge (Department of Extra-Mural Studies) and Greenwich University (where he was Head of Economics Division). He is joint editor of *International Papers in Political Economy*, has edited or served on the editorial boards of a number of journals and is a member of the Council of the Royal Economic Society. He has edited a number of books and is the author of several others including *The Post-Keynesian Approach to Economics: an Alternative Analysis of Economic Theory and Policy* (1992) and *Money, Pricing, Distribution and Economic Integration* (1996). He has published widely in journals and books in post-Keynesian economics, macroeconomics, monetary policy and applied econometrics.

Nicholas Barr obtained his BSc (Econ) at the London School of Economics and his PhD at the University of California, Berkeley. He has been a member of the economics department at the LSE since 1971. His writing includes *The Economics of the Welfare State* (3rd edition, 1998), *Student Loans: the Next Steps* (1989) and (as editor) *Labor Markets and Social Policy in Central and Eastern Europe: the Transition and Beyond* (1994). He spent two periods of leave at the World Bank, from 1990–92 as a member of the Central and Southern Europe human resources division, working on the design of income transfers and health finance in Poland, Hungary, Czechoslovakia, Yugoslavia, Bulgaria, Romania and Russia, and in 1995–96 as one of the principal authors of the *World Development Report 1996: from Plan to Market*.

Rod Cross was educated at Wigan Grammar School, LSE and the University of York. Currently a Professor of Economics at the University of Strathclyde, he previously held academic posts at the University of Manchester, Queen Mary College and the University of St Andrews. He is the author of *Economic Theory and Policy in the UK* (1982), and editor of *Unemployment, Hysteresis and the Natural Rate Hypothesis* (1988) and *The Natural Rate of Unemployment: Reflections on 25 Years of the Hypothesis* (1995). He has published journal articles dealing mainly with hysteresis and unemployment, the Duhem thesis and transition in Central Europe. He was consultant to the Polish National Bank in the early years of liberalization and an occasional member of the Treasury Academic Panel.

Sami Daniel was born in Basrah, Iraq and obtained his BSc (Econ) and MSc (Econ) at the LSE where he also worked as a research assistant. He is Associate Dean of the Faculty of Human Sciences at Kingston University, having been Head of the School of Economics and Politics there from 1971–87. He has taught at Middlesex University and (as visiting fellow) Queen Mary College and the University of Konstanz. He was the first national secretary of the Association of Polytechnic Teachers in Economics (1971–79) and the first economist from the former polytechnic sector to serve on the Council of the Royal Economic Society. He served with Maurice Peston and Bernard Corry on the CNAA Economics Board. His major area of research interest is the economics of organizations.

Ciaran Driver has degrees in Electrical Engineering and Systems with a PhD in Economics. He was a research assistant at Queen Mary College, University of London, 1971–3 and subsequently lectured at a number of London polytechnics. From 1983–86 he worked as economic advisor at the National Economic Development Office. He has taught economics at Imperial College since 1987 and was appointed Reader in 1996. His books include: *Investment Expectations and Uncertainty* (with David Moreton, 1992) and *Investment, Growth and Employment: Perspectives for Policy* (1999) (edited with Paul Temple), published by Routledge. His published work deals mainly with capital investment and structural change.

John Grahl is Professor of International Business at the University of North London. Until September 1998, he was Reader in European Economic Integration at Queen Mary and Westfield College, University of London. He is the author of many books and articles on the European Union and other aspects of European political economy. His most recent book, *After Maastricht: a Guide to European Monetary Union* was published by Lawrence and Wishart in 1997.

Hugh Gravelle graduated from Leeds University with a degree in accountancy. He joined the recently established economics department at Queen Mary College in 1969. After learning economics by teaching a class on Maurice Peston's first year undergraduate course (which started with an elementary derivation of von Neumann–Morgenstern cardinal utility) he was successively Lecturer, Senior Lecturer, Reader, Professor and Head of Department. In 1996 he moved to the University of York to take up a research post in the Centre for Health Economics. He works on the application of microeconomic theory to problems of public policy and has published widely in public sector economics, economics of law, and health economics. He is also the co-author, with ex QMC colleague Ray Rees, of *Microeconomics*, which is now in its second edition and has been translated in several languages.

Eliakim Katz is Professor of Economics at York University in Toronto, Canada. He was a colleague of Maurice Peston and Bernard Corry while a lecturer at Queen Mary College 1973–78. Maurice Peston was his PhD supervisor.

Mike Marshall is Senior Lecturer in Economics at the University of East London. He has published articles on contemporary economic and social policy in *Journal of Economic Issues, International Journal of Applied Economics*, and *Review of Social Economy*. He co-edited (with Philip Arestis), and contributed to *The Political Economy of Full Employment* (Edward Elgar, 1995).

Robin Matthews is Professor of International Business Policy at Kingston University Business School. He has worked at the Confederation of British Industry and as a business consultant to many companies in the UK. He has lectured and taught in many countries. Since the early 1990s, he has been involved on a number of projects in the Russian Federation. Currently his research and extensive publications are in the area of international business and in the multidisciplinary applications of complexity to organizations.

Barry Moore is a Fellow in Economics at Downing College Cambridge. He has made over fifty contributions to journals including the *Economic Journal*, *Economica* and *Cambridge Journal of Economics*. He is an internationally recognized authority on the evaluation of government policies concerned with regional and urban economic regeneration. He has acted as advisor to the OECD and the House of Commons Committee on Welsh Affairs, and consultant to the European Commission, as well as many organizations in both the private and public sectors. He joined the Department of Applied Economics in Cambridge in 1970, and in 1985 became Assistant Director of Research in the Department of Land Economy in the University of Cambridge. His recent research has been concerned with understanding the growth and development of clusters of high technology firms, academic-industry links and innovation in small firms.

Paul Ormerod was born in Rochdale, Lancashire in 1950. He read economics at Christ's College Cambridge and obtained an MPhil in economics and econometrics from St Catherine's College Oxford in 1973. From 1973–80 he worked as a macroeconomic modeller and forecaster at the National Institute of Economic and Social Research, London. He worked briefly at *The Economist* newspaper group before becoming Director of Economics at the Henley Centre for Forecasting in 1982. He left Henley in 1992, and now runs Post-Orthodox Economics. He was Visiting Professor of Economics at Queen Mary College from 1983 to 1991, and since then he has been Visiting Professor at Manchester University. In 1979, he edited the proceedings of the state-of-the-art conference on macroeconomic modelling and forecasting (*Economic Modelling*). More recently, he has been working on complexity and non-linear systems. In 1994, he published the *Death of Economics*, which has been translated into ten languages. In 1998, he published *Butterfly Economics*.

Ray Rees was born in Port Talbot, Wales in 1943. He obtained his BSc (Econ) degree at the London School of Economics in 1964 and the MSc there in 1965. He has been Professor of Economics at the University of Munich since 1993. He was among the first group of four economists hired by Maurice Peston to launch the Department of Economics at Queen Mary College in 1966. His books include: *Public Enterprise Economics* (1975, 1984), *Economics: a Mathematical Introduction* (1993), *Mathematics for Economics* (1995), and (with Hugh Gravelle) *Microeconomics* (1981, 1992). He has published papers in the areas of economics of public enterprise; privatization and regulation; theories of the firm; oligopoly, collusion and competition policy; asymmetric information, agency and insurance markets; and models of the household.

Max Steuer came to the LSE from the United States as a graduate student, and joined the staff in 1959. The School was and is his main focus. Long leaves were at the University of Pennsylvania as Visiting Professor in 1968, and as Chairman of the Economics Department at the University of Ghana from 1971–74. He has done consulting work for the Treasury, the Bank of England and the Department of Trade and Industry. He actively promoted the one-year taught MSc in Economics at the LSE and coined the phrase, and taught, 'Methods of Economic Investigation'. He developed the structured PhD Programme in Economics at LSE and teaches the Seminar in Research Strategy. Publications include *Mathematical Sociology* (with Janet Holland), *The Impact of Foreign Direct Investment on the United Kingdom* (various authors, HMSO) and *Culture and Optimality* (STICERD). He is currently Dean of the Graduate School at LSE, a co-director of the Centre for the Philosophy of the Natural and Social Sciences, and associated with the City Policy, Architecture and Engineering Programme at LSE.

David Wall was born in Bootle, England in 1940 and obtained his BSc (Econ) at the LSE in 1962. After three years in the graduate school at LSE he joined the faculty at the University of Sussex in 1965, where he taught until 1996. In 1969–70 he was a Postdoctoral Fellow at the University of Chicago and has held visiting positions at the University of Wisconsin–Milwaukee, Nuffield College Oxford, Macquarie University, the World Bank and the Australian National University. He has served as a consultant to several international organizations and as an advisor to various governments. In 1996 he was appointed to a Visiting Professorship at the School of Oriental and African Studies of the University of London, and he also took up appointment as Consultant to the OECD Development Centre and to the Chatham House China Task Force at the Royal Institute of International Affairs. His publications include *The Third World Challenge* (1967), *The Charity of Nations* (1973), *China's Long March to an Open Economy* (with Kiichiro Fakasaku, 1994) and *China's Opening Door* (with Jiang Boke and Yin Xiangshuo, 1996).

Adrian Ziderman is Professor of Economics at Bar Ilan University, Israel and editor of the *International Journal of Manpower*. He was born in the UK and holds Economics degrees from Cambridge University (1959), Stanford University (1961) and a PhD (1973) from the LSE, where Maurice Peston was his thesis supervisor. He has held academic posts at Stanford University, the LSE, the University of British Columbia, Tel Aviv University and Bar Ilan University where he was Head of the Economics Department and Director of the Economics Research Institute, and has worked as Senior Economist at the World Bank (1987–91). He has acted as consultant to international agencies, as well as government departments and agencies in the UK, Israel, Kenya, Mozambique, South Africa, Tanzania, Thailand, Turkey and Zambia. He is the author of some sixty papers in academic journals and has published four books, including *The Utilisation of Educated Manpower in Industry* (with Mark Blaug and Maurice Peston, 1969), *Manpower Training: Theory and Policy* (1978) and *Financing Universities in Developing Countries* (with D. Albright, 1995).

Introduction

Sami Daniel, Philip Arestis and John Grahl

This is the third of three volumes published to celebrate Bernard Corry's and Maurice Peston's contributions to British academia in general, and to economics in particular. Bernard and Maurice have had a major influence on the development of economics as a discipline in the UK: not just economics as an academic discipline but the way it is taught. In the 1960s both moved from the London School of Economics (LSE), where they had been Readers, to what was then Queen Mary College (QMC), University of London, now Queen Mary and Westfield College (QMW). They set up, and subsequently developed and expanded, a successful Economics Department; they both stayed at QMW until their retirement. Over the years they have acquired enormous respect and admiration from colleagues throughout the world.

Maurice and Bernard have much in common in addition to being the famous QMC and QMW Economics Department double act. They were both East End boys, both were briefly evacuated in the Second World War, both were students at the LSE (Bernard saw the last year of the School Certificate, Maurice the first of the A level). They both did national service after graduating. They both taught at the LSE and (as Visiting Professors) at the University of California at Berkeley. At the LSE they formed part of the famous M^2T (Methodology, Measurement and Testing) Seminar for the Young Turks of the time.[1] Their academic interests coincide in two very important areas: they have both maintained a longstanding interest in macroeconomics and in economic policy. They have both served as Economic Advisors (Bernard on a part-time basis, Maurice on full-time as well as part-time stints). Both are Labour Party members of long standing. They both played an important role in the development of economics in the new university sector through their work for the Council for National Academic Awards (CNAA): they both served as chairmen of its Economics Board (see Daniel, 1999 in this volume), and gave their support to the fledgling Association of Polytechnic Teachers in Economics (APTE). They both took early retirement at the same time, becoming very active Emeritus Professors (Bernard was Dean of the Faculty when theoretically on a half-time contract). They officially retired within a year of each other. They jointly edited the volume of essays in honour of Lord Robbins (Peston and Corry, 1972).

When it came to organizing a festschrift for Bernard and Maurice, it was clear that most potential contributors would wish to contribute to a joint festschrift: so now they share something else. They are the only academics to our knowledge to have a joint three-volume festschrift.

BERNARD CORRY

Bernard Corry was born in east London in 1930, and, apart from a brief period of evacuation during the Second World War, went to school there – at Leyton County High School. He read for the BSc (Econ) on a state scholarship graduating in 1951, and worked on his doctorate at the LSE, supported by a University of London scholarship. His PhD, awarded in 1958 (see Corry, 1962) was on the 'Macroeconomic Thought of the Classical Political Economy', which signalled two lifelong interests he pursued with enormous fervour. He was a tutor at the LSE in 1954–56, before being offered a temporary assistant lectureship at the University of Durham in 1957–58. After a year he was given tenure as a lecturer. His return to the LSE in 1958 as assistant lecturer thus represented, initially, a demotion. One reason for the return was that he had been teaching more or less everything at Durham.[2] Soon, however, he was promoted to lecturer (1961) and reader (1964). At the LSE he was now able to specialize in the history of thought and macroeconomics. His seminar (with Kurt Klappholz) on Smith, Ricardo and Marshall, and his lecture course on Swedish Monetary Theory were very popular with undergraduates. In 1968 he moved to QMC as Professor of Economics. There he helped Maurice to shape the Department of Economics and, in particular, to establish the MSc programme and the Graduate School. The Graduate School won wide recognition for its quality and its thorough preparation in contemporary economics. Bernard was the driving force – both as a teacher and as overall organizer. One early signal of his success was in gaining substantial support from the Social Science Research Council in scholarship funds. He was Head of the Department of Economics at QMC (1974–85) and Dean of the Faculty of Social Sciences in the years 1974–77 and 1988–91.

His two specialisms, history of thought and macroeconomics, were enriched by a third major interest, labour economics, initially sparked by his interest in income distribution[3] and work on regional mobility.[4] It was not surprising, therefore, that between 1968 and 1972 he was Senior Economic Adviser at the Department of Employment and Productivity, advising Barbara Castle on regional labour markets and (now again fashionable) minimum wages. Over the years, Bernard published extensively in all these three areas.

He was an important member of the CNAA Economics Board right from its inception, chaired it for a number of years (he was Chairman between 1974 and

1982), and the success story of economics in the ex-polytechnic sector is due to a very large extent to his efforts to give academic respectability to the then new sector. More significantly, though, he has been an extremely close friend of the Departments of Economics throughout the university sector, acting as external examiner, chairman of visiting CNAA parties to validate new degrees, reading papers to staff seminars and merely visiting departments to advise and see his many friends. Economics departments in the new universities owe Bernard a great deal for his contributions to their work. They benefited enormously from Bernard's encouragement, kindness and constructive criticism (particularly on the importance of research and its tight link to teaching). Whether they listened to him as much as they should, is of course another story! As chairman of visiting CNAA panels and the chair of the Economics Board of the CNAA, his influence was substantial, both at the formal sessions and in the after dinner visits to bars and pubs! That involvement helped the CNAA institutions at that early and critical stage of their development. His humane and flexible approach was extremely helpful.

Those of us lucky enough to have been taught by Bernard, are grateful for his teaching. His ability to teach skilfully is, of course, well known. His colleagues report that Bernard scored consistently top marks on the internal teaching assessment by the students of the Department of Economics. His friendly concern with students, both undergraduate and postgraduate, his encouragement of discussion, particularly 'after hours', not only made for excellent staff student relations, but left deep intellectual marks and helped shape many a burgeoning economist.[5]

For many years Bernard was the main force at the Association of University Teachers in Economics (AUTE) annual conference, now the Royal Economic Society (RES) conference. He was Secretary of the AUTE from 1960 to 1978, and later its Chairman from 1980 to 1985. Bernard's work for the AUTE conference, with the smallest amount of secretarial assistance, was Herculean. He occupied himself with every aspect of the event: the venue and accommodation, attracting papers and inviting special lecturers, timetabling, publicity, even catering arrangements. The AUTE conference rapidly became what, in its new form it remains, the largest UK symposium of the economics profession. Bernard was also the key figure in publishing the output as AUTE Conference volumes, which have now been replaced by the special conference volume of the *Economic Journal*. His interest in the polytechnics was also reflected in this work – he encouraged large numbers of polytechnic economists to contribute to the annual AUTE conferences, thus getting many of them started on active research and publication. And, of course, he encouraged and helped the Association of Polytechnic Teachers in Economics (APTE) which made him Honorary Vice-President and then Honorary President. Another professional development on which Bernard played a pioneering role, was the establishment of specialist research groups. He established, with Social Science Research Council (SSRC) financial backing, the labour economics research group. That innovation developed into, and remains, a key platform for communication and debate among economists in Britain. Both in his specialist work in labour economics and macroeconomics, and in his design of the masters programme at QMC, Bernard was keen to strengthen the empirical basis of research in economics and to promote a closer and more continuous interaction between theory and evidence.

MAURICE PESTON

Maurice Peston was also born in 1930 in London. In fact he is almost a local in relation to QMW. He was educated at Hackney Downs School before graduating in Economics at the London School of Economics, and doing graduate work at Princeton University. He had been a reader before he left the London School of Economics in the mid-1960s to start up the Department of Economics at QMC, becoming a Professor of Economics and the first head of that department in 1965. Under his and Bernard's guidance the department grew and achieved its balance of high quality research and good teaching for which it is internationally famous.

Maurice started his academic career as a microeconomist (he enjoyed the problem-solving nature of the subject, and was particularly interested in public finance), although three of his early publications were the famous papers on balanced budget multipliers, one of which he wrote with his friend William Baumol[6] (see Peston, 1954, Baumol and Peston, 1955, Peston, 1958). But his deep interest in macroeconomics is reflected in his *Review of Economic Studies* paper on the aggregation problem (Peston, 1959), a paper of which he is justly proud. Here he argued that the aggregation problem was not a problem of indices or of measurement: 'economic theory at any level of aggregation exists on a par with economic theory at any other level, and if an aggregation problem exists, it is because economic theory at some level is unsatisfactory' (Peston, 1959, p. 59). The conclusion of the article reads almost like a manifesto.

> Instead of being concerned with rules which allow macro variables to be derived from (or at least related to) micro variables, the analysis of aggregates ought to be concerned with the invention and improvement of macrotheory. Thus if a macroeconomic equation . . . is found to be invalid, it is not because its variables are incorrect aggregates of micro-variables, but because it includes some irrelevant variables, excludes some relevant ones, and incorrectly postulates how these variables behave. The aggregation problem as understood at present is no help towards this end. Indeed, it acts as a straightjacket on economic theory at all levels. (Ibid., p. 63)

Maurice was among the first to make use of sophisticated computer models. In the early 1970s he initiated an extremely successful project in the application of optimal control techniques in economics – some of us know the project well enough for in the late 1970s we benefitted substantially from it. This work was of paramount importance in terms of its policy implications. It recognizes that whilst policy can have powerful effects on the level and pace of economic activity, there are constraints in both its implementation and impact. The policy maker is thought to have a number of objectives and instruments, but there are penalties when the objectives are not achieved. This work had an early influence on British economic policy and also on subsequent developments in the area of economic policy. It was pioneering both in the application of dynamic control theory to questions of economic policy and in its use of advanced techniques of time series analysis.

Amongst his many contributions, Maurice was Economic Adviser to the Treasury[7] from 1962 to 1964, to the Ministry of Defence between 1964 and 1966, and to the House of Commons Select Committee on Nationalised Industries from 1966 to 1970. In the 1970s he became economic adviser to Labour in government and opposition :[8] he was variously Special Adviser to the Secretary of State for Education and Science from 1974 until 1975, and Adviser on Prices between 1976 and 1979. He was awarded a peerage in 1987 and became Lord Peston of Mile End and thus directly active in politics: Opposition Spokesman on Energy and on Education and Science in 1987, and concerning Treasury matters from 1990 to 1992. He was also spokesman on industry for the Opposition in the House of Lords.[9]

Maurice's wide range of activities includes being a member of the SSRC and Chairman of its Economics Board from 1976 until 1979, a Council Member of the Royal Pharmaceutical Society of Great Britain since 1986, and Chairman of the Office of Health Economics since 1991. Since 1972 he has been editing the highly successful journal *Applied Economics* and more recently *Applied Financial Economics* and a third one under the title *Applied Economics Letters*. But he always found time to indulge his passionate support for Arsenal Football Club. This keen interest in football resulted in a long stint (initially as member, and later Chairman) on the football Pools Panel.

As Chairman of the Economics Board of the CNAA between 1967 and 1973 Maurice contributed substantially to the development of economics degrees in the then Polytechnic sector, bringing a helpful and constructive approach. With the late Tom Evans, he organized the CNAA conference on *Recent Developments in Economics* in 1971 which had a great impact on the teaching and development of economics in the then polytechnic sector. He chaired the final session of the 5-day conference which created the Association of Polytechnic Teachers in Economics (which elected him, a year later, as its first Honorary President). Those of us who were on the receiving end will never forget Maurice's firm chairing of CNAA visits to departments of Economics. As a chairman he commanded respect, admiration, not to mention some trepidation! The continuing quality of economics education in the new universities is in no small measure the consequence of Maurice's sterling work in this regard.

CONTRIBUTORS TO THE FESTSCHRIFT

The contributors to these volumes include people who first knew Bernard and Maurice as colleagues (David Currie, Meghnad Desai, Pat Dillon, Charles Goodhart, Hugh Gravelle, Brian Henry, Haizhou Huang, Eli Katz, Morris Perlman, Ray Rees, Max Steuer and Adrian Ziderman), as their students or research assistants (Philip Arestis, Mike Anyadike-Danes, Nick Barr, David (Danny) Blanchflower, Ken Burdett, Rod Cross, Sami Daniel, Miriam David, Ciaran Driver, Joe Ganley, John Grahl, Peter Groenewegen, Sam Hollander, David Laidler, Gerry Lyons, Rob Matthews, Barry Moore, Eric Pentecost, Alan Speight and David Wall), or through professional contact (Keith Bain, Peter Howells, Murray Glickman, Steve Nickell, Mike Marshall, Patrick Minford, Bob Nobay, Paul Ormerod, David Peel and Frank Skuse). Many of these people have also got to know them in many other ways. And we all regard them as dear friends. We offer these essays in their honour, and in recognition of their many achievements and contributions.

VOLUME THREE

The application of economics to policy has been a central concern of both Bernard Corry and Maurice Peston throughout their careers. This third volume of the festschrift in their honour is focused on policy issues.

The first group of papers bears on policy in labour markets and on the problem of unemployment. *Barry Moore* presents an empirical study of the reabsorption of redundant workers in local labour markets. He traces the path (into employment, self-employment, inactivity or training) taken by workers made redundant in five local labour markets as a result of closures in aerospace, coal, steel and synthetic fibres. Probit analysis is then used to measure the way in which a worker's characteristics, family circumstances and financial predicament influence the probability of continuing unemployment and the path through redundancy.

Mike Marshall develops a critique of what has become the conventional wisdom informing employment policy in Western Europe – the belief that rigidities and imperfections have produced excessively high wage costs, restrictive practices and poor productivity. Marshall observes that the main New Right project of the 1980s and 1990s has been to attack these rigidities by intervention to curb vested interests and distributional coalitions and by a restructuring of the state's role in the economy. As against this orthodoxy, Marshall suggests that, although the UK labour market has become more flexible in a number of ways, the 'market solution' has not produced widespread or clearly acceptable improvements in performance. He goes on to argue that the orthodox approach to reforms ignored the power of insider pressures for rent-sharing. 'Institutional rigidities' are in fact necessary to the functioning of labour markets: they reduce uncertainty, guide expectations and generate a necessary minimum of trust.

Robin Matthews examines the 'stakeholding' approach to the employment relation which has recently attracted a great deal of attention as a potential alternative to more orthodox positions. He discusses strategic decision making within the enterprise as a cooperative game and explores a range of solution concepts and their implications for strategy and pay-offs. Corporate culture is linked to alternative specifications of transferable utility and recommendations for corporate governance are derived.

While the next group of papers are also centrally concerned with policy questions in general and with unemployment in particular, they also raise important methodological issues. *Paul Ormerod*, in a contribution which takes as its starting point Maurice Peston's long period as the editor of *Applied Economics*, calls into question the reliance of conventional economics on econometrics. In the analysis of time-series, the impressive battery of tests which accompany econometric equations have no unambiguous meaning, especially when the equation is repeatedly respecified in order to satisfy the tests. The phenomenon of out-of-sample 'parameter drift' is universal. The application of non-linear signal processing techniques suggests very strongly that macroeconomic series have little or no deep structure. This view confirms Irving Fisher's 70-year-old hypothesis that the business cycle is inherently unpredictable because, in modern terminology, the dimension of the problem is too high relative to the available number of observations. Ormerod concludes that the instability of estimated equations using macroeconomic data arises from an inherent property of the data itself Although we may obtain approximations over short time periods, such equations will inevitably break down.

Ciaran Driver's contribution takes its inspiration from Maurice Peston's well-known essay, 'When is a problem of economic policy solvable?'. Peston had suggested that 'a diminution in the commitment to full employment . . . may reduce the average level of investment and increase its variance'. Driver shows that increased risk may indeed lead firms to reduce investment. Since it is also likely that loosening the commitment to full employment increases risk, and that investment is important for employment growth, it follows that abandoning full-employment policy makes job creation more problematic. Driver is thus led to endorse Peston's view that 'a problem of economic policy is solvable when politicians can be persuaded to solve it', in this case by emphasizing capacity rather than capital intensity. A necessary condition is a move away from the supposedly 'realistic' position that intervention can do little to improve employment outcomes.

Rod Cross examines the prevalent view of standard economic analysis that temporary shocks have only temporary effects. Appealing both to the history of thought and to a model where a heterogeneous population of firms react in asymmetrical ways to expansionary and contractionary shocks, he discusses the properties of (i) *heterostasis*, (ii) *remanence*, (iii) selective memory of non-dominated extremum shocks. Finally, he uses this framework to provide a history of equilibrium unemployment in the UK, unemployment equilibria being haunted by hysteresis.

The third group of papers are concerned with policy questions other than employment. *Patricia Apps and Ray Rees* explore the topical question of how to tax couples, In the traditional literature the problem was posed in terms of whether a progressive income tax should be based on the individual incomes of the partners or on their combined income. The starting point for Apps and Rees is that the theoretical literature on optimal taxation is insufficiently developed to provide a satisfactory treatment of the issue, essentially because of the way in which the household is modelled. Using a more complex representation of the household, as typically containing two adults and where the alternative to labour market supply is not only pure leisure but also household production, they investigate the question with linear tax models. They argue that generalizations of their results should be perfectly tractable.

Hugh Gravelle looks at the problem of regulating pharmaceutical suppliers. The *ex post* value added scheme proposed by Loeb and Magat has the virtues of simplicity and transparency and leads to efficient outcomes under certain market and technological conditions. Gravelle investigates what happens when these conditions are not satisfied. His analysis suggests that the key informational problem is to discover the therapeutic value of the drug in question. Even in an unregulated market this is imperfectly measured by the producing firm's revenues. Imperfect agency makes the revenue measure even more problematic. It remains the case that therapeutic assessment is required for any mechanism which is intended to provide suitable rewards for information. Efficient direct regulation of or subsidy to investment requires in addition information about the innovation technology.

A different regulatory issue is examined by *Max Steuer*. There are well-established conventions for the timing of payments for many transactions. For example, students usually pay their fees in advance, newspapers and many other consumer goods are paid for at the time of purchase, labour is usually paid for when the work is completed. Steuer argues that recent EU policy, attempting to change payment conventions to benefit consumers, is misconceived. There is a welfare loss in changing the timing of payment because the root cause for the need for different timing according to circumstances is the cost of enforcing contracts. With uncertainty about the exact nature of goods and services, and potential costs in securing payment, payment in advance or payment after the event can both create surpluses in the right circumstances compared to payment at the time of purchase. These surpluses can then be divided between buyers and sellers. Hence the right timing-of-payment convention becomes a stable institution which cannot be invaded by an alternative convention. A policy which attempts to legislate against a surplus-generating convention will result in welfare loss.

In the closing section, three papers consider economic policy in the context of transition and development. *David Wall* shows that emergent China is not only a major importer of external capital in the form of FDI, it has also become an important supplier of capital on world markets. Wall examines the nature and distribution of these outflows. There are considerable problems with the available data, but he is nevertheless able to document a well-defined pattern of investment across countries and to detect specific investment patterns driven by the desire to secure access to raw materials, to secure access to proprietary technology, to develop new markets and to penetrate trade barriers. He concludes that China has become a major overseas investor and that it is playing a growing role on this stage. Many Chinese enterprises are already major multinational companies and many more will be joining their ranks in the near future.

Nicholas Barr discusses pension reform in Central and Eastern Europe. The income transfer systems inherited from the command economy are not well adapted to the needs of a market economy. Pensions were too low, were paid to too many people and cost too much. The root of the problem is a very low pensionable age, but it is aggravated by the very weak administrative capacity of the social insurance authorities. Frequently this meant that they had no record of individual contributions. Barr sees three approaches to a solution: to raise the retirement age and equalize it for men and women, to modernize the administration of benefits and improve the collection and enforcement of contributions. In addition, private pensions, though not a panacea, may act as a complement to state pensions while assisting in the development of capital markets.

Finally, *Eliakim Katz and Adrian Ziderman* discuss training policy in developing countries. They argue that both the specific rationale for intervention and the methods which are used will vary with the level of development and with institutional change. The direct public provision of training services, for example, may be correct if enterprises themselves have a limited capacity to do so, but is not in general justified merely by externalities which lead to a gap between the social and private benefits of training. Because economic environments differ, there can be no single prescription for training policy; instead the role of the government in training markets has to be based on local conditions and informed by careful economic analysis. This last recommendation is certainly in agreement with the approach to policy formation always adopted by Bernard Corry and Maurice Peston.

ACKNOWLEDGEMENTS

Special thanks must go to the contributors for their willingness to respond to our comments and suggestions with forbearance and good humour. Thanks are also extended to Shirin Yassin of the Faculty of Human Sciences at Kingston University, June Daniels and Christine Nisbet of the Department of Economics, University of East London, for their secretarial assistance. We are also grateful to Joan McSweeney, Secretary to the Economics Department of QMW for her help, and to Eilis Rafferty of QMW Library for bibliographic information. Finally, Edward Elgar and his staff, particularly Jane Croft and Ian Garbutt, provided excellent support in the preparation of the three volumes.

NOTES

1. The late Chris Archibald, Kurt Klappholz, Kelvin Lancaster, Richard Lipsey, Max Steuer and Jim Thomas spring to mind. The late Bill Phillips was the only 'established' member of the department who was invited to attend the seminar.
2. For a very interesting and entertaining account of his early years as an economist see the interview he had with Keith Tribe, published as Chapter 13 of Tribe, K. (1997), *The Making of Economists*, Cambridge University Press.
3. See Corry (1966). This article developed from teaching interests.
4. His work with Jennifer Roberts on unemployment and regional mobility was 'pipped to the post' by Oliver (1964). Although their contribution was significantly different from Oliver's, and although they continued work on it and extended the time period covered (see Corry and Roberts, 1967) the two authors decided not to submit their paper for publication: those were the days when there was no pressure to publish! But their work led to interest in activity rates (see Corry and Roberts, 1970; Corry and Roberts, 1974 and their report, Roberts and Corry, 1973).
5. He inspired many satirical student sketches performed in the sixties at the LSE by a group called the Red Robbins Ensemble. Its repertoire included a song about him to the tune of the Drunken Sailor which included the lines: 'Hey up and up he rises . . . give the man a Chair here'. He also 'featured' in one of its sketches, a spoof of him talking about his list of the world's top ten economists.
6. Maurice has great affection for William Baumol whom he met at Princeton. He follows his work very closely, and felt strongly enough about it to write in the same area: see for example: Peston (1957), following up Baumol (1956); Peston (1967), following Baumol's work on revenue maximization; and Peston (1980) which clarified the distinction between cost and volume terms, and the relative price effect, a class of problems he first encountered at the Treasury in 1962 as Clarke's Law, but which became associated with William Baumol, as in, for example Baumol and Bowen (1965).
7. Among the many papers he wrote at the time, one recently received the attention it deserves. It advocated the introduction of student loans (but *not* student payment of fees!).

8. His work as Economic advisor was lauded by Roy Hattersley at the recent conference at QMW in celebration of Maurice's work. One story in particular is worth repeating here:

> I was appointed Shadow Education Minister in what I can only describe as desperate circumstances. Ted Short gave up the job at 3 o'clock on a Thursday afternoon. I was appointed an hour later. At 6 o'clock, at a meeting of the Parliamentary Labour Party, I learnt, to my surprise, that I was to lead for the Opposition on the Monday afternoon in a debate entitled 'Framework for Expansion'. That, though I did not know it at the time, was the name of a new Education White Paper. With forty-eight hours to prepare, I naturally turned to Maurice Peston. He was – somewhat to my annoyance – transfixed by the statistical note with which it ended.
>
> I recall now him explaining with a combination of incredulity and glee that the government had got its figures wrong. Far from the Education budget expanding, in real terms there would be contraction over the next two financial years. He tried to explain the position to me, at one point exclaiming, 'But you did Part I Statistics'. I told him that I had been referred and that I had to take Part I Statistics a second time at the end of my final year. In despair, he wrote me a passage which explained the accounting errors and urged me to read it to the House of Commons.
>
> It was a sign of my confidence in Maurice Peston's judgement that I did just that. The result was consternation all round. Norman St John Stevas – winding up the debate for the government – spoke for, I fear, both sides of the House when lie expressed astonishment that I should, 'Take on the Secretary of State in an area where she is so strong and he is obviously so weak'. It was generally agreed that I had made an ass of myself.
>
> After the debate I asked Maurice Peston how I might retrieve the situation. 'Say it again', he told me. 'For we are right and she is wrong'. I recall rather resenting the plural pronoun. But it seemed too late to start telling people it was Peston who miscalculated not me. So I wrote letters to newspapers. I included the paragraph in handouts and I went on radio programmes and read out the statement again. On the following Friday morning, Stuart McLure – Editor of the *Times Educational Supplement* and doyen of education journalists – phoned to express his interest in my persistence. He had no doubt that I was wrong. But the nature of the error, which I persisted in repeating, intrigued him. He was, he said, going to ask for a ruling from the one man who really understood these things – Maurice Peston.
>
> I can quote almost verbatim the leader which appeared on the following week in the TES. It concluded, 'Seven days ago we accused Roy Hattersley of miscuing. Today we have to concede that he potted black. It was Margaret Thatcher who got her sums wrong.' My statistical experience having at last been acknowledged, I phoned round all the newspapers to demand that they made up for their earlier, and totally unjustifiable, lack of faith. Some of them actually made amends. So I wrote to Margaret Thatcher asking her to concede that she was wrong. I still await the reply.

9. Roy Hattersley gives an interesting account of the effect of Maurice's direct manner on the prospects of his political career:

> He is an essentially serious man. But he has always chosen to hide the strength of his feelings under the pretence of flippancy and sometimes even cynicism. I regard that as an admirable quality – much to be prized in an age of conspicuous piety. It may be, however, that Maurice's slightly cavalier attitude towards objects of veneration – ideas, institutions and individuals – has in the recent past worked to his disadvantage. I recall, back in 1970, going with him to see a football match at Stamford Bridge. One of the directors, now a Labour peer, but then no more than a world famous actor, told Maurice Peston, in suitable lovey fashion, that he had longed for years to meet him. Maurice replied that the man had never heard of him until they met that afternoon. I have no doubt that his manner has offended a large number of other peers. I can think of no other reason why he has not become a member of the government.

REFERENCES

Baumol, W.J. (1956), 'Acceleration without magnification', *American Economic Review*, **46**.

Baumol, W.J. and W.G. Bowen (1965), 'On the performing arts: the history of their economic problem', *American Economic Review*.

Baumol W.J. and M.H. Peston (1955), 'More on the multiplier effects of a balanced budget', *American Economic Review*, **45**, 140–48.

Corry, B.A. (1962), *Money, Saving and Investment in English Economics*, 1800–1850, London: Macmillan.

Corry, B.A. (1966), 'The role of technical innovation in the theories of income distribution', *American Economic Review*, **56** (2) (Proceedings).

Corry, B.A. and J.A. Roberts (1967), 'Inter-regional migration and unemployment: 1950–63', LSE Economics Department, mimeo.

Corry, B.A. and J.A. Roberts (1970), 'Activity rates and unemployment: the experience of the United Kingdom 1951–66', *Applied Economics*, **2**.

Corry, B.A. and J.A. Roberts (1974), 'Activity rates and unemployment – some further results', *Applied Economics*, **6**.

Daniel, S. (1999), 'CNAA economics: the development of economics in the new universities', in S. Daniel, P. Arestis and J. Grahl (eds), *The History and Practice of Economics: Essays in Honour of Bernard Corry and Maurice Peston*, volume 2, Cheltenham: Edward Elgar.

Oliver, F.R. (1964), 'Inter-regional migration and unemployment: 1951–61', *Journal of the Royal Statistical Society, Series A*, 42–69.

Peston, M.H. (1954), 'A note on the balanced budget multiplier', *American Economic Review*, **46**, 129–30.

Peston, M.H. (1957), 'Acceleration and magnification', *American Economic Review*, **47**.

Peston, M.H. (1958), 'Generalising the balanced budget multiplier', *Review of Economics and Statistics*, **48**, 288–91.

Peston, M.H. (1959), 'A view of the aggregation problem', *Review of Economic Studies*, 58–64.

Peston, M.H. (1967), 'Changing utility functions', in M. Shubik (ed.), *Essays in Mathematical Economics in Honour of Oscar Morgenstern*, Princeton, NJ: Princeton University Press.

Peston, M.H. (1980), 'The ratio of public to private expenditure and the relative price effect', *British Review of Economic Issues*, 46–51.

Peston, M.H. and B.A. Corry (eds) (1972), *Essays in Honour of Lord Robbins*, London: Weidenfeld and Nicolson.

Roberts, J.A. and Bernard Corry (1973), 'Changing composition of the labour force: 1950–72', *SSRC Archives*.

Selected publications of Bernard Corry and Maurice Peston

BERNARD CORRY

Corry, B.A. (1958), 'The theory of government expenditure in classical economic policy', *Economica.*

Corry, B.A. (1959a), Malthus and Keynes, *Economic Journal.*

Corry, B.A. (1959b), 'A testimonial from Ricardo, *Economica.*

Corry, B.A. (1962), *Money, Saving and Investment in English Economics, 1800–1850*, London: Macmillan.

Corry, B.A. (1966), 'The role of technical innovation in the theories of income distribution', *American Economic Review*, **56** (2) (Proceedings).

Corry, B.A. (1972), 'Lauderdale and public debt', in M.H. Peston and B.A. Corry (eds), *Essays in Honour of Lord Robbins*, London: Macmillan.

Corry, B.A. (1975), 'Should economists abandon hope?', *History of Political Economy.*

Corry, B.A. (1978), 'Keynes in the history of economic thought', in A.P. Thirlwall (ed.), *Keynes and Laissez-faire*, London: Macmillan.

Corry, B.A. (1986), 'Keynes's economics: a revolution in economic theory or economic policy?', in R.C.D. Black (ed.), *Ideas in Economics*, London: Macmillan.

Corry, B.A. (1996), 'The politics of the natural rate of unemployment', in R. Cross (ed.), *The Natural Rate after Twenty-five Years.*

Corry, B.A. (1997a), 'Unemployment in the history of economic thought', in B.A. Corry (ed.), *Unemployment and the Economist*, Cheltenham: Edward Elgar.

Corry, B.A. (1997b), 'Keynes's use of the term "involuntary employment": a historical perspective', in P. Arestis, G. Palma and M. Sawyer (eds), *Capital Controversy, Post-Keynesian Economics and the History of Economic Thought*, London: Routledge.

Corry, B.A. and D. Laidler (1967), 'The Phillips relation: a theoretical explanation', *Economica.*

Corry, B.A. and J.A. Roberts (1970), 'Activity rates and unemployment: the experience of the United Kingdom 1951–66', *Applied Economics*, **2**.

Corry, B.A. and J.A. Roberts (1974), 'Activity rates and unemployment – some further results', *Applied Economics*, **6**.

Corry, B.A., J. Nugent and D. Saunders (1982), 'Female unemployment in the UK', in C. Ungerson (ed.), *Sexual Divisions*, London: Tavistock.

Corry, B.A., P. Ormerod and J. Rigg (1990), *The Economic Impact of the Arrival in the UK from Hong Kong of 50,000 Heads of Households and their Dependants*, Henley Centre.

MAURICE PESTON

Baumol, W.J. and M.H. Peston (1955), 'More on the multiplier effects of a balanced budget', *American Economic Review*, **45**, 140–48.

Blaug, M., M.H. Peston and A. Ziderman (1967), *Utilization of Educated Manpower: Preliminary Report*, Edinburgh: Oliver and Boyd.

Peston, M.H. (1954), 'A note on the balanced budget multiplier', *American Economic Review*, **44**, 129–30.

Peston, M.H. (1957), 'Acceleration and magnification', *American Economic Review*, **47**.

Peston, M.H. (1958), 'Generalising the balanced budget multiplier', *Review of Economics and Statistics*, **40**, 288–91.

Peston, M.H. (1959a), 'A view of the aggregation problem', *Review of Economic Studies*, 58–64.

Peston, M.H. (1959b), 'On the sales maximisation hypothesis', *Economica*, **26**, 128–36.

Peston, M.H. (1960), 'Returns to scale', *Oxford Economic Papers*, (NS) **12**, 133–40.

Peston, M.H. (1967), 'Changing utility functions', in M. Shubik (ed.), *Essays in Mathematical Economics in Honour of Oscar Morgenstern*, Princeton University Press.

Peston, M.H. (1969), 'Aspects of the pricing policy of nationalised industries', in J. Margolis and H. Guiton (eds), *Public Economics: An Analysis of Public Production and Consumption and their Relations to the Private Sector*, St Martin's Press.

Peston, M.H. (1971), 'Tax mix and effective demand', *Public Finance*, **26**, 493–6.

Peston, M.H. (1972), 'Correlation between targets and instruments', *Economica*, **39**, 427–31.

Peston, M.H. (1973), 'Note on tax changes and fluctuations in national income', *Journal of Political Economy*, **81**, 1467–70.

Peston, M.H. (1974), *Theory of Macroeconomic Policy*, Oxford: Philip Allan (2nd edition: 1982).

Peston, M.H. (1979), 'When is a problem of economic policy solvable?', *Thames Papers in Political Economy*, Autumn.

Peston, M.H. (1980a), 'The ratio of public to private expenditure and the relative price effect', *British Review of Economic Issues*, 46–51.

Peston, M.H. (1980b), *Whatever Happened to Macroeconomics*, Manchester University Press.

Peston, M.H. (1981), An aspect of the crowding out problem', *Oxford Economic Papers*, **31**, 19–27.

Peston, M.H. (1982), *The British Economy: an Elementary Macroeconomic Perspective*, Oxford: Philip Allan (2nd edn 1984).

Peston, M.H. and R.E. Quandt (1986), *Prices, Competition and Equilibrium*, Oxford: Philip Allan.

Peston, M.H. and T.M. Whitin (1954), 'Random variations, risk and returns to scale', *Quarterly Journal of Economics*, **68**, 603–12.

Peston, M.H. and B.S. Yamey (1960), 'Intertemporal price relationships with forward markets: a method of analysis', *Economica*, **27**, 355–67.

Peston, M.H., E. Katz and H.S.E. Gravelle (1976), 'Public sector pricing with foreign demand', *Applied Economics*, **8**, 1–10.

PART I

Labour Markets and Employment

1. The post-redundancy experience and the dynamics of local labour market adjustment

Barry Moore*

1 INTRODUCTION AND CONTEXT FOR THE ANALYSIS

This paper presents the results of a study investigating the post-redundancy experience of workers made redundant within the context of five major redundancy programmes taking place in the early 1990s. It is in many ways a suitable contribution to a volume dedicated to Maurice Peston and Bernard Corry. The research was funded by the Department for Education and Employment to examine the relationship between an individual's personal and family characteristics and the propensity to become and to remain unemployed, or be hired by another organization following redundancy. It is therefore concerned with public policy and the dynamics of labour market adjustment, which are areas of longstanding interest for both Maurice and Bernard either directly or indirectly. Certainly, in the three decades since I was appointed as Maurice's research assistant in the then new Department of Economics at Queen Mary College (QMC), his most important contribution as an economist has been in helping shape public policy, particularly in the area of education and training. His interest in training goes back to research carried out in the Unit for Research on Higher Education in the 1960s, where among others he worked on training with Adrian Ziderman, also one of the first to be appointed at QMC. In this context, I was fortunate to work at QMC and to have Maurice's support in joining Wynne Godley in the Department of Applied Economics at Cambridge to work on policies related to regional unemployment and the dynamics of adjustment in local labour markets. Bernard Corry is of course of special importance to me, as he is for generations of students at LSE and QMC, in providing inspirational teaching in economics and in particular with his lectures on the development of economic analysis. In research our interests have rarely overlapped except in respect of labour market analysis, where our common

* The chapter derives from a wider study undertaken by the author and David O'Neill for the Department of Education and Employment, 1994/95.

interest has been that of migration and labour market adjustments to disequilibrium. In a recent contribution he argued 'Policies have concentrated on changing the characteristics of those without work to have greater incentives to find their place in the demand for labour. The alternative strategy of altering the structure of demand for labour to place people without work in jobs has only briefly surfaced in the history of economic thought', (Corry, 1997). It is perhaps appropriate that the research presented in my paper should bear on this important issue and provide some support for a more balanced approach to the predicament faced by the unemployed called for in Bernard's overview of unemployment.

A review of the literature revealed a dearth of survey-based statistical analysis that specifically sought to explore the dynamics of adjustment in the local labour market, to disentangle the relative importance of different factors on the destination of redundant workers and to chart the 'labour market itinerary' followed in the post redundancy period. Jones (1989) used logit analysis to assess the experience of redundant steelworkers at the BSC plant in Shotton during 1980–81 and at Shotton, Consett and Llanelli in 1985. Mackay (1972) also provided important insights into the post redundancy experience in the late 1960s labour market shake-out. Finch (1996) examined the re-employment experience of former aerospace employees within the local economy in and around Preston in the northwest of England.

The new data used in the analysis derives from a major programme of research into the post redundancy experience of workers made redundant in five major locations in the UK. These included British Aerospace closures, one in Hatfield the other in Preston, the British Steel closure at Ravenscraig, the closure by British Coal of three collieries in Mansfield and the closure of ICI Fibres at Harrogate. These closures and the subsequent redundancies occurred in the period 1991–93 when the UK economy was experiencing a severe recession and employment in many sectors had been declining since 1990. At the same time conjunctural factors, such as the cuts in defence spending, were having important implications for employment in defence-related industries such as the aerospace sector.

The next section briefly describes the nature and context of each of these closures, Section 3 sets out the research methodology, Section 4 presents the conceptual framework and Sections 5 and 6 present the main results including the analysis of the post redundancy path and the probit modelling.

2 THE NATURE AND CONTEXT OF THE CLOSURES

2.1 British Aerospace (Hatfield, Dynamics Division), Hertford and Harlow Travel to Work Area (TTWA)

The BAe Dynamics Division (Hatfield site) covered some 800 acres of land in the Hatfield area. The site contained an airfield and a large area of covered workspace which was mainly devoted to the development of guided weapons and the manufacturing of Airbuses. As at January 1992, over 3000 people were employed at the site and survey data reveals that 90 per cent of respondents lived within 25 miles of the site.

Increased competition in the aerospace industry necessitated that BAe rationalize their production processes. In short, this was to be achieved by closing down a number of sites and concentrating production in the remainder. In February 1992, a redundancy programme was announced that would reduce staff numbers at Hatfield by a third before the year was out. In September 1992, it was announced that the decision to completely close the site (and transfer operations to Chadderton, Bristol and Woodford) by the end of 1993 had been taken. Thus, the redundancies commenced in April 1992 and continued on a monthly basis until the effective closure of the site in December 1993. Table 1.1 provides summary information on the timing and scale of the redundancies.

Table 1.1 The timing and scale of the redundancies at BAe, Hatfield

Date	No. employed	No. of redundancies
April 1992	3362	–
July 1992	2810	552
December 1992	2268	542
July 1993	1106	1162
December 1993	22*	1084
Total	–	3340

Note: * Staff necessary to carry out financial wind up and site maintenance.

Source: AVRO International Aerospace.

2.2 British Aerospace (Strand Road Preston, Military Aircraft Division), Preston TTWA

The BAe Warton Unit consisted of three sites within Lancashire: Preston (Strand Road), Salmesbury Aerodrome, and Warton Aerodrome. In 1989, 14 460 people were employed at the three sites, and, from BAe records, it is estimated that 50 per cent of Warton Unit employees lived in the Preston TTWA. The Strand Road site covered 27 acres and contained one million square feet of covered workspace which was mainly devoted to advanced computer controlled manufacturing activities. Aerospace related manufacturing activity had taken place at the Strand Road site since 1921 and the site was becoming increasingly expensive to maintain and offered little opportunity for expansion.

In 1990 BAe announced it's 'Restructure Programme'. The main thrust of the programme was the rationalization of the Military Aircraft Division –

mainly in response to changes in demand for defence products and also to meet the need for cost reductions to ensure competitiveness in a market characterized by the increased usage of the competitive tendering process. The rationalization process included plans to close the Strand Road site (which in 1990 employed 4500) by the end of 1993. The redundancies commenced in July 1991 and the closure of the site was completed in October 1993. The timing of the redundancies and job losses are shown in Table 1.2.

Table 1.2 Timing of redundancies and jobs lost at BAe, Strand Road, Preston (July 1991–October 1993)

Month	1991	1992	1993
January	–	104	1
February	–	25	2
March	–	28	10
April	–	165	22
May	–	206	153
June	–	191	71
July	173	87	47
August	1	31	61
September	275	62	17
October	95	22	43
November	492	30	–
December	36	74	–
Cumulative total	1072	2097	2524

Source: British Aerospace, Warton Aerodrome.

Redundancy payments were made under the 'special early release programme' (SERP). Thus a one-off redundancy payment, dependent on age and years of service, was payable for an amount not exceeding 104 weeks pay and all those over 50 were entitled to a pension. In addition all those made redundant were eligible to use the 'New Start' outplacement service (which included 'Job Search' and 'Business start-up' courses) supported by BAe and Lancashire Enterprises and funded, in part, by the European Social Fund.

2.3 British Coal (Rufford, Shirebrook and Clipstone collieries), Mansfield TTWA

Traditionally, the Mansfield TTWA relied heavily on coal mining for employment opportunity. As late as 1984 over 29 per cent of the Mansfield TTWA workforce in employment were employed in mining (Coalfield Communities Campaign). The three collieries that are the focus of this study are all situated within the Mansfield TTWA. Despite their close geographical proximity to Mansfield town, both Clipstone and Rufford are within the Newark and Sherwood District, and Shirebrook is within the Bolsover District.

In October 1992, British Coal, faced with a reduction in demand for coal resulting primarily from the switch to gas by power stations, announced the forthcoming closures of 31 of its collieries with the associated loss of over 25 000 jobs. The resulting political debate caused a retrenchment of this policy and the number of collieries facing closure was reduced to 10. Despite this, by February 1994 33 pits had been closed. Clipstone, Shirebrook and Rufford closed during the October 1992–February 1994 period and the timing of the closures and associated redundancies are detailed in Table 1.3. It is estimated that 77 per cent of employees at the three collieries were resident in the Mansfield TTWA.

Table 1.3 Timing of redundancies and jobs lost at British Coal, Mansfield

Colliery	Date of closure	Jobs lost
Clipstone	April 1993	997
Shirebrook	May 1993	1402
Rufford	November 1993	764
Total	–	3163

Source: British Coal Enterprise.

As part of the redundancy package, all those made redundant were eligible to take advantage of the Jobs and Career Change Scheme (JACCS) operated by British Coal Enterprise (BCE). JACCS is, basically, a comprehensive outplacement scheme. The JACCS services offered through British Coal Enterprise's centralized and on-site facilities included *inter alia*, a confidential counselling, vacancy search and display, self-marketing programmes, financial seminars, secretarial support and, where appropriate, funding for retraining in a variety of skills linked to the job market. The above services are available to all those made redundant by British Coal. The only caveat is that they must be accessed within six months of redundancy.

2.4 ICI Fibres, Harrogate TTWA

ICI Fibres employed over 2000 staff at the beginning of the 1980s. The gradual rundown of the site over the decade meant that by 1990, shortly before the closure of the site was announced, there were 400 people employed at the site. ICI records reveal that over 75 per cent of these workers were resident in the Harrogate TTWA.

In January 1991 the closure of ICI Fibres was announced. The closure necessitated 220 redundancies; the remaining 180 staff agreed to take early retirement. The first tranche of redundancies was scheduled for May 1991 and small numbers of staff were made redundant each month between then and May 1993 when the site was closed.

2.5 British Steel, Ravenscraig, Lanarkshire TTWA

The Ravenscraig integrated steelworks was built in 1954 and commissioned in 1957. The works occupied 400 hectares in the south west of the Motherwell District, some 1.5 miles east of Motherwell town centre and 16 miles from Glasgow city centre. In 1974 there were 5700 people employed at Ravenscraig. From the late 1970s onwards, British Steel began contracting out much of the work from Ravenscraig which had been previously undertaken by company employees. As such, by the beginning of the 1990s, the workforce at Ravenscraig had been reduced to just over 3000; with 89 per cent of the workforce resident in the Lanarkshire TTWA.

In May 1990, British Steel announced its intention to close the Hot Strip Mill at Ravenscraig. The Mill closed in February 1991, with the loss of 770 jobs. In the same month British Steel announced the forthcoming closure of one of the two remaining blast furnaces at Ravenscraig. The closure followed in July 1991, resulting in 1100 redundancies. Although British Steel had made a commitment at the time of privatization in 1987 to continue steel making in Ravenscraig until at least 1994, they had added the proviso that the continued operation of the plant was subject to favourable market conditions. Unfortunately, market conditions were unfavourable and in January 1992 the final closure of Ravenscraig was announced. In June 1992 the last operating blast furnace at Ravenscraig closed representing the loss of 1220 jobs (see Table 1.4).

Table 1.4 Timing of redundancies and jobs lost at British Steel Ravenscraig, Lanarkshire (February 1991–June 1992)

Description	Date	Jobs lost
Hot Strip Mill closure	February 1991	770
Blast furnace closure	July 1991	1100
Final closure	June 1992	1220*
Total	–	3090

Note: * includes 70 jobs at Hunterston.

Source: British Steel, Motherwell District Council, LDA.

The Treaty of Paris makes a number of specific provisions for redundancy entitlements that directly benefit those engaged in steel making. In addition, the EEC also have in place a system offering benefits to former steel workers under the 'Iron and steel employees re-adaptation scheme'. This scheme is designed to encourage the rationalization of steel and iron making throughout Europe. As such, the redundancy entitlements of those made redundant from Ravenscraig were somewhat atypical and are worth enumerating.

(a) EEC funded (and DTI delivered) training for 52 weeks. Those participating receive full pay (equivalent to their British Steel salary) during the training period.
(b) Those moving into employment at a wage less than their previous earnings receive a 'top up' to 90 per cent of their British Steel income.
(c) Those moving into unemployment are eligible to weekly payments of 90 per cent of their British Steel earnings for up to one year.
(d) Those becoming self employed receive 100 per cent of their British Steel salary for the first year and 80 per cent of their British Steel salary for the second year.
(e) A one-off redundancy payment.
(f) Those over 50 years old receive an enhanced pension and a negotiated severance package.
(g) Access to a comprehensive counselling package.

Obviously, eligibility for the above benefits is dependent on length of service. It is also worth adding, that, for the eligible, the above benefits must be accessed within 18 months of being made redundant. Given the characteristics of our sample, detailed in Appendix A, the vast majority of those surveyed appear to have been eligible for the above redundancy package.

3 METHODOLOGY

The methodological approach was largely survey based (all the surveys were conducted between July 1994 and June 1995), and this was supplemented with the use of official statistics pertaining to the local labour markets under consideration. For each case study there was a survey of redundant workers. In all, 9475 questionnaires were issued and 2677 were returned representing a 28 per cent response rate.

It was decided that, where possible and desirable, all those made redundant would be sampled to ensure that the actual sample was large in relation to the population, thus allowing analyses of the importance of differences in the population and differences in the post-redundancy experience.

The questionnaire was designed to gather extensive information on both characteristics that may influence the post-redundancy experience and the actuality of the post-redundancy experience itself. Considerable care was taken to ensure that the information gathered as a result of the survey would be amenable to the application of probit analysis. Given the largely factual nature of the questionnaire and the extent of the survey, it was decided that it would be undertaken via post with a telephone and face-to-face follow up where necessary.

Table 1.5 The redundant worker surveys – sample sizes

Case study	Questionnaires issued	Questionnaires returned	Strike rate (%)
Hertford	2335	782	33
Preston	1000	422	42
Mansfield	3030	810	27
Harrogate	210	99	47
Lanarkshire	2900	564	19
Total	9475	2677	28

Table 1.5 details the scale of the survey work undertaken with respect to the redundant workers. It is worth noting that the overall response rate of almost 30 per cent is exceptionally high for a survey of this type. However, there is one caveat worth mentioning: the possibility of non-response bias. Certain cohorts are less likely to respond to a survey than others. For example, individuals who move out of the local area may be more difficult to contact and will, therefore, have a lower response rate. Given that the more geographically mobile tend to be members of the higher occupational groups, it is possible that biased estimates of some parameters (the propensity to unemployment, for example) may result.

4 FACTORS INFLUENCING THE POST-REDUNDANCY EXPERIENCE

A review of the theoretical literature indicates a wide variety of factors to be of potential importance in influencing the post-redundancy experience. In developing the statistical analysis these factors have been grouped into six broad categories;

- Personal factors; age, gender.
- Household factors; marital status, number of dependants and so on.
- Human capital factors; qualifications, skill level, and so on.
- Wealth factors; savings, mortgage, and so on.
- Policy factors; assistance received post-redundancy and so on.
- The external local labour market; unemployment levels.

Figure 1.1 shows these categories.

An important feature of the methodology is the recognition that the factors noted above influence the *dynamics* of change in the post-redundancy period and the path taken by redundant workers. Thus the framework of analysis distinguishes six possible destinations for redundant workers immediately following redundancy – unemployment, training, outplacement, employment, self-employment, inactivity – and all but outplacement are identified as final destinations at the end of some specified period of time. The empirical work was

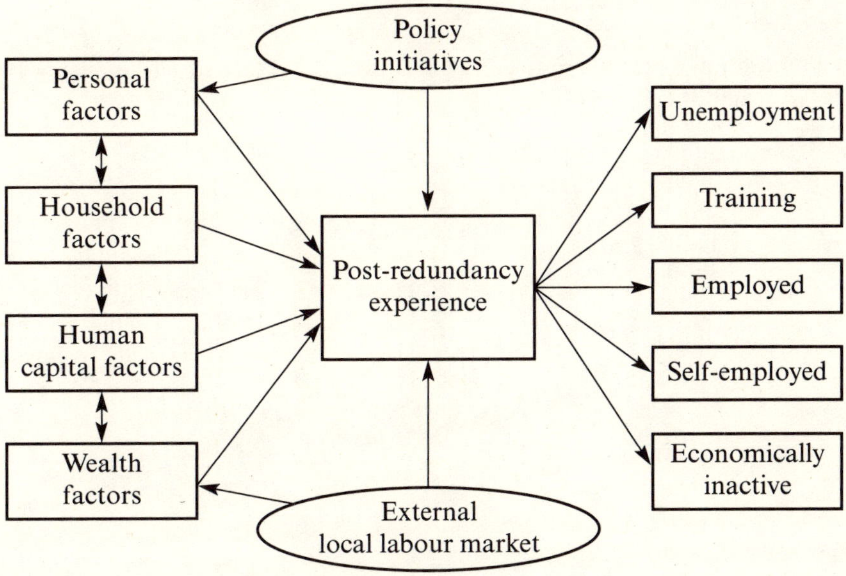

Figure 1.1 Factors influencing the post-redundancy experience

also designed to assess how much time was spent in intermediate destinations *en route* to the final destination.

5 THE POST-REDUNDANCY PATH

The five surveys of redundancies were each carried out for different lengths of period following the start of the redundancy programme.

Figure 1.2 presents summary information concerning the timing and scale of the redundancies in each of the five case study areas in relation to date at which the surveys took place. As can be seen, the Lanarkshire redundancies ended a relatively long time (25 months) before the date of the survey, while the Mansfield and Hertford redundancies ended a relatively short time (9 and 8 months, respectively) before the time of the survey. The Lanarkshire and Harrogate redundancies occurred, on average, almost three years prior to the survey while the Mansfield redundancies occurred just over a year prior to the survey. The overall average lag is 23 months. The information on lags is useful in that the parameters that are the focus of this study may well be

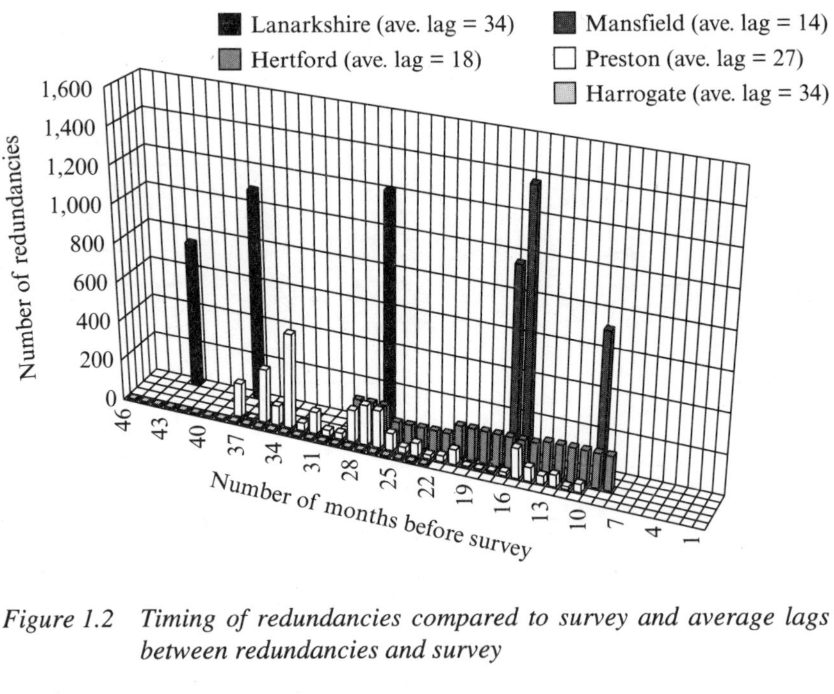

Figure 1.2 Timing of redundancies compared to survey and average lags between redundancies and survey

determined, in part, by the passage of time. Basically, the labour market's natural adjustment processes will, generally, take time to work, suggesting that the longer the lag between the redundancies and the survey, the more complete the adjustment process will be. This suggests that, *ceteris paribus*, differences in parameters between case studies will in part be determined by differences in the average lag.

Figure 1.3 shows the post-redundancy experience of the combined sample. The first vertical section of the diagram shows the immediate destination of those workers made redundant between 2/91 and 12/93. The second vertical section shows the proportion of time the redundant workers spent in their intermediate destinations – a period of time that began, depending on when they were made redundant, between 2/91 and 12/93. The third vertical section shows the destination of the redundant workers at the time of survey – 7/94 and 2/95 being the months in which the survey work was undertaken.

One-third of those responding to the surveys entered unemployment immediately following the redundancies. At the time of the survey, after an average lag of 23 months, the propensity to enter unemployment had fallen to 20 per cent. Interestingly, of the 906 people who entered unemployment immediately following the redundancy only 288 were still unemployed at the time of the survey. Given that the average lag between redundancy and survey was 23 months, of all those entering unemployment immediately following a large scale redundancy an average of 4.9 per cent leave the count every month (13.9 per cent every quarter) during the following two years.

Almost a fifth of the samples (19 per cent) entered employment after the redundancies and a further 3 per cent became self employed giving a total reabsorption rate of 22 per cent. At the time the surveys were conducted, after an average lag of 23 months, the reabsorption rate had almost tripled to 59 per cent: 52 per cent employment, 7 per cent self employment.

Table 1.6 presents summary information concerning the destination of redundant workers for each of the case studies and overall. As can be seen, the propensity to unemployment immediately following redundancy was below that of the total sample in Lanarkshire, Mansfield and Harrogate. In the case of Lanarkshire and Mansfield this is no doubt due to attractiveness of the training/outplacement components of the redundancy package. In the case of Harrogate, the high skill level of the workforce was probably an important factor. Additionally, the relative age and the size of the redundancy payments made available to the Harrogate workforce no doubt contributed to the low propensity to enter unemployment by increasing the attractiveness of economic inactivity. It is worth noting that the 'immediate' propensity to unemployment excludes those who, for a variety of reasons (for example, holidays, registration inertia),

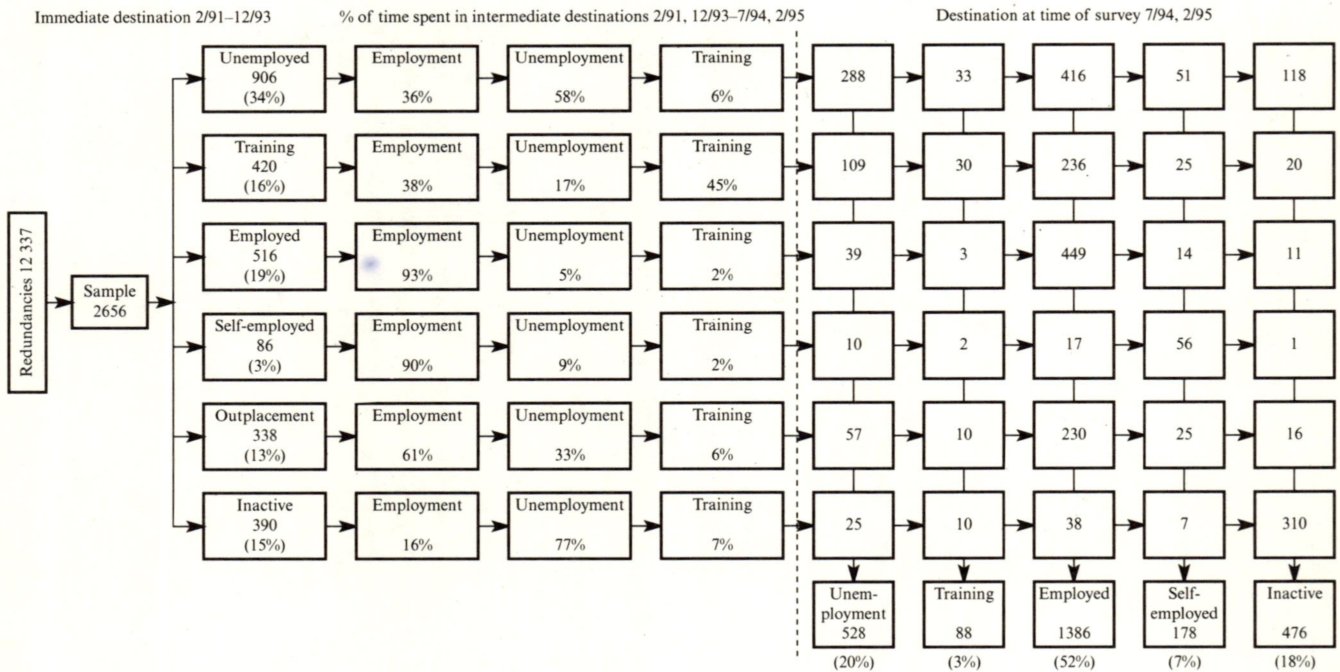

Figure 1.3 The path through redundancy – combined sample

do not join the claimant count immediately but for whom unemployment is, eventually, the first formal post-redundancy destination that they enter. This is likely to bias the immediate propensities to unemployment downwards.

Table 1.6 The propensity to sign on and the reabsorption rate

Study	Average lag between redundancy and survey (months)	Final redundancy (m/y)	Propensity to unemployment		Reabsorption rate: employment (self-employment)	
			Immediate	At survey	Immediate	At survey
Hertford	18	12/93	53	19	29 (3)	58 (6)
Preston	27	10/93	46	14	8 (3)	27 (6)
Mansfield	14	11/93	25	20	20 (4)	60 (8)
Harrogate	34	5/93	29	11	27 (11)	43 (16)
Lanarkshire	34	6/92	12	25	12 (1)	52 (4)
Total sample	23	N/A	34	20	19 (3)	52 (7)

Note: All surveys took place in July/August 1994 except for Harrogate (February 1995).

At the time of the surveys, the propensities to unemployment of the case study samples had converged somewhat. Harrogate remained considerably below average in this respect – indicative, again, of the highly skilled ICI workforce. The propensity to unemployment of respondents to the Preston survey was also relatively low, although this was in part due to the demographics of the workforce and their high propensity to become economically inactive.

The immediate reabsorption rate is well below average in both Preston and Lanarkshire. In the case of the latter, this is again due to the popularity of the training option offered within the redundancy package. The low immediate reabsorption rate for the Preston study is due to the high propensity to become unemployed combined with the fact that 42 per cent of those surveyed became economically inactive following redundancy. Both Hertford and Harrogate experienced high immediate reabsorption rates – in the case of Harrogate this is attributable to the high skill level of the workforce and, in the case of Hertford, this is due to both the robustness of the local economy and the relatively high level of skills amongst the workforce.

The reabsorption rate at the time of the survey is relatively low in Preston again indicative of the popularity of economic inactivity amongst those made redundant. In Mansfield the reabsorption rate exceeds the average. Why this should be so is not immediately apparent, although the success of BCE's outplacement programme in placing 68 per cent of those that quoted it as a first destination is potentially important.

6 STATISTICAL MODELLING OF FACTORS INFLUENCING THE PROPENSITY OF REDUNDANT WORKERS TO BECOME UNEMPLOYED

To explore the relative importance of factors influencing the propensity to become unemployed both bivariate and multivariate probit analysis was carried out (only the latter is presented in this paper). This approach has been used by Jones (1989), Moore and O'Neill (1995, 1996) and by Finch (1996).

The model is a standard probit of the form

$$z = c + \beta_1 x_1 + \ldots + \beta_n x_n + \varepsilon$$

$y = 1$ if $z > 0$, $y = 0$ if $z \leq 0$ where:
c = constant
$\beta_1 \ldots \beta_n$ = coefficients of the independent variables (factors)
$x_1 \ldots x_n$ = independent variables (factors)
ε = normally distributed error term
y = whether an individual is unemployed or not (if y is 1 = unemployed, if y is 0 = not unemployed)

A stepwise addition process was then applied to the selected factors. The first factor selected had the highest log likelihood ratio amongst those with a level of statistical significance of 0.00 per cent in the bivariate regressions (in the case of propensity to unemployment immediately following redundancy this was 'Location; Lanarkshire'). All the other factors were then added to the equation in turn and the one which produced the highest statistical significance of all previous factors and itself was retained in the equation. This process was reiterated until none of the excluded variables made a significant contribution to the explanatory powers of the equation. Throughout the stepwise procedure due regard was also paid to the log likelihood ratio and the correlation matrix. This process aims to produce the best predictor of unemployment probability with the fewest number of factors possible.

The results of the multivariate regression analysis at the time immediately following redundancy and at time of survey (on average 23 months later) are presented in Table 1.7. With respect to *personal factors*, gender and age were both significant as factors influencing the propensity to unemployment. Males were more likely to become unemployed than females at the time of redundancy. Redundant workers in the 25–39 age group and those in the 60+ group were

Table 1.7 Multivariate regression analysis of factors correlated with the propensity to unemployment

Factors	Immediately following redundancy		At time of survey (lag = 23 months)	
	Coefficient	Significance	Coefficient	Significance
Constant	–0.46	0.22	–0.99	0.00
Location				
Lanarkshire	–0.29	1.13	N/S	N/S
Preston	N/S	N/S	–0.48	0.00
Hertford	0.24	0.09	N/S	N/S
Personal				
Male against female	0.27	1.85	N/S	N/S
Age: 25–39	–0.26	0.29	–0.17	3.86
Age: 50–59	0.31	0.07	0.28	0.15
Age 60+	–0.26	0.25	–0.28	3.72
Household				
Single	0.26	0.25	0.27	0.61
Partner with FT job at time of survey	0.19	1.70	N/S	N/S
Partner employed elsewhere at time of redundancy	N/S	N/S	–0.20	0.32
Human capital				
No NVQ (academ.)	0.14	4.68	0.15	2.71
Technical (SOC3)	0.23	0.89	N/S	N/S
Clerical (SOC467)	N/S	N/S	–0.61	0.00
Skilled manual SOC5)	0.36	0.00	N/S	N/S
Semi/unskilled (SOC89)	0.26	3.43	N/S	N/S
Length of employment	–0.54	0.17	N/S	N/S
Pay £150–249 pw	N/S	N/S	0.20	0.35
Financial capital				
LA/Housing assoc.	0.35	0.21	0.30	0.18
Other debts: none	–0.23	0.02	N/S	N/S
Other debts: £2–4k	N/S	N/S	0.23	0.65
Log likelihood	– 1167		–989	

Notes

All coefficients are significant at the 95 per cent level of confidence. The least significant coefficient is 'No NVQ' which only becomes significant at the 95.32 per cent level of confidence (that is, 100 – 4.68 = 95.32).

NS = not significant

significantly less likely to become unemployed than other age cohorts, whereas those in the 50–59 group were significantly more likely than other age groups to become unemployed. With respect to the former, it is likely that the lower propensity to unemployment for the 60+ cohort may reflect the greater tendency for those in this group to become economically inactive. The positive coefficient for the 50–59 group may reflect employer bias against recruiting relatively more expensive elderly workers by comparison with younger age groups. As far as the redundant workers *domestic situation (household factors)* is concerned, being single or having a partner with a job raises the probability of being unemployed at time of redundancy and at time of survey, following redundancy. For redundant workers with partners in full time employment, there is a higher probability of being unemployed immediately following redundancy but the reverse is true some two years later at the time of survey. Perhaps surprisingly the number of dependants does not emerge as a statistically significant factor. A number of indicators of *human capital* emerge as statistically significant. Thus redundant workers with no NVQs have an above average probability of being unemployed as do technical, skilled manual and semi-skilled manual workers. This contrasts with those in clerical occupations where there is a negative relationship. Shortness of time with the employer is another indirect measure of human capital that is significant and the negative relationship indicates that the shorter the period of work with the employer the lower the probability of being unemployed. However this negative relationship tends to reflect a move by long-serving workers into inactivity rather than employment, no doubt because length of service and age are positively correlated. Finally, relatively low wage earners are associated with an above average probability of unemployment. The importance of a number of *financial capital* factors was tested for including redundancy payments, housing status and size of mortgage. Those in local authority accommodation or Housing Association rented accommodation experience an above average probability of being unemployed as do those with non-mortgage debts of between £2–4k. Those with no debts have a lower probability of being unemployed.

7 CONCLUSIONS

This paper has explored the post-redundancy experience of workers made redundant in five different locations. Results have been presented for the combined sample of 2656 workers made redundant in the period 1991–93. The analysis of the dynamics of adjustment in the local labour market shows that after about two years the initial proportion of unemployed falls from about one-third of redundant workers to one-fifth. Immediately following redundancy about one-fifth of the sample had found employment but within two years this figure had risen to just over one-half. Of those that initially went into unemployment following redundancy 13 per cent were unemployed two years later. The impact on self employment was relatively small with 7 per cent of the sample in this category at the time of survey and 18 per cent became economically inactive. Of the 29 per cent that went into training or outplacement some 61 per cent subsequently found employment.

Of the different factors identified as influencing the destination of redundant workers, gender, age, household status, human capital and financial capital and location were all found to be important. The multivariate analysis suggested that being male, aged 50–59, single or with a partner with a job, relatively low human capital and living in rented local authority housing were characteristics raising the probability of being unemployed following redundancy.

SELECT BIBLIOGRAPHY

Atkinson (1985), *Flexibility, Uncertainty and Manpower Management*, IMS Report no. 89.

Beatty and Fothergill (1994), 'Registered and Hidden Unemployment in Areas of Chronic Industrial Decline: The Case of the UK Coalfelds', Paper presented at the Regional Studies Association conference.

British Coal Enterprise Ltd (1994), *Helping Create Jobs: A Review of Activities.*

Bryson, A. and S. McKay (eds) (1994), *Is it Worth Working*, PSI.

Campbell and Duffy (1992), *Local Labour Markets: Problems and Policies.*

Carmichael (1978), 'Local labour market analysis.. its importance and a possible approach', *Geoforum*, **9**.

Carmichael (1981), 'The labour-market behaviour of employers: a framework for analysis and a case study of a local labour market', in Martin (eds), *Regional Inflation and Unemployment.*

Cockerham, J. (1994), 'Redundancies in Great Britain: results from the Spring 1992 to Spring 1993 Labour Force Surveys', *Employment Gazette.*

Cole, S. (1987), 'The economic costs of plant closures', in *Project Appraisal* **2**.

Cole, S. (1994), 'A community accounting matrix for Buffalo's East Side neighbourhood', in *Economic Development Quarterly.*

Corry, B.A. (1997), 'Unemployment in the history of economic thought', in B.A. Corry (ed.), *Unemployment and the Economist*, Cheltenham: Edward Elgar.

Derbyshire County Council (1992), *Colliery Closures: Impact Study.*

EAP Consultants (1992), *Impact Study of the Closure of BAe's Strand Road Plant.*

Eggington (1988), 'Regional labour markets', *Bank of England Quarterly Bulletin* **28** (3),

Employment Department, 'Estimating the impact of major redundancies on local unemployment', Internal paper.

Finch, J. (1993), *New Start Data Base Description and Preliminary Analysis – an Interim Report.*

Finch, J. (1996), 'The re-employed experiences of former Aerospace employees', Discussion Paper 96–02 Department of Economics, University of Aberdeen.

Coal Industry (1985–9), *Economy and Society*, **19** (1).

Glyn (1986), 'Colliery results and closures after the 1984–5 coal dispute', *Oxford Bulletin of Economics and Statistics*, **50**.

Green, Owen and Hasluck (1991), 'The Development of Local Labour Market Typologies: Classification of Travel-to-Work-Areas', Employment Department Research Paper no. 84.

Gudgin, Fothergill and Brunskill (1979), *New Manufacturing Firms*, Regional Employment Growth, Research Series 39, London: Centre for Environmental Studies.

Gujarati (1988), *Basic Econometrics*.

Guy, M. (1994a), *Grimethorpe: Redundant Miners Survey*.

Guy, M. (1994b), *Parkside: Redundant Miners Survey*.

Guy, M. (1994c), *Silverhill: Redundant Miners Survey*.

Guy, M. (1994d), *Dole not Coal: Redundant Miners Survey*.

Guy, M. (1994e), *Taff Merthyr: Redundant Miners Survey*.

Harris et al. (1987) *Redundancy and Recession*.

Hinde, K. (1995), *Evaluating the Economic Impact of Unemployment Following Plant Closure: The Case of North East Shipbuilders Ltd in Sunderland*.

Hinde, K. (1994), 'Labour market experiences following plant closure: The case of Sunderland's shipyard workers', *Regional Studies*, **28** (7),

Jenkins et al. (1981), 'Labour market closure and recession', Occasional Paper no. 19, University College of Swansea.

Jones, D.R. (1989), After redundancies – labour market adjustment and hysteresis effects', *Oxford Bulletin of Economics and Statistics*, **51** (3),

Lancashire County Council (1994), T*he Aerospace Industry in Lancashire*.

Layard, Nickell and Jackman (1991), *Unemployment*.

Lee, Burns, Newby and Winterton (1985), 'The Restructuring of the British Coal Industry', *Cambridge Journal of Economics*,

Liao, T.F. (1994), *Interpreting Probability Models, Logit, Probit and Other Generalised Linear Models*, Sage Publications.

Mackay et al. (1971), *Labour Markets Under Different Employment Conditions*.

Mackay et al. (1980), *Redundancy and Displacement*, Department of Employment Research Paper no. 16.

Manufacturing, Science Finance Union (1991), *British Aerospace PLC: A critique of corporate policy*.

Manufacturing, Science Finance Union (1994), *MSF aerospace review: technology, the key to the future*.

Martin and Tyler (1990), 'Local disparities in unemployment and real wages in Great Britain', *Cambridge Economic Review*.

Minford and Stoney (1991), 'Regional policy and market forces: a model and an assessment, in Bowen and Mayhew (eds), *Reducing Regional Inequalities*,

MMC (1983) *National Coal Board*, London: HMSO, Cmnd 8920.

Moore, B. and P. Townroe (1990), *Urban Labour Markets: A Review of Urban Research*, Department of the Environment, HMSO.

Moore, B. and D. O'Neill *The Impact of Redundancies on Local Labour Markets and the Post Redundancy Experience*, Research Studies RS23, Department for Education and Employment.

Motherwell District Council. *The Effect of Steel Closures*.

NUM (1984), *The Economic Case Against Pit Closures*.

Österland (1989), 'Declining industries, plant closing and local labour markets', in Albrechts, Moulaert, Roberts and Swyngedouw (eds), *Regional Policy at the Crossroads: European Perspectives*,

PA Cambridge Economic Consultants (1994), *Cross Programme Placing Rates: A Review of Literature and Recommendations for Future Research.*

Reilly (1992), 'An analysis of local labour market wage differentials', *Regional Studies* **3**.

Robinson (1970), *Local Labour Markets and Wage Structures.*

Rowthorn, R. and T. Ward (1979), How to run a company and run down an economy; the effects of closing down steel-making in Corby', *Cambridge Journal of Economics.*

Stevens, J. (1992), *The Impact of Scottish Steel Closures l990–1996*, Fraser of Allander Institute.

Thurow (1976), *Generating Inequality.*

Witt (1990), *When the Pit Closes – the Employment Experiences of Redundant Miners*, Coal Communities Campaign.

APPENDIX A THE REDUNDANT WORKER SAMPLES

A1 Introduction

A1.1 This section provides summary information on the redundant worker samples under the headings of personal, household, human capital and wealth factors. The displacement and supplier company samples are not defined here for reasons of confidentiality.

A2 Describing the Redundant Worker Samples

A2.1 Table 1.8A provides statistics on the sample sizes of the five case studies.

Table 1.8A Redundant worker survey – sample sizes

	Hertford	Preston	Mansfield	Harrogate	Lanarkshire	Total
Sample size	782	422	810	99	564	2677
% of total sample	29	16	30	4	21	100

Personal factors

A2.2 Table 1.9A provides details of the personal factors specific to the samples.

Table 1.9A Redundant worker survey – personal factors (%)

	Hertford	Preston	Mansfield	Harrogate	Lanarkshire	Total
Gender						
Male	85	94	99	65	95	92
Female	15	6	1	35	5	8
Age						
18–24	6	1	2	1	4	3
25–39	36	9	61	19	34	38
40–49	20	12	29	15	29	23
50–59	24	52	8	56	23	24
60+	15	26	1	8	10	11

A2.3 The case studies involved established companies in traditional industries and this is the main reason behind the bias of the samples towards males. In terms of age, Mansfield (British Coal) had the youngest workforce, while Preston (BAe) and Harrogate (ICI) had the oldest workforces.

Household factors

A2.4 Table 1.10A provides details of the household factors specific to the samples.

Table 1.10A Redundant worker survey – household factors (%)

	Hertford	Preston	Mansfield	Harrogate	Lanarkshire	Total
Domestic						
Single	22	16	12	13	21	18
Couple	79	83	87	87	78	82
Dependants						
0	56	66	28	62	43	47
1–2	34	25	58	34	44	43
3–4	8	5	13	3	10	9
5+	0	1	1	0	1	1
Distance from site						
< 4 miles	34	48	49	58	50	45
5–9 miles	21	18	33	17	28	26
10–24 miles	35	33	16	17	19	25
25+ miles	9	1	1	5	2	4

A2.5 The Hertford (BAe) site had the widest effective travel to work area, while Mansfield (British Coal) had the smallest effective travel to work area.

Human capital factors

A2.6 Table 1.11A provides details of the human capital factors specific to the samples.

Table 1.11A Redundant worker survey – human capital factors (%)

	Hertford	Preston	Mansfield	Harrogate	Lanarkshire	Total
Length of employment						
1–4	23	2	3	5	9	10
5–9	32	4	13	14	10	17
10–24	31	66	68	26	59	54
25+	12	28	15	54	22	19
Position (SOC)						
Managerial (1)	16	14	14	24	14	15
Professional (2)	7	2	1	17	3	4
Technical (3)	27	17	22	19	13	21
Clerical, sales, secretarial (4, 6, 7)	14	12	3	31	8	10
Skilled manual (5)	29	38	44	4	33	35
Semi/unskilled manual (8,9)	6	18	13	3	28	15
Academic qualifications						
Degree+	12	3	3	32	8	8
A level equivalent	8	5	3	18	14	8
O level equivalent	45	24	47	30	27	39
None	31	62	43	17	48	44
*Vocational qualifications						
NVQ4	23	9	11	41	32	21
NVQ3	52	43	35	24	46	47
NVQ2	10	5	14	13	12	12
NVQ1	1	1	1	0	2	1
Other	2	0	3	1	0	2
None	29	48	45	35	27	39

Note: * More than one response possible – figures may not sum to 100.

A2.7 In terms of all the four human capital measures shown here, the Harrogate (ICI) workforce were by far the better endowed. The Preston (BAe) and Mansfield (British Coal) workforces were in possession of far fewer objective indicators of skill.

Wealth factors

A2.8 Table 1.12A provides details of the wealth factors specific to the samples.

Table 1.12A Redundant worker survey – wealth factors (%)

	Hertford	Preston	Mansfield	Harrogate	Lanarkshire	Total
Redundancy payment						
< £10 000	55	23	1	15	4	22
£10 000–24 999	27	38	38	24	51	37
£25 000–49 999	13	34	56	32	39	36
£50 000+	3	4	3	27	3	4
Housing tenure						
Private rented	9	4	3	2	8	6
LA/HA rented	13	2	3	0	33	12
Live with relatives	2	0	1	0	1	1
Own property	13	33	11	21	6	14
Mortgage < £20 000	19	42	39	35	27	32
Mortgage £20 000+	42	17	42	38	21	34

A2.9 In line with their relatively high periods of tenure the Harrogate (ICI) workforce enjoyed the highest redundancy payments.

2. Flexible labour markets and economic performance: a critique of eurosclerosis deregulation strategies[1]

Mike Marshall

INTRODUCTION

As Keynesianism became discredited in the 1970s and 1980s, neoclassicism, in a variety of forms, increased its influence. As it did so a neoclassically inspired strategy of greater 'flexibility' came to the fore. In the US, the neo-conservative backlash manifested itself as Reaganomics, and the experience of the US became important for Europe because Reaganomics was influential in the spread of so-called liberal productivist ideas to Europe in the form of 'eurosclerosis' theories.

From the New Right perspective, flexibility has been seen exclusively in terms of removing or reducing the 'institutional rigidities' that prevent the full operation of market forces and the ability of economic agents to respond to price movements. Not surprisingly, since most analyses have been inspired by, and based upon, the analysis of Olson (1982), the need for greater flexibility became associated with attacks on certain vested interests (trade unions) and corporatist strategies and policies. The policy strategy suggested by such flexibility theories is one of deregulation, tax and welfare cuts, and a general restriction on governmental activity. These policies certainly found favour with the post-1979 Thatcher government in Britain.

Conservative governments of the 1980s and 1990s in the UK have sought to limit institutional interventions in free markets and many reforms have focused directly on the labour market, or were expected to improve the economy by changing the labour market. At a policy level, this particular flexibility thesis[2] makes several arguments. First, wages are too high and too rigid, thereby pricing workers out of jobs and creating unemployment. (Here powerful trade unions and centralized collective bargaining arrangements are seen as the main problem.) Second, wage differentials are too small, hindering labour mobility and efficient structural adjustment. Third, legally based labour rights are too extensive, leading to high labour costs. Finally, social security systems encourage voluntary unemployment and act as a disincentive to work.

The neo-liberal solution of deregulation then implies a restoration of market forces with arguments for economic efficiency complementing libertarian arguments in favour of a return to individual autonomy and an abandonment, or at least severe curtailment, of the collectivist institutions of the welfare state. The vision guiding the reforms has been that of a more flexible labour market, where wages depend more on company performance than on the 'going rate', where labour is highly mobile and where firms respond rapidly to market signals. In short, it is a vision of a labour market resembling that of the decentralized US rather than the more regulated and institutionally structured labour markets of Western European countries. In what follows, this analysis of the labour market will be subjected to critical examination.

Given their long-standing interest in macroeconomic performance and their healthy scepticism of neo-conservatism, these are issues that have been of great concern to both Maurice Peston and Bernard Corry. The latter in particular, as a former Senior Economic Advisor to the (then) Department of Employment and Productivity and someone with a long and distinguished academic contribution to the study of unemployment, part-time work and other labour market-related issues, has illustrated such a concern. Both of them I think, even if they do not agree with all the arguments presented below, will share the author's general scepticism regarding the rationale and effects of the labour market policies carried out in the UK in the 1980s and 1990s.

FLEXIBILITY, WAGES AND UNEMPLOYMENT

A major criticism of European labour markets, compared to the US, is the occurrence of real wage rigidity in the face of shocks; for example, falls in the demand for labour, resulting in decreases in the quantity employed, rather than falls in the price of labour. Real wage rigidity is an accusation particularly made of the UK. Estimates of the percentage change in real wages in response to a one per cent rise in unemployment give figures of only –0.4 per cent for the UK, with –1.2 per cent for the US and a much higher –2.6 per cent for Germany (Anderson and Mayhew, 1994). Those who claim that the labour market is rigid argue that workers do not adjust wage demands or expectations quickly in response to changing demand conditions and do not adjust them by enough to restore equilibrium. This implies the need to lower worker expectations and to remove or remould the institutional mechanisms that cause inflexibility and labour immobility.

There is considerable debate, however, over the influence of real wages on the level of unemployment. In contrast to the predictions of a free market model, empirical evidence fails to show a direct relationship between unemployment and real wages, especially since 1979. According to Standing (1986), wage cuts would only have a small and slow effect on employment, so that wages would have to fall a great deal to induce a substantial cut in unemployment.

The objective of labour market deregulation is to generate a higher level of employment by securing equilibrium between supply and demand. However, the evidence is that the labour market is in unstable equilibrium, only held in balance by high levels of unemployment, and that low pay is a major cause of labour market instability. For example, almost 40 per cent of the vacancies notified to Job Centres are in the distribution, hotels and catering and repairs sectors, although this accounts for only 20 per cent of total employment. The evidence suggests that, except possibly in periods of exceptionally high unemployment, in the low pay segments of the labour market there is a substantially greater degree of unsatisfied demand for labour, meaning that compared with other sectors, wages are too low. Recession brings supply more into line with demand by destroying alternative job opportunities. Thus, as Michie and Wilkinson (1994) have argued, rather than low pay being an answer to unemployment, high levels of joblessness are a precondition for many people accepting low paid jobs, which they quit when job prospects improve.

Moreover, deregulation policies in themselves are unlikely to resolve the European unemployment crisis. The effects of flexibility initiatives, although pursued by the government with the target of reducing unemployment, are somewhat ambiguous. Enterprises are as likely to use their additional degrees of freedom to reduce costs as to expand output and investment. Market rigidities are not the only barrier to expansion, equally important are the effect of major uncertainties linked to structural change. Flexibility strategies in themselves do not clarify the future pattern of market demand or reduce the risks of long-term investment. They make it easier to deploy new technology, but it is more likely that technology will be used to shed labour than enhance output (Grahl and Teague, 1989).

Whilst there was a relative improvement in inflation and growth rates, overall the transition from unemployment to employment worsened in the 1980s. This can be seen by the proportion of the jobless out of work for more than a year, which rose from 29 per cent in 1979 to 36 per cent in 1990. OECD data for durations of unemployment for other European countries show that the UK did not do better than the EU countries in altering the share of the unemployed who are long term. The reforms that succeeded in making work more attractive relative to joblessness for men did not succeed in moving them into employment rapidly, though they may have done so for women (Blanchflower and Freeman, 1994).

Also, as we saw throughout the 1980s, the creation of jobs does not necessarily promote a proportionate reduction in unemployment, and a reduction in the unemployment figures does not necessarily mean an increase in permanent full-time work. Certainly in the 1980s there was an increase both in the activity rate and the numbers in part-time work. Those taking up part-time work, the only growth area of employment in the last decade, have largely been female new entrants bypassing open unemployment. Consequently, each increment in employment has been associated with something like a 0.6 per cent change in unemployment, with the problem of long-term unemployment growing.

Furthermore, labour flexibilization may well increase cyclical fluctuations in unemployment. Fixed-term contracts provide increased flexibility by lowering firing costs. European governments have encouraged the use of such contracts, first, by reducing social security contributions for youth training under temporary contracts, and second, by relaxing the restrictions on the use of fixed-term contracts in non-temporary activities. Temporary jobs seem to be one of the most important ways in which firms have strived for increasing employment flexibility, particularly in Spain. The interest in Spain has been triggered by two main factors: first, since the early 1970s, it has had the worst unemployment record in Europe; second, in 1975 it inherited a very rigid labour market from Franco's regime. In 1984, the government introduced fixed-term labour contracts with low firing costs for all activities, temporary or not. This scheme now comprises one-third of all employees. The results seems to have been that labour demand became more responsive to output fluctuations during the period 1985–88. It seems that initially, with a rise in temporary employment, there is a lowering of average wage costs and a fall in unemployment. However, after a while, increases in labour costs occur, and if aggregate demand falls, unemployment rises with the brunt of this adjustment borne by temporary workers. In Spain, the unemployment rate rose from 16 per cent to 23 per cent between 1991 and 1993. What has been achieved is flexibility at the margin, affecting certain groups of workers, but not the core of permanent employees (Bentolila and Saint-Paul, 1992; Bentolila and Dolado, 1994). This has tended to create a dual labour force at the firm level.

Labour flexibility policies then try to reduce barriers to wage flexibility, to remove the institutional arrangements which increase employment-related costs to the employer and prevent workers pricing themselves into jobs: but how secure are such arguments? The efficiency wage hypothesis (Akerlof and Yellen, 1986) asserts that the wage rate affects the quality of work, or the effort applied by the worker. Higher pay can lead to higher morale and higher productivity. It is more efficient for the firm to offer a wage rate above the market clearing level, thus negating government policies to promote employment by moving closer to a labour market equilibrium. Furthermore, according to the fair wage effort hypothesis, workers proportionately withdraw effort as their actual wage falls below the fair wage. This model predicts that if a perceived fair nominal wage does not rapidly change in proportion to shifts in nominal aggregate demand, then aggregate demand shocks will produce cyclical variations in unemployment, thereby producing demand-generated business cycles (Akerlof and Yellen, 1990).

FLEXIBILITY, TRADE UNIONS, COLLECTIVE BARGAINING AND ECONOMIC PERFORMANCE

Despite the high unemployment during the 1980s, growth of real wages was high in the UK, indicating that the Thatcher reforms did not produce a better trade-off between inflation and unemployment. OECD data shows that from 1979 to 1989 real hourly earnings in manufacturing increased by 2.6 per cent in the UK compared with 1.4 per cent in OECD Europe, despite the above average rate of unemployment in the UK (Blanchflower and Freeman, 1994).

As regards wage bargaining, the neo-liberal preference is for local deals. However, under such bargaining, pay is increasingly influenced by local profitability. Where firms are operating in imperfect markets, the implications are profound since monopoly power in the product market produces a rent, and workers are able to boost earnings by enjoying a share of this rent. Changes did occur in the 1980s which boosted efficiency, productivity and profits, at least in manufacturing. However, the 'insiders' were rewarded with higher real wages, whilst, simultaneously, the number of unemployed grew (Metcalf, 1994). Thus, the consequence of local bargaining in conditions of imperfect competition seems to be 'rent sharing' by employed workers and a reduction of 'outsider' influences on wage determination and a corresponding worsening of the trade-off between wage inflation and unemployment (Holmlund and Zetterberg, 1991; Metcalf, 1993).

Wage setting in Europe seems to be significantly affected by insider employees, protected by high labour turnover costs and specific skills. Wages are the outcome of a bargaining process whereby firms and their employees share the economic rent captured by firms on goods markets. By reducing labour turnover costs, legal changes encouraging the use of temporary contracts should have reduced the power of insiders in the wage bargain. However, they may, ironically, have increased it, at least in those countries where protection for permanent employees is still high. The wage bargain is largely in the hands of the core of permanent, full-time employees, and the empirical evidence suggests that these insiders may be able to obtain higher wages because the presence of a buffer of flexible employees lowers the likelihood that insiders will lose their jobs. Thus, temporary employment may increase, not decrease, the share of income captured by permanent employees. This is confirmed in the case of Spain, and to a lesser extent by the experience of other European countries (Bentolila and Dolado, 1994).

The higher labour turnover associated with fixed-term contracts may also have a negative impact on long-term productivity. The evidence from Spain is that while greater employment fluctuation may have reduced the cyclicity of labour productivity, productivity growth has actually fallen in Spanish manufacturing industry (Bentolila and Dolado, 1994). The reason for this may be that the short tenure inherent in fixed-term contracts discourages investment in human capital on the part of both firms and workers. Alternatively, fixed-term workers may exert less effort than permanent employees.

Labour mobility is allegedly becoming increasingly important as the structural adjustment of industry and effective responses to external shocks are seen as necessary conditions for renewed economic expansion. Labour immobility, it is alleged, will cause regional variations in unemployment which will not only be less efficient and cause more social problems than evenly spaced unemployment, but also generate a higher average unemployment rate nationally.

A perceived immobility of labour implies the need for wider differentials between occupations and between growing and declining regions and sectors. Thus collective agreements which set rates of pay across labour markets with differing supply and demand conditions have been targeted as a source of rigidity. It could be the case, however, that a more relevant signal to workers is the existence of vacancies in an area. Most evidence suggests that labour immobility is more likely to be a result, rather than a cause, of unemployment (Grahl and Teague, 1989).

The relationship between the extent of labour mobility and the allocative efficiency of the labour market is not straightforward. Frequent job changes involve transaction costs for both workers and employers, but some mobility is obviously necessary if employers are to adjust their labour input to their needs, and if workers are to get the jobs that maximize their income. International comparisons show that there is no optimal amount of labour mobility (OECD, 1986). In the US short tenure jobs are coupled with high employment growth; in Japan good overall employment growth is achieved with lifetime employment. Low external job mobility does not necessarily imply inefficiency, it might be merely a consequence of better matching between employers and employees, and high levels of firm-specific training.

In the second half of the 1970s productivity growth was lower in unionized than in non-union companies. This gap was narrowed, and quite possibly eliminated or even reversed, during the 1980s. Averaged over the 1980s, unionized companies had a superior productivity growth record than their non-union counterparts. Labour productivity has continued to grow rapidly in the 1990s reflecting the sharper fall in employment than output. The differential growth in unionized workplaces in the first part of the 1980s was probably a consequence of changes in work organization. Unionized plants were more likely to have experienced a change in work practices because they were more likely to have had initial restrictions on managerial discretion *vis-à-vis* restrictive practices.

Over the 1980s and 1990s, the productivity performance is probably attributable to the interaction of greater product market competition, high unemployment and a declining power, and a reduced willingness of workers to resist managerial initiatives and changes in work systems. As Metcalf (1993) has emphasized, much of this productivity growth, particularly in unionized workplaces and companies, came from unrepeatable sources. Given this fact, it is arguable that the best hope for further improvements in labour productivity rates lie with greater investment in physical and human capital and a move from adversarial towards cooperative industrial relations.

Trade unions may be a key institutional rigidity in the eyes of neo-liberals, but there is a respectable position to be argued about the possible beneficial effects of unions on productivity. Unions can communicate the preferences of workers directly to management. By voicing worker discontent and establishing job rights according to seniority, quit rates can be reduced, and the incentives for firm-specific training increased. Unions may also provide a channel through which labour can draw management's attention to changes in working methods or production techniques. This argument may be more pertinent in countries where there is consensus in industrial relations. By increasing the economic rewards from employment and by providing mechanisms for grievance expression, unions may directly improve productivity by increasing morale, motivation and effort. These arguments have some empirical support, and they undermine the rationale of flexibility policies which aim to repress the role of trade unions and collective bargaining.

Given the key role ascribed by many to capital accumulation in the growth process, it is not surprising that the impact of the industrial relations system on investment in new technology, process and product innovation, research and development and in human capital, has been a major focus of attention. The theoretical arguments cut both ways. On the one hand, union pressure on pay will cause firms to invest more heavily so as to reduce their need for expensive labour. On the other hand, union presence might lower investment directly or indirectly. The direct effect occurs if unions delay the installation of new machinery or operate inflexible work rules inhibiting the fullest use of the machinery. Any indirect effect is less easy to spot. When a company invests in a new project, unionized workers may capture ('tax') some of the returns in the form of higher pay because, once the capital is installed or the R&D is done, the process cannot easily be reversed, thereby weakening the company's bargaining position.

Any link between unionization and investment, then, cannot be established *a priori*; it is an empirical matter. The evidence, however, is conflicting. Machin and Wadhwani (1991) found a positive relationship between union recognition and the introduction of technical change between 1981 and 1984. They explained this by three factors operating in the early 1980s. First, unionized workplaces had higher pay than non-union workplaces, which directly encouraged greater investment. Second, unionized workplaces experienced more organizational change, particularly the elimination of restrictive practices, than non-union workplaces. These changes frequently went hand-in-hand with more investment. Third, the union 'voice' has a background role in the higher investment via more formalized consultative practices. On the other hand, Denny and Nickell (1992) found, for 1980–84, that union recognition depressed investment, but this was offset as density rose. However, even 100 per cent density did not completely counter the negative recognition effect.

The evidence then is mixed. Cross-section evidence suggests that unionized organizations have a superior investment performance, whilst time-series studies have tended to indicate a depressive effect. However, at worst, one can say that there is no clear evidence that unionization has adversely affected investment in the UK in the 1980s and early 1990s. Moreover, if anything, unionized workplaces use more, and invest more in, advanced capital equipment and human capital than do their non-union equivalents (Metcalf, 1993, 1994).

As regards the latter, Michie and Wilkinson (1994) have argued that low pay, and the resulting labour force instability it creates, are major obstacles to effective training and personnel policies. When unemployment is high the pressure on management is relaxed. When the labour market tightens, firms are reluctant to train because labour turnover is high and potential recruits are reluctant to take training seriously because of the poor job prospects. Entry to low-paying trades is often a last resort, and entrants quit at the first opportunity. Consequently, investment in training shows a poor return to both employer and employees. The tighter labour market of the late 1980s led to a spate of new company policies and collective agreements to improve the relative pay of low-paid and part-time workers, to extend fringe benefits to part-timers, to introduce job evaluation and to train, motivate and involve workers at the lower end of the job hierarchy. However, these reforms were confined to the leading firms and sectors where unions are well-established. The vast majority of low paid workers were not included. Moreover, with the subsequent growth of unemployment, the pressure on firms to improve their personnel policies so as to increase pay, productivity and quality of service receded. In the early 1990s major employers, such as the Burton Group, casualized jobs, cut pay and worsened conditions of work.

Deregulation strategies, of course, could be viewed as an implicit subsidization of low paying firms. Low pay can serve as a substitute for more effective productive and marketing strategies and for new technology. Dependence upon low-paid labour becomes a means by which inefficient producers and obsolete technologies can compete and survive (Deakin and Wilkinson, 1991/2). The presence of a large reserve of flexible labour can discourage competition between firms on the basis of improved production, technology and marketing. In this manner, low wages and low productivity become self-reinforcing. Strong unions, on the other hand, provide incentives to employers to find other means of flexibility than simply trying to expand the pool of low-security–low skill–low-paid jobs.

If the empirical evidence on unionization and investment is not uniform, then that on trade unions and profitability is. All the major relevant studies show a significant negative association between unionization and financial performance or profitability in the UK (Metcalf, 1994). The implications of this, however, are not so clear cut. On the one hand, if this is purely a distributional matter then, depending on one's viewpoint, this could be seen as a satisfactory redistribution of income from capital to labour. On the other hand, if the lower profitability results in less investment in R&D and in physical and human capital, this will damage the dynamic prospects of the company, and would tend to worsen job creation and retard economic performance.

The evidence is far from conclusive, but there are some indications that the implications for long-run economic performance are not significant. This seems to be the case where unions are simply creaming off some of the firms' supernormal profits in the form of higher pay. It also appears that this link between unionization and financial performance became weaker as the 1980s progressed (Metcalf, 1993).

THE SOCIAL CONSEQUENCES OF FLEXIBILITY

The moves towards flexibility in the UK labour market seem to have produced the marked rises in inequality that have been observed for some time in the US. Blanchflower and Freeman's work (1994) indicates: a general increase in inequality of earnings; greater regional and industrial earnings differentials for nominally similar workers; and that most of the rise in earnings inequality occurred for workers with similar measured skills – which is not what we would expect from a better functioning labour market.

Over the 1980s and 1990s, earnings of the higher paid have increased more rapidly than those of the lower paid, and the growth of non-manual pay has outstripped that of manual workers. At the lowest decile for manual males, the increase in real pay from 1979 to 1992 was 4 per cent, while at the highest decile for non-manual it was 53 per cent. For females these increases were 10 per cent and 60 per cent respectively. This change in the structure of earnings, Michie and Wilkinson (1994) have argued, can be explained by three main factors. First, the decline in employment in manufacturing was mainly concentrated in the middle range of the earnings distribution. Second, the increase in employment was concentrated in sectors such as banking, insurance, finance and business, where earnings are relatively high, and in hotel, catering and other such services, where earnings tend to be low. The disappearance of jobs from the middle of the earnings distribution and the increase at each end would explain at least part of the widening of the earnings distribution. Third, there was a tendency for the earnings of the relatively higher paid to grow rapidly and those of the low paid to increase relatively slowly.

It is generally accepted that trade unions are likely to be associated with more compressed wage structures. The pay distribution is less dispersed for union than for non-union workers. The decline of union strength has been associated with a huge increase in pay inequality among both individuals and workplaces between 1980 and 1990. The decline in the share of plants with recognized unions accounts for a fifth of the coincident rise in earnings inequality.

Work on the US has found that 21 per cent of the 1978–88 rise in the standard deviation of log earnings can be attributed to falling union density (Gregg and Machin, 1994). Gosling and Machin (1993) explored this issue for the UK. In 1980 the standard deviation of the log real semi-skilled earnings was 0.028 (or 10.2 per cent of the non-union mean) lower in unionized plants. By 1990 this gap had widened to 0.066. These results come about from a rise in inequality in both the union and non-union sectors, but the rise is much larger in the non-union sector. The impact of the decline in unionization amounts to 18 per cent of the 1980–90 rise in the variance of semi-skilled earnings or wage inequality.

UK governments have added to the regressive effects of their labour market policies on the income distribution by their tax and social welfare policies. The elimination of higher rate tax brackets, the change towards indirect taxation, and increases in national insurance contributions have favoured the rich. Meanwhile there have been cuts in social benefits, and a tightening of eligibility criteria. In 1989, social benefits were a smaller proportion of GDP than in 1979, despite an increase in the number of pensioners of around one million, a similar increase in those without work and claiming benefits and an increase in the recipients of family credit of 250 000. Redistribution has therefore been from the poor to the rich, and within different categories of the poor. Between 1979 and 1989, the share of household income of the bottom two-fifths fell from 24 per cent to 19 per cent, while that of the top two-fifths increased from 58 per cent to 64 per cent (Michie and Wilkinson, 1994).

Furthermore, in the UK the Wages Councils used to provide a system of minimum wages. The ratio of the minimum to the average wage in the Wages Councils sectors, however, declined during the 1980s, from over 0.8 to around 0.65, reflecting a failure to uprate minimum wages in line with average pay in these sectors. The standard deviation of log hourly earnings in the Wages Councils sectors, a measure of wage dispersion, clearly rose through the decade. Machin and Manning (1992) regressed this measure on the log of the minimum/average wage ratio, and found this coefficient to be significantly negative. This variable can account for somewhere between 9 per cent and 20 per cent of the rise in dispersion amongst these low pay sectors over the period 1979–90. Despite the problems of governmental interference, declining numbers of wage inspectors, and continuing difficulties in transmitting information to covered workers, the repeal of the last remaining 26 Wage Councils by the 1993 Employment Rights and Trade Union Reform Act seems destined to further erode the economic position of the most economically vulnerable members of the employed workforce, and to further exacerbate existing inequalities.

As has been extensively commented upon, much of the employment creation of recent times has taken the form of part-time, and other atypical, jobs. For example, according to recent Labour Force Survey (1995) figures, 550 000 new jobs were created in the UK between spring 1993 and autumn 1995. Of these fully 60 per cent were part-time. Significantly, however, given that 85 per cent of part-timers are female, half the increase in part-time work was taken by males, many perhaps trying to both acquire work experience and to find a way into full-time employment. However, the more casual and insecure low paid employment becomes, the greater the difficulties faced by those who are either fully or partially unemployed in finding a permanent route back into full-time employment (Deakin and Wilkinson, 1991/2). An expansion of part-time work has not been sufficient to meet the employment needs of the UK.

Moreover, government policy has clearly changed the environment in which part-timers work. For example, the abolition of Wages Councils referred to above has meant that more part-time workers earn beneath the threshold for paying national insurance contributions, thereby undermining their future benefit entitlement. Part-timers employed by subcontracted firms in privatized sectors of the economy have found themselves getting lower rates of pay than they received for doing equivalent work in the public sector, with worse terms and conditions of employment. There has been a reduction in the extent of national industry-wide pay agreements, which may previously have set a floor to wages paid to part-time (largely female) workers. Certainly a statistical analysis of 13 OECD countries has indicated that centralized wage fixing arrangements seem to be strongly associated with high relative earnings for women (Whitehouse, 1992). It seems clear then, that this changing labour market environment has left women vulnerable to the expansion of low paid and unregulated employment. Labour market deregulation seems to have been based on a competitive and job-enhancing strategy of lower wage costs. Such a strategy naturally has had a differential impact on low-income female part-time workers.

As Freeman (1995) points out, the social costs of flexibility can be high. In the US, increased wage flexibility has meant sharply rising inequality and falling earnings for the lowest paid. By the early 1990s low paid American workers received less in purchasing parity terms than low-paid European workers, and poverty has risen, especially among younger families with children. Falling wages for the less skilled, however, did not lead to increases in their employment or working hours. The US may have had a lower rate of unemployment than Europe in the decade since the early 1980s, but the social costs in terms of falling living standards, worsening income inequalities and rises in crime have been great, and the US has still not resolved the employment problems of the unskilled.

Similar problems and ironies clearly exist in the UK also. For example, families on benefits have no incentive to take part-time, low-paid and insecure work, and 'entry jobs' are increasingly taken by those with a working partner. The bizarre and unwanted consequence is an increase in the numbers of families dependent on welfare support simultaneous with a growth in those with two or more earners. Long-run poverty among families effectively denied access to earned income proceeds apace with a form of job creation apparently decreasingly effective in reducing the unemployment count and with increasing inequality of labour incomes (Gregg and Wadsworth, 1995).

CONCLUSION

Overall, although not uniformly, labour flexibility has increased (Beatson, 1995; ACAS, 1988). The labour market in the UK has become more flexible in a number of ways. The membership and power of trade unions has been significantly reduced, less than half of employees now have their pay determined by collective bargaining, wage determination has become more decentralized, employment levels may have become more sensitive to demand conditions in the 1980s and 1990s, some increase in functional flexibility has taken place; part-time work and self-employment have increased, UK employers face relatively few legislative constraints compared to their rivals. However, has there been a transformation in economic performance? The Thatcherite reforms succeeded in their goals of weakening union power and they may have marginally increased employment (via the creation of part-time jobs) and wage responsiveness to market conditions and they may have increased self-employment. However, the reforms failed to increase the responsiveness of real wages to unemployment. They were associated with a slower transition from non-employment to employment for men. There was a devastating loss in full-time jobs for male workers and they produced substantial increases in wage inequality that are hard to justify on the grounds of improved competitiveness.

If one accepts that the liberalization policies have not produced widespread improvements in economic performance, then two very different conclusions can be drawn. One interpretation has been that the Thatcherite policies did not go far enough and/or they did not have sufficient time to succeed. As we approach the end of 1996, however, we still await the 'economic miracle'. The other interpretation is that the reforms were based on an incorrect understanding of how the labour market operates. In particular, the reform package failed to recognize the power of insider pressures for rent-sharing and related policies that segment decentralized labour markets in periods of less than full employment. From this perspective, reforms that liberalize markets may require exceptionally tight labour markets to succeed. Blanchflower and Freeman's (1994) interesting and controversial view is that the Thatcher reforms might have done wonders in the 1950s and 1960s, but could not deliver their promised results in the 1980s and 1990s because of the high rate of unemployment. This hypothesis suggests that the success of market-enhancing policy reforms does not depend solely on the reforms themselves, but also on the broader economic environment. It also implies that in a world subject to business cycle and other fluctuations, placing all of one's eggs in the decentralized labour market of competitive theory may be far from ideal.

The deregulation strategy has suggested attacks on trade unions and collective bargaining and, where the latter exists, changing its form to make it more related to local conditions. However, as has been seen, the links between unions, investment and productivity are complex and, at the least, the evidence is not unequivocally supportive of the neoclassical case. Furthermore, Freeman (1995) and Gregg and Wadsworth's (1995) work raises major questions about the social acceptability of the whole approach.

Moreover, in this context it is worth reflecting on the logic of the flexibility strategy. Is it really the best way forward to further cut and limit benefit entitlement so that families on benefit take the low-paid, insecure part-time jobs on offer? Also what about the overall implication of using unemployment as a disciplinary device whilst at the same time worsening the trade-off between unemployment and inflation?

As we have seen, the break-up of the traditional system of industrial relations has seen fewer workers covered by collective agreement, more decentralized bargaining, and pay increasingly sensitive to individual and workplace performance and local labour market conditions. In terms of the transformation of pay-setting institutions then, the government achieved virtually all it set out to do, yet unemployment rose to a post-war high. As Metcalf (1994) has argued, there seem to be two possibilities here. Either the government was wrong concerning the link between pay-setting institutions and employment outcomes, in which case the emphasis on individual and company performance and the undermining of collective organization should be reversed. Or, alternatively, the government got it right about pay-setting institutions. This, however, would seem to cast major doubts on macroeconomic policy during the Thatcher period. After all, extremely high unemployment rates are not normally taken to be a criterion of economic success, let alone compelling evidence of an 'economic miracle'.

As Metcalf (1993) concluded in his survey of the relationship between industrial relations and economic performance, surely we can come up with a better system of industrial relations and collective bargaining than one that requires excessively high levels of unemployment to get wage inflation under control?

There has by no means been a blanket acceptance of the prescriptions of the flexibility thesis across Europe. Even the OECD has counselled caution, noting that public policy needs to steer a middle course, one which avoids having an adverse effect on efforts to improve skills, redesign jobs, and redeploy workers within an enterprise; and which also avoids causing further segmentation of the labour force between those with secure career employment and those with casual dead-end jobs (OECD, 1990) .

The UK has had the only government fully committed to the prescriptions of this type of flexibility thesis, and consequently has implemented a full assault on industrial relations, labour market institutions, employment legislation, and the EU Working Hours Directive (with its unacceptable rigidities of 48-hour weeks and paid holidays). This blind acceptance of the doctrines of the flexibility thesis ignores the fact that many such labour market institutions were set up to protect labour from exploitation and are essential if workers are to preserve acceptable standards of living and working conditions. Moves to increase labour flexibility in this way are unlikely to be in the best interests of working people and suggest increased conflict and confrontation.

Neoclassical based pro-flexibility views, in fact, are simplistic and ignore the fact that certain 'institutional rigidities' are essential to the working of markets (Neilson, 1991). They are needed to reduce uncertainty, guide expectations and generate a necessary minimum of trust (Hodgson, 1988). Flexibility in some areas requires stability ('rigidity') in others. The experience of corporatist economies such as Sweden and Austria in the 1970s and 1980s provides convincing support for this thesis, as does that of Japan, since much of Japanese success has been based on 'flexible rigidities' (Dore, 1986).

NOTES

1. The author wishes to acknowledge the research assistance provided by Nicola Allison (then of UEL) the preparation of an earlier draft of this chapter.
2. There are of course, a number of other flexibility theses, most notably those concerning the flexible firm and flexible specialization. No discussion of these is offered in this chapter.

REFERENCES

Akerlof, G.A. and J.L. Yellen (eds) (1986), *Efficiency Wage Models of the Labour Market*, Cambridge: Cambridge University Press.

Akerlof, G.A. and J.L. Yellen (1990), 'The fair wage-effort hypothesis and unemployment', *Quarterly Journal of Economics*, **105** (2), 255–83.

Anderton, B. and K. Mayhew (1994), 'Comparative analysis of the UK labour market', ch. 1 in R. Barrell (ed.), *The UK Labour Market: Comparative Aspects and Institutional Developments* NIESR, Glasgow, Cambridge: Cambridge University Press, 15–50.

Advisory Conciliation and Arbitration Service (ACAS) (1988), *Labour Flexibility in Britain: The 1987 ACAS Survey*, Occasional Paper no. 41, London: ACAS.

Beatson, M. (1995), *Labour Market Flexibility*, Employment Department Research Series, no. 108.

Bentolila, S. and J. Dolado (1994), Labour flexibility and wages: lessons from Spain', *Economic Policy*, **18**, April, 53–99.

Bentolila, S. and G. St-Paul (1992), 'The macroeconomic impact of flexible labour contracts, with an application to Spain', *European Economic Review*, **36** (5), 1013–47.

Blanchflower, D.G. and R.B. Freeman (1994), 'Did the Thatcher reforms change British labour market performance?', ch. 2 in R. Barrell (ed.), *The UK Labour Market*, Cambridge: Cambridge University Press, 51–92.

Deakin, S. and F. Wilkinson (1991/2), 'Social policy and economic efficiency: The deregulation of the labour market in Britain', *Critical Social Policy*, **33**, 40–61.

Denny, K. and S. Nickell (1992), 'Unions and investment in British manufacturing industry', *British Journal of Industrial Relations*, **29** (1), 113–22.

Dore, R. (1986), *Flexible Rigidities: Industrial Policy and Structural Adjustment in the Japanese Economy 1970–1980*, London: Athione Press.

Freeman, R. (1995), 'The limits of wage flexibility to curing unemployment', *Oxford Review of Economic Policy*, **11** (1), 63–72.

Gosling, A. and S. Machin (1993), 'Trade unions and the dispersion of earnings in UK establishments, 1980–90', Centre for Economic Performance, London School of Economics, no. 140.

Grahl, J. and P. Teague (1989), 'Labour market flexibility in West Germany, Britain and France', *West European Politics*, **12** (2), 91–111.

Gregg, P. and S. Machin (1994), 'Is the UK rise in inequality different?', ch. 3 in R. Barrell (ed.), *The UK Labour Market*, Cambridge: Cambridge University Press, 93–125.

Gregg, P. and J. Wadsworth (1995), 'A short history of labour turnover, job tenure, and job security, 1975–93', *Oxford Review of Economic Policy*, **11** (1), 73–90.

Hodgson, G.M. (1988), *Economics and Institutions*, London: Polity Press.

Holmlund, B. and J. Zetterberg (1991), 'Insider effects in wage determination: evidence from five countries', *European Economic Review*, **35** (5), 1009–34.

Machin, S. and A. Manning (1992), 'Minimum wages, wage dispersion and employment: evidence from the UK wages councils', Centre for Economic Performance, London School of Economics, no. 80.

Machin, S. and S. Wadhwani (1991), 'The effects of unions on investment and innovation: evidence from WIRS', *Economic Journal*, **101**, 324–30.

Metcalf, D. (1993), 'Industrial relations and economic performance', *British Journal of Industrial Relations*, **31** (2), 255–83.

Metcalf, D. (1994), 'Transformation of British industrial relations? Institutions, conduct and outcomes 1980–90', ch. 4 in R. Barrell (ed.), *The UK Labour Market*, Cambridge: Cambridge University Press, 126–57.

Michie, J. and F. Wilkinson (1994), 'The growth of unemployment in the 1980s', ch. 1 in J. Michie and J. Grieve Smith (eds), *Unemployment in Europe*, London: Academic Press, 11–31.

Nielson, K. (1991), 'Learning to manage the supply-side: flexibility and stability in Denmark', ch. 15 in B. Jessop, H. Kastendiek, K. Nielson and O.K. Pederson (eds), *The Politics of Flexibility: Restructuring State and Industry in Britain, Germany and Scandinavia*, Aldershot: Edward Elgar, 282–313.

Olson M. (1982), *The Rise and Decline of Nations*, New Haven: Yale University Press.

Organisation for Economic Co-operation and Development (OECD) (1986), *Flexibility in the Labour Market – The Current Debate*, Paris: OECD.

Organisation for Economic Co-operation and Development (OECD) (1990), *Labour Market Policies for the 1990s*, Paris: OECD.

Standing G. (1986), *Unemployment and labour market flexibility: The United Kingdom*, ILO: Geneva.

Whitehouse, G.(1992), 'Legislation and labour market gender inequality: an analysis of OECD countries', *Work, Employment and Society*, **6** (1), 65–86.

3. Firms' strategies and cooperative games: elements of a stakeholding approach[1]

Robin Matthews

INTRODUCTION

Maurice Peston and Bernard Corry are distinguished not only by their achievements as scholars and teachers, but by making government and organizations more effective. The list of their achievements is long. A small but significant part of both their careers was their work in shaping economics and business courses in polytechnics. They saw that, for the most part, the difference between these institutions, founded by the Labour Government in the mid 1960s, and the universities of the time, was one of social class rather than quality and where this was not the case they sought to remedy the situation. But entry barriers are continuously resurrected. Corroborating Ricardo, revival currently takes the form of a putative super league, supported most vociferously by the most marginal members who stand to gain the least economic rent: but the effort of Peston and Corry has created effective competition for any such cartel.

Misapplication of economic theory has become almost sacred in governments and organizations. To doubt the efficacy of market solutions always and everywhere has become heresy. Impervious to standard textbook analysis of international trade, competitiveness has become a goal in itself, manifested in *downsizing, reengineering, lean manufacturing* and *core businesses*. Metaphor has become a substitute for analysis. Who can contradict these tropes except by advocating their implicit opposites, *overgrown, disintegrating, obese*, and *focusing upon the unessential*? This paper develops one aspect that is implicit in the approach of Maurice Peston and Bernard Corry: organizations, which include governments as well as firms, in the public and the private sector, have multiple objectives, and their achievement is determined, and should be judged by, the distribution as well as the size of their payoffs. Stakeholding is substituted for competitiveness and its foundations are sought.

In this chapter decision making in firms is analysed through the application of cooperative games. The aim is to examine the effect of different specifications of the utility functions of decision makers on the realization of potential payoffs. Payoffs are interpreted as rents that can be distributed among stakeholders as transferable, but not necessarily monetary, utilities. A number of related questions are posed: *Of the profile of possible strategies, which are likely to occur? Will they result in the realization of potential payoffs? What actions can the firm adopt to increase the possibility of potential payoffs being achieved?*

In a cooperative game the set of decision makers includes not only managers and workers, but also other stakeholders; stockholders, alliance partners, creditors and the community in general. The outcome is a specification of the coalitions that are formed. In contrast to noncooperative games which focus on individuals as the primitives, the focus of cooperative games is upon coalitions and the joint actions that they take. Actions are taken by coalitions, but they emanate from the preferences of individual members with respect to the set of expected consequences. The division of payoffs between stakeholders is at least as significant as their absolute size since the utility functions of the multiple decision makers in the firm determine outcomes.

Plan of the Chapter

The chapter is organized as follows: the first section sets out a general payoff function and describes the alternative specifications of transferable utility that are used; in the second section the strategy of the firm is specified as a cooperative game; in the third, solution and efficiency concepts, Nash equilibrium, Shapley values and the core are described; the fourth part discusses the effect of different specifications of transferable utility. In conclusion, wider aspects of stakeholding are outlined.

Although the approach is novel, it has a number of related foundations in the history of thought: (i) the theory of the firm (Holmstrom and Tirole, 1989; Tirole, 1990; Conner, 1991), especially the dichotomy between firms and markets (Coase, 1937; Penrose, 1959; Richardson, 1996), and governance (Williamson, 1970, 1975; Hart, 1996); (ii) linear economic models (Koopmans, 1951; Dorfmann, Samuelson and Solow, 1958; Gale, 1960); and (iii) cooperative games (von Neumann and Morgenstern, 1944; Myerson, 1991; Moulin, 1988; Aumann, 1989). The literature on stakeholding is extensive (Crossland, 1956; Kay and Silberston, 1995; Hutton, 1995; Gamble and Kelly, 1996; Coates, 1996; Minns, 1996; Mandleson and Liddle, 1996).

THE STRATEGIC PAYOFF FUNCTION AND UTILITY

The firm is treated as a cooperative game with N agents or decision makers. Any subset of N is a coalition, and there are 2^N such coalitions. Agents include all stakeholders; workers managers, customers and stockholders. To each coalition,

$C, T, \subseteq N$, is associated a single number, or payoff, $Z(C)$, that is available to the group. Payoffs are transferable and can be measured in money, or in psychic terms (quality of life, security, a good environment) and distributed to stakeholders as transferable utilities.

Payoffs

In any period the determinants of total payoffs, Z, viewed as potential rather than actual values (hence the inequality), can be expressed as

$$Z \leq \{[P], [\theta_S], [\theta_{-S}]_{\text{all } S \in N}; [A], [N], [C]; [H], [E], [\Omega]\} \tag{3.1}$$

The function can be divided into three sets of related variables:

1. *decision variables*: θ_S, and θ_{-S}, are decisions and actions reflecting expected utilities in the preference relation $[P]$. θ_S refers to decisions taken by S, an individual or group, and θ_{-S} those of others, $-S$. Corporate culture and mission are located in the domain of decision variables. They influence *activity variables*, and their impact is conditioned by *environmental variables*.
2. *activity variables*: $[A]$, $[N]$, and $[C]$, respectively, denote value adding activities, their number, and the coalitional structure of an entire economy or an organization. $[A]$ is a matrix of activities which corresponds to the production functions or value chains of firms, that generate payoffs. The number of activities, $[N]$, describes the size, and scope of the economy, or organization. The way in which basic activities are grouped into firms or partitions within firms is described by $[C]$. Joint actions taken by coalition members determine the size and division of payoffs.
3. *environmental variables*: these are summarized by $[E]$, $[H]$, and $[\Omega]$. $[E]$ denotes expectations about the external environment, $[H]$ is an irreversible state variable reflecting the history and path dependence of the system. $[\Omega]$ is a stochastic factor, incorporating shocks, or noise, emphasizing the non-deterministic nature of expression (3.1).

The payoff function can be described as an open text, in contrast to many of the partial and deterministic models developed in strategy, which focus on a restricted set of relationships, and assume an unbroken chain of cause and effect. The payoff function is seen as a network of interrelationships. Strategies are formed interactively at many levels; whole economies, organizations, divisions within organizations, business units within divisions, and so on. Organizations rise and fall, and are continually revised and recombined as a result of competition, integration, and coordination. Learning and adaptation results in the emergence of new industries and products, and the development of new niches.

Three Types of Utility

Preferences [*P*], the product of the utility of outcomes, and the subjective probabilities of their occurrence, express agents' expected transferable utilities. Motivation for decisions is determined by preferences. Consider three types of utility: (i) *instrumental*, (ii) *conditional*, and (iii) *symbolic*. The discussion develops the ideas of Nozick (1995).

Instrumental utilities

Instrumental utilities relate strategic actions directly to expected payoffs, and are the product of the utility associated with the outcome, and the subjective probability of it occurring. Expected payoffs are not influenced by the choice of action itself. Instrumental utility, expected by decision maker *S*, depends only upon the subjective probability *S* attaches to a set of particular outcomes, and is independent of any action that another agent, –*S*, may take. If θ_S is an action taken by agent *S* having *M* possible outcomes O_m, expected instrumental utility is,

Definition (expected instrumental utility): $\mathrm{EIU}(\theta_S) = \Sigma_{(m \in M)} \text{prob}\,(O_m)\, U(O_m)$. (3.2)

Expected conditional utility

Expected conditional utility reflects strength of belief in outcomes. It describes a conjecture by *S* that the probability distribution of outcomes can be influenced by the decisions, θ_S, that she takes. Expected conditional payoffs are the product of the utility associated with a particular outcome, and the subjective conditional probability of that outcome occurring. Suppose, to use an illustration taken up later in the paper, that mutual gains from cooperative behaviour are to be had, and *S* conjectures that the probability of cooperative action by (–*S*) is increased if she demonstrates the desire to cooperate by her own actions: suppose also that she believes that faced with similar alternates he (–*S*) will act similarly. Expected conditional utility, $\mathrm{ECU}(\theta_S)$, is,

Definition (expected conditional utility): $\mathrm{ECU}(\theta_S) = \Sigma_{(m \in M)} \text{prob}\,(O_m \mid \theta_S)\, U(O_m)$ (3.3)

Symbolic utilities

Symbolic utilities arise when a probable outcome of an action is associated with another outcome to which the individual attaches utility. *S* may cooperate for a number of reasons; perhaps she attaches utility to having a reputation for being a trustworthy partner, making a prestigious product, or being associated with a charismatic leader, or a worthwhile objective. Expected symbolic utility, $\text{ERU}(\theta_S)$, is

$$\textit{Definition (expected symbolic utility)}: \text{ERU}(\theta_S) = \Sigma_{(m \in M)} \text{prob}\,(O_m)\, U(O_m + R) \quad (3.4)$$

where R is the event that agent S associates with outcome O_m.

High-powered market-like incentive schemes are often destructive of cooperation and learning in organizations, (Teece and Pisano, 1994), so in their stead, the importance of culture and mission is stressed. The culture of an organization is characterized by the probabilities of particular types of behaviour and the strength of belief that members have about the likelihood of their occurring. Instrumental utility implies that S imagines the probabilities of another's behaviour are unaffected by her own choices: actions by $-S$ are unaffected by the decisions of S and vice versa. In the scenario of expected conditional utility the likelihood of a cooperative outcome seen from the point of view of S is determined by her own choices. Furthermore S may believe that she can increase the probability of cooperative behaviour on the part of others by demonstrating cooperative behaviour herself. Conditional utility suggests *reciprocity* in decision making: S chooses an action based on her beliefs about the actions of other players. The concept of symbolic utility is connected with the notion of a corporate mission. Mission statements, however banal they may appear in practice, reflect attempts to link corporate objectives with outcomes that are *significant* to the individual. *Reciprocity* and *significance* are important features of stakeholding.

THE FIRM AS A COOPERATIVE GAME

Consider a firm, or any organization for that matter, that has N agents. Agent is a general term that may correspond to key decision makers acting as individuals, or as members of a subset or coalition, C. Coalitions may be thought of as business units, or reporting centres, or functional areas, or as groups of stakeholders who share the firm's payoffs. Payoffs are transferable utilities or rents that are created by agents; (i) as individuals creating value themselves, which accrue to themselves, a_{ij} $(i = j)$, and (ii) as interdependent entities who generate synergies, a_{ij} $(i \neq j)$. The problem of interdependence is simplified by viewing agents as producing joint outputs, those that have value in themselves, and those which create value in others. The total value created by a coalition is $Z(C)$, and by a grand coalition of all agents, $Z(N)$.

$$Z(C) \leq \Sigma_{(i,j \in C)} a_{ij} \text{ all } C \subseteq N. \tag{3.5}$$
$$a_{ij} \geq 0 \text{ all } i,j.$$

The Activity Matrix

The term activity roughly corresponds to a process, defined for example as 'a collection of linked activities that take one or more input and creates an output of value to the customer' (Hammer and Champy, 1993, p. 35): activities are discrete sets of value chains that can be linked to the rest of the organization by coalition behaviour.

The organization is illustrated as an activity matrix in Figures 3.1(a), and 3.1(b). Payoffs to the grand coalition in 3.1(a) are 10, ($z\{1,2\} = 10$). Payoffs to single member coalitions, ($z\{1\} = 2$, $z\{2\} = 2$), are *security levels*, assumed to be the lowest that can be forced on individual agents: $z(\varnothing) = 0$.

Interdependence is two way: one activity potentially creates value in others: similarly, it permits other businesses to create value. This might be described as the yin and yang of business synergy: neither would be possible if the organization were *unbundled*, or partitioned in such a way that businesses were effectively isolated. In the organization matrix, synergies are off diagonal elements ($s \neq i$, $s \neq j$): inward synergies, a_{is}, are the contributions to value added in business s by other activities in the coalition C, and outward synergies, a_{sj}, the contribution of s to other businesses. Total synergy in activity s is the sum of the two:

$$\sigma^s = \Sigma_{(i,s \in C)} a_{is} + \Sigma_{(j,s \in C)} a_{sj} \quad \text{all } C \subseteq N,\ i,j \neq s. \tag{3.6}$$

The marginal contribution of a business is its value as a stand alone unit, a_{ss}, plus the value of inward and outward synergies within a coalition:

3	2
2	3

(a)

4	9	2
3	5	7
8	1	6

(b)

Figure 3.1 Activity matrices

$$m(a^s) = \Sigma_{(i,s\in C)} a_{is} + \Sigma_{(j,s\in C)} a_{sj} + a_{ss} \quad \text{all } C \subseteq N,\ i,j \neq s. \tag{3.7}$$

In Figure 3.1(b), synergies created by activities one two and three to the matrix as a whole (the grand coalition) are (22, 20, 18) respectively, and the marginal value of each activity to the grand coalition is (26, 25, 24). In economic terms the marginal value of an activity is its contribution to economic rent of a particular coalition; the difference to the rental of a coalition if it were withdrawn from the coalition. Thus in Figure 3.1(a), the marginal contribution of each activity as a one agent coalition is $z\{1\} - z\{\varnothing\} = 3$, and $z\{2\} - z\{\varnothing\} = 3$, and a two-agent coalition marginal contribution are, $z\{1,2,\} - z\{1\} = 8$, $z\{1,2\} - z\{2\} = 8$: synergies created by each activity are 2.

The significance of treating synergies as joint outputs should be noted. Suppose every activity or coalition of activities is increased by a scalar, $\lambda > 0$, then its rental is increased by $\lambda\, Z(C)$: there are constant returns to each coalition (*linearity*). Equally, when activities, or coalitions are linked, there may be increasing or diminishing returns to cooperation. Following Arrow's treatment of externalities (1969), the organization matrix encompasses a subtle distinction, between constant returns (additivity and divisibility of payoffs) to particular activities or coalitions, and the possibility of increasing returns, or superadditivity (if synergies are positive), when they are combined.

Generalization

The organization matrix can be extended as a metaphor to whole economies, or even sets of economies, and the economic process seen as one of forming and reforming coalitions. The value of the whole, $Z(W)$, becomes the sum of these contributions:

$$Z(W) \leq \Sigma_{(i,j \in N)}\, a_{ij}. \tag{3.8}$$

N is large, and so therefore is the number of potential coalitions. A snapshot is an apposite description of inequality (3.8). Coalition behaviour is not random though: it is conditioned by cultural factors expressed in the utility functions specified above.

The given conditions illustrated in the payoff function, that underlie the organization matrix, form a landscape. The metaphor can be extended in evolutionary terms which resembles Kauffman's exposition of Boolean networks (Kauffman, 1993, 1995). Evolution means the formation of coalitions of increasing economic value or rent – a rugged fitness landscape, in which hills are created by synergies when they are positive and chasms when they are negative. Radical improvements are easier at first, but later longer jumps are necessary across the matrix if improvements are to happen. Major advances become more difficult, and waiting times increase, as bigger efforts are required to reach more distant optima. The landscape itself is rarely static since elements in the payoff function are ever changing. So the game is seldom repeated exactly.

Convexity

Activity matrices which satisfy the condition that the bigger the coalition joined by an activity, the bigger the contribution, are described as convex: there are increasing returns to cooperation. Both matrices in Figure 3.1 exemplify convex organizations. The structure of the firm, considered as a cooperative game, is convex if the larger the coalition that agent S joins, the larger his, or her, marginal contribution. For any two coalitions, C and T, in an organization with N agents, convexity implies that for all $C, T \subset N \backslash \{s\}$,

$$C \subset T \Rightarrow Z(C) \cup \{s\} - Z\{C\} \leq Z(T) \cup \{s\} - Z(T). \tag{3.9}$$

Marginal contributions in Figure 3.1(a) have been illustrated and values for successively larger coalitions in the three-agent matrix in 3.1(b) are calculated above, and can be seen to increase as coalition size increases. If the nature of the cooperative game in the firm is described in terms of an activity matrix, a sufficient but not necessary condition for convexity is that all elements in the matrix be non-negative.[2]

Transforming the Activity Matrix into a Cooperative Game

Figure 3.2(a) represents the transformation of the data in Figure 3.1(a) into a cooperative game: players have the alternative of forming single member or two member coalitions. Joint cooperation (C,C) leads to payoffs (5,5); cooperation by just one player (C,D), or (D,C), leads to payoffs (3,5), and (5,3), respectively; joint failure to do so (D,D), to (3,3).

Non-cooperative outcomes result in inefficiency in the sense of failure to realize potential value added. Having no costs of forming coalitions, the game in 3.2(a) has no dominant strategy: each player is indifferent between cooperation, (C), and non cooperation, (D). Suppose generating gains from cooperation incurs costs that are borne by the player generating synergies. Neither security levels, nor benefits from mutual cooperation are changed by the introduction of transactions costs, but their inclusion transforms the game into a *prisoners dilemma*, since unreciprocated cooperation brings greatest net benefits. In Figure 3.2(b), transactions costs are 2, giving payoffs, (5,5) = (3 + 4 – 2, 3 + 4 – 2) to cooperation: but assuming that all costs are borne by the *donor*, higher payoffs accrue to a coalition member who receives benefits but does not incur the costs of creating them: (C,D) = (3 – 2, 3 + 4) = (1,7), and (D,C) = (7,1). Transactions costs are 2 so that net synergy benefits of 2 requires a gross benefit of 4. In Figure 3.2(c) a more extreme set of costs (5) and benefits (7) is illustrated. In general terms, A_{ST} and A_{TS}, the off diagonal elements in 3.1(a), are the difference between expected gross benefits (b_{ST} and b_{ST} respectively), and costs (c_S and c_S respectively): $A_{ST} = b_{ST} - c_S$ and $A_{TS} = b_{TS} - c_T$, where the expressions on the right hand side, are found in Figure 3.2(d). Costs and benefits are assumed to be symmetric, so $b_{ST} = b_{TS}$ and $c_S = c_T$. Referring to

	C	D
C	5,5	3,5
D	5,3	3,3

(a)

	C	D
C	5,5	1,7
D	7,1	3,3

(b)

	C	D
C	5,5	–2,10
D	10,–2	3,3

(c)

	C	D
C	Security payoffs (*S*, –*S*) plus cooperative gains minus transactions costs $(A_S + b_{TS} - c_S) = A_{SS}$ $(A_T + b_{ST} - c_T) = A_{TT}$	*S*'s security payoffs minus *S*'s transactions costs $(A_S - c_S)$ *T*'s (that is, –*S*) security payoffs plus cooperative gains from *S* $(A_T + b_{ST})$
D	*S*'s security payoffs plus cooperative gains from *T* $(A_S + b_{TS})$ *T*'s (that is, –*S*) security payoffs minus *T*'s transactions costs $(A_T - c_T)$	Security payoffs (*S*, –*S*) (A_S) (A_T)

(d)

Figure 3.2 Cooperative games

off-diagonal elements in Figure 3.1(c) to Figure 3.2(c), we have, $A_{ST} = b_{ST} - c_S = A_{TS} = b_{TS} - c_T = 7 - 5$. Note that given positive transaction costs, $(A_S + b_{TS} - c_S) < (A_S + b_{TS})$ and $(A_S) > (A_S - c_S)$, so under the assumptions the game takes a prisoners' dilemma form.[3]

It is assumed in making the transformation from the activity matrix to a cooperative game that neither player can be forced below his or her stand alone value (the minimum security level), if they fail to cooperate. The area XKY in Figure 3.3 describes the set of feasible solutions, given the minimum security level assumption: so in the case of mutual cooperation, if payoffs are realized, feasible payoffs lie on the line segment XY. Equal distribution of payoffs is illustrated by the line OV: an increase or decrease in the slope of this line symbolizes a distribution of payoffs in favour of one player or the other.

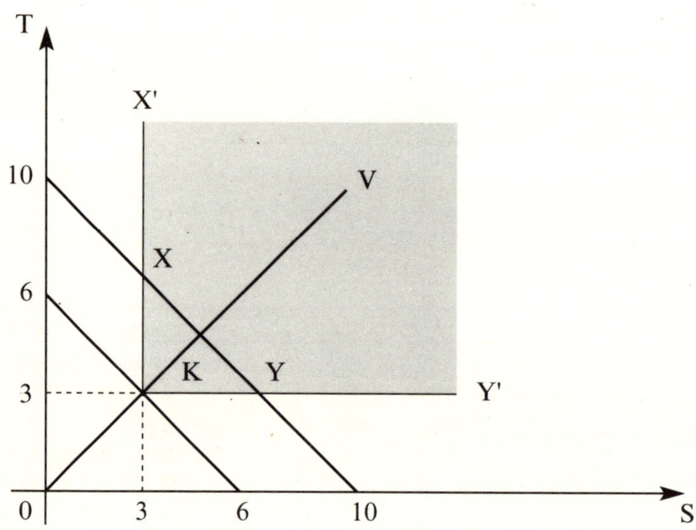

Figure 3.3 Illustrating a two activity game

UTILITY AND THE REALIZATION OF THE FIRMS' PAYOFFS

This section begins by describing the significance of different specifications of transferable utility for three equilibrium concepts, Nash equilibrium, Shapley value, and the core, for the efficiency of coalitions, defined by their capacity to realize potential payoffs. *Will payoffs, illustrated in Figure 3.1, be realized? Do security levels alone determine Z*? The argument, throughout the section refers to a convex game, as defined in (3.9).

Solution Concepts

Nash equilibrium is the best known and most frequently used solution concept in game theory: it describes a situation in which no single player can obtain a higher payoff by changing his or her strategies, provided no other player changes theirs. Define a strategy selection by s as θ_s, and for other players as θ_{-s}, and a profile of k (i = 1, ..., k) possible strategies, $(\theta^s_i, ..., \theta^s_{i-1}, \theta^{s'}_i, \theta^{s'}_{i+1}, ..., \theta^s_k) = \theta_k$, for each of the s players. $A^{s'}$ is a Nash equilibrium if,

$$\textit{Definition (Nash equilibrium)}: z\{\theta^{s'},\theta^{-s}) \geq z\{\theta^s|\theta^{-s}\} \text{ all } \theta^s \subseteq \theta_k. \tag{3.10}$$

The Shapley value is one way of distributing payoffs. It ascribes to each agent a payoff that is equal to his or her expected marginal contribution to a random coalition in the game. A random coalition C, not containing agent s, is achieved conceptually by arranging all the N players in a line (1, 2, ..., N), assuming all N! arrangements are equally likely, and placing in C all which precede s. If x_s is the payoff to an individual agent, the Shapley value is formally defined as,

$$\textit{Definition (Shapley value)}: x_s = \Sigma_{(C \subseteq N-s)} C!(N-C-1)!N!^{-1} [Z(C \cup \{s\}) - Z\{C\}]. \tag{3.11}$$

Since $[Z(C\cup\{s\}) - Z\{C\}]$ is the marginal contribution of agent s, to coalition C, the Shapley value is the weighted sum of his or her marginal contributions; the weights being the mathematical expectation of the coalition occurring randomly. Further the sum of these expected marginal contributions is equal to the value of the grand coalition, $Z(N)$. Hence the Shapley value is Pareto efficient, in that no other outcome can leave all agents better off.

In a two-person game, as illustrated in Figure 3.2(a), Shapley values are easy to calculate. Permitted values of C, $(C \subseteq N - s)$, are 0 and 1. For $C = 0$, $C!(N - C - 1)!N!^{-1} = 0!(2-1)!2!^{-1} = 1/2$, and for $C = 1$, $C!(N - C - 1)!N!^{-1} = 1!0!2!^{-1} = 1/2$. Corresponding marginal values are 3 and 7, giving $(x_1, x_2) = (3/2 + 7/2, 3/2 + 7/2) = (5,5)$.

The core is defined as the set of feasible payoffs which no coalition can improve upon, by making both players better off.

$$\textit{Definition (The core)}: \Sigma_{(s \in N)} X_s = Z(N) \text{ and } \Sigma_{(s \in N)} X_s \geq Z(C) \text{ all } C \subseteq N, \tag{3.12}$$

The core, given the data in Figure 3.2(a), is any weighted sum (by k, $1 \geq k \geq 0$) of the allocations, (3, 7), and (7, 3). Core allocations are, of course, Pareto efficient. Clearly also the Shapley value is contained in the core.[4]

Drawing on (3.11), (3.12), and the inequality, (3.1), a new definition is introduced for the purposes of the paper. Considering the firm as a cooperative game, if potential payoffs in the activity matrix are realized, the solution and the associated allocation of payoffs is efficient.

Definition (Efficiency as realization): $Z = Z(N)$, and $\Sigma_{(s \in N)} x_s$. (3.13)

Four levels of efficiency, of increasing strictness, can be identified: (i) *viability*; (ii) *superadditivity*; (iii) *convexity*; (iv) *the core*. Given the assumption that no activity can be coerced into accepting less than its stand alone value, the weakest condition for improvement satisfying is *viability*. Any level of organization is *viable* if two conditions are met: (i) positive added value; and (ii) it must be worth more than the sum of the constituent activities: for $(i = j)$ $Z \geq \Sigma_{(i,j \in N)} a_{ij}$. Superadditivity (in the strong sense) requires the strong inequality $Z > \Sigma_{(ij \in N)} a_{ij}$.

Core solutions are efficient in that potential payoffs (given the assumption that there are no changes within the payoff function) are fully realized. In a convex game, Shapley values are part of the core, and therefore efficient. One attraction of Shapley values is that they represent the distribution of payoffs according to the expected marginal contributions of agents (Myerson, 1980, 1991). In a changing landscape, measuring the surplus in terms of profit, viability is probably all that can be asked of an organization.

Efficiency as Realization of Payoffs

There is an important distinction between *existence* and *realization*. The assumption that activity matrices are convex ensures that both the Shapley value, and the core, *exist*. Further, the Shapley value occupies a central position in the core: it is the convex hull of the marginal contributions. *Existence* is used in a mathematical sense: it is an a priori proposition that the assumption of convexity is a necessary and sufficient condition for the core (which also contains the Shapley value). This is logically prior to, but distinct from, the assertion that a particular outcome, will be *realized*.

In the next section, different predictions are set out, in the following alternative specifications of:

(i) The utility functions of decision makers; instrumental, conditional, and symbolic utility.

(ii) The number of repetitions of the game; essentially the distinction is between a finite or infinite number of repetitions.
(iii) Changes in the data underlying the variables in the payoff function.

The argument is that *realization* is contingent upon the preferences of decision makers: expressed by expected *instrumental, conditional* and *symbolic utilities*. An underlying assumption is bounded rationality; Simon (1980) takes into account the cognitive limitations of both knowledge, and computational capacity.

For the purposes of the argument, specifications (i) and (ii) are collapsed. If conditions are not expected to change in the foreseeable future, this amounts to asserting that a large, if not infinite, number of repetitions of a given game are expected, so the condition corresponds approximately to an infinitely repeated game: conversely, if changes are expected, few, if any, repetitions are implied.

These remarks are illustrated in Figure 3.3. Core allocations lie on the line segment XY: it can be seen from the activity matrix, and the transformation into a cooperative game (Figures 3.1(a), and 3.2(a)), that this is feasible and Pareto optimal, since both players cannot be made simultaneously better off if payoffs lie on this line segment. The Shapley value is given by the coordinates of L (5,5), which, in Figure 3.3, is also a Nash equilibrium solution.

Implications

Now the questions posed at the beginning of the paper are addressed: *Of the profile of possible strategies, which are likely to occur? Will they result in the realization of potential payoffs? What actions can the firm adopt to increase the possibility of potential payoffs being achieved?* Following expressions (3.2)–(3.4), payoffs are interpreted as expected transferable utilities of outcomes summarized by the organization matrix. Because the organization matrix is a changing landscape, the main concern is with games that are expected to have limited repetition. Implications for infinitely repeated games are merely sketched. Different specifications of utility in (i), (ii) and (iii) above result in different predictions about realized potential payoffs, in the form of a solution along XY, where (3.13) is satisfied.

Given purely instrumental utilities, decision makers in a finite game are generally assumed to choose a dominant strategy, resulting in a non cooperative outcome. Outcomes that depend on others are seen beyond one individual's influence. Potential payoffs from cooperation may not be realized. This describes a variety of real world situations: failure to realize synergies in alliances and mergers, non-cooperation in preservation of exhaustible resources (forests and fishery), *free riding*, and prisoners dilemma issues generally; all illustrate solutions in which security levels alone determine Z.

The introduction of expected conditional utility leaves payoffs unchanged but reflects altered beliefs. As the payoff function implies, strategy is an interactive process. Formulation and implementation is influenced at many levels within the firm, and outcomes depend upon external responses. In contrast to the situation under instrumental utility, conditional utility reflects the belief that interactions and reactions by others can be influenced by the individual's actions. The case for stakeholding in terms of efficiency is that mutual gains from cooperative behaviour are to be had, if *S* conjectures that the probability of cooperative action by others, –*S*, can be enhanced by her own behaviour. The likelihood of cooperation may similarly be increased if organizational objectives are linked to those of individual stakeholders. The observations about expected conditional and symbolic utilities are summarized in Figure 3.4. Other circumstances are also summarized.

Attempts to manipulate corporate culture reflect efforts to create conditional expected utilities conducive to the creation of quality, trust, and synergy. They reflect ways of sidestepping the dilemma of designing incentive compatible mechanisms (Hurwicz, 1972; Ledyard, 1978, 1987; Radner, 1982). Symbolic utility is often summarized in mission statements, and enunciations of strategic

	PAYOFFS REALIZED?		
	Instrumental utility	**Conditional utility**	**Symbolic utility**
Finite game: changes in the payoff function: zero transactions costs.	Perhaps	Yes	Yes
Finite game: changes in the payoff function: positive transactions costs.	No	Yes	Yes
Infinite game: no changes in the payoff function: zero transactions costs.	Yes: if threats are realistic	Yes	Yes
Infinite game: no changes in the payoff function: positive transactions costs.	Yes: if threats are realistic	Yes	Yes

Figure 3.4 Results for different specifications of utility

intent, that link corporate goals to personal objectives valued by individual stakeholders: much of the symbolism of advertising, leadership, and human resource management has the same purpose. Firms seem to recognize implicitly the importance of conditional utility for *reciprocity*, and the *significance* of symbolic utility: hence the emphasis on culture and strategic intent. In practice, though, they are ignored by many top managers, trapped in the illusions of competitiveness, downsizing, reengineering, and habitually reneging on implicit contracts with stakeholders to increase rents accruing to stockholders.

Much of the discussion of the importance of corporate culture, and strategic intent is unsatisfactory, useful only as a tranquillizing facade for the abrasive talk of competitiveness. Unconvincing and empty of real content, it often amounts to tautology, or wishful thinking: *successful companies have the right culture – how do we know they are successful? Because they have the right culture*. Sometimes it seems that competitive advantage measured by transferable payoffs or rent, can be got merely by dreaming. The argument of popular texts seems circular (see for example, Hamel and Prahalad, 1994; Bartlett and Ghoshal, 1994). The link between culture and strategic intent and symbolic and conditional utilities (i), helps to identify ways of realizing potential payoffs by cooperation.

PREFERENCES	EXPECTED PAYOFFS FROM COOPERATION	TARGET
INSTRUMENTAL UTILITIES	$\Sigma_{(m\in M)}$ prob(O_m) $U(O_m)$	prob$U(O_m)$: the probability of outcome m occurring
CONDITIONAL UTILITIES	$\Sigma_{(i\in N)}$ prob$(O_m\vert\theta_s)$ $U(O_i)$	prob$(A_{TS}\vert c_S)$, and prob$(A_{ST}\vert c_T)$: the conditional expected probabilities by θ_S, (θ_{-S}) of mutually cooperative actions.
SYMBOLIC UTILITIES	$\Sigma_{(m\in M)}$ prob(O_m) $U(O_m + R)$	R: events symbolically connected, by S $(-S)$ with outcome i.

Figure 3.5 Target variables for cooperative behaviour

Culture can be defined in terms of artefacts (Levi-Strauss, 1968) or in managerial terms as mental programming (Hofstede, 1980, 1983). As an artefact, one aspect of culture is reflected by the organization matrix and the views which stakeholders take of expected instrumental utilities associated with it. Here culture is defined in terms of the probability of certain kinds of behaviour (see Figure 3.5). Willingness to incur the transactions costs (c_T, c_S) of creating synergy, demonstrates a commitment to a cooperative culture, and increases the likelihood of reciprocal behaviour by others, (prob($A_{TS} \mid c_S$), and prob($A_{ST} \mid c_T$)). Among stakeholders, cooperative behaviour can take many forms: one is to demonstrate that the distribution of payoffs is seen as fair. Further a collaborative culture is founded on repetition of cooperative behaviour, even though the organization landscape in which it takes place may be continually changing. In terms of the demonstration and repetition effects, by establishing a history of non-cooperative behaviour, leaders of stakeholder groups, who are obviously mendacious do a lot of damage.[5]

The implicit assumption in much discussion of corporate governance is that the shareholder is the preeminent stakeholder. The analysis in the paper suggests otherwise. Realization of monetary and non-monetary payoffs, and in particular creation of long-term rents for shareholders, depends on the distribution as well as the size of payoffs.

CONCLUDING REMARKS

A stakeholder approach to corporate governance is associated with the sustainability of organizations, and has three elements summarized here. *Viability* relates to stockholders and is a necessary condition. It implies positive or economic rent in money terms and superadditivity. Competitive advantage defined as a rate of return commensurate with risk is an alternative way of expressing this. Competition on stock markets as well as product markets is real and an incentive to efficiency, whether or not the more expansive justifications of competitiveness are to be believed.[6] Viability is a weaker condition than convexity, requiring only that in the ever changing organizational landscape some synergies are realized.

Sufficient conditions also require *reciprocity*, an acceptable balance between stakeholders' interests, and *significance*, some congruence between the individual values of agents stakeholders as decision makers at various levels, and the goals of organizations. Sustainability also requires trust, commitment and imagination: qualities that are unlikely to be forthcoming unless employees, customers and the community in general, feel they have a stake, both in terms of its payoffs, and in identifying with its goals. Employees matter, but so do citizens. As Shell learned at Brent Spar, Greenpeace was able to substitute scientific validation by the widely held assumption that big companies are untruthful.

Interest has been reawakened in the stakeholder economy by unease about the dominant role of the City and anxiety as the fashion for lean production and reengineering destroys roles and jobs, even in the most successful corporations, whilst enhancing payoffs to equity holders and senior executives, who reward themselves with stock options. Opponents of stakeholding insist that it is undefinable. Actually the meaning is clear, and very close to the conditions for the sustainability of organizations. Sustainability implies a capacity not just to attain competitive advantage, but recreate it on a continuous basis. In the short term, it may be a matter of luck, and being in the right place at the right time (Coloroll, Queens Moat Hotel and many of the spectacular retail successes of the 1980s), or being protected against new competition (the privatized utilities), but some degree of permanence requires the three conditions, which also define stakeholding.

Given the changing landscape, borrowing Alfred Marshall's terminology, the representative firm is a transient entity. At a macro level, the capitalist system (or market economy), in its present form, is unlikely to represent the culmination of history and civilization. A modest requirement for its durability was provided by Keynes and remains true:

> For my own part I believe there is social and psychological justification for significant inequalities of wealth, but not for such large disparities as exist today. There are valuable human activities which require the motive of money making ... But it is not necessary for the stimulation of these activities and stimulation of these proclivities that the game should be played for such high stakes as at present. (Keynes, 1936, p. 374)

Often, employees feature only as a cost, and share prices can be boosted by downsizing and lean production. The customary platitude 'our employees are our most valuable resource' is a corporate delusion. Top executives renege upon implicit commitments to staff about security of employment, and conditions of work.

Much of management thinking is schizophrenic. The machismo of reengineering, without compassion, coexists with a new feeling for culture and strategic intent; concepts that are merely ornaments in company reports, unless they are understood in terms of *reciprocity* and *significance*. Corporate culture, defined in terms of the probability of certain kinds of behaviour, refers in particular to the norm that cooperation between stakeholder groups will be mutually reciprocated, and rewarded; strategic intent relates to symbolic utility, and is achieved by linking the organization's goals with those of its stakeholders.

The definition of competitive advantage focuses on the surplus to shareholders: but sustainability depends on the distribution of payoffs as well as their absolute level. Given persistent unemployment, the costs destroyed by one enterprise through downsizing and so on reappear in another – as unemployment, and social security charges: diminished expectations of work mean that they also surface as health expenditures and crime. In Britain half of the population lives in households that receive means tested benefits (Field, 1995). Benefits of economic growth in the United States over the last fifteen years have accrued mainly to just one per cent of the population. Governments seem incapable of satisfying income expectations, or assuaging anxieties. Mr Blair seems to understand that the surest way of becoming unpopular is to get elected. Hence the importance of the revival of interest in stakeholding.

NOTES

1. For a fuller discussion of the issues in the chapter and proofs of the various propositions see Matthews (1994, 1995, 1996).
2. Convexity requires that $m(a^s) \geq 0$ all $C \subseteq N$. $m(a^s) = \Sigma_{(j \in C, j \neq s)} (b_{sj} - c_{sj}) + \Sigma_{(i \in C, i \neq s)}(b_{is} - c_{is}) + a_{ss}$. The argument is not substantially affected when it is noted that mutual cooperation in a coalition is the efficient outcome if the expressions in brackets are positive for all $i,j,s, \subseteq C$.
3. For a proof of this and other propositions in the section see Matthews (1996).
4. These are dealt with by folk theorems, trigger strategies, enforceable outcomes, and so on.
5. In 1995 for example, when Yorkshire Water failed to deliver water in many places, the salary of the Chairman, including stock options, increased by a factor of around 5. For this and many examples see Paul Foot (1996).
6. In some versions of the myth, global pirates are said to roam international stock markets, seeking firms who fail the superadditivity test and reducing aspirations of a job for life to mirage.

REFERENCES

Arrow, K.J. (1974), *The Limits of Organizations*, New York: Norton.

Arrow, K.J. (1970), 'Economic organization: issues pertinent to the choice of market vs non market allocation', in R. Haveman and J. Margolis (eds), *Public Expenditure and Policy Analysis*, New York: Columbia.

Aumann, R.J. (1989), 'What is game theory trying to accomplish', in K.J. Arrow and S. Honkapohja (eds), *Frontiers of Economics*, Oxford: Basil Blackwell, 8–55.

Axelrod, Robert (1984), *The Evolution of Cooperation*, New York: Basic Books.

Bartlett, C.A and S. Ghoshal (1989), *Managing Across Borders: The Transnational Solution*, Boston, MA: Harvard.

Bartlett, C.A. and S. Ghoshal (1994), *Changing the Role of Top Management: Beyond Strategy to Purpose*, Harvard Business Review.

Binmore, K. (1992), *Fun and Games*, Lexington, MA: D.C. Heath and Company.

Buckley, Peter J. and Jonathan Michie (1996), *Firms Organizations and Markets*, Oxford: Oxford University Press.

Campbell, A. and K.S. Luchs (1992), *Strategic Synergy*, Oxford: Butterworth-Heinemann.

Coase, R.A. (1937), 'The nature of the firm', *Economica*, **IV**. 386–405.

Coates, David, (1996), 'New Labour or old', *New Left Review*, **219**, 62–78.

Connor (1991), 'The Resource Based Theory of the Firm', *Journal of Management*, **17** (1), 121–54.

Crosland, C.A.R., (1956), *The Future of Socialism*, London: Cape.

Dorfman, R., P.A. Samuelson and R. Solow (1958) *Linear Programming and Economic Analysis*, New York: McGraw Hill.

Edwards, J., John Eatwell, Murray Milgate and Peter Newman (eds), (1990), *The New Palgrave: A Dictionary of Economics*, London: Macmillan.

Field, Frank (1995), *Making Welfare Work: Reconstructing Welfare for the Millennium*, Institute of Community Studies.

Foot, Paul, (1996), 'I will embarrass you now by saying that I always thought you should be Chancellor of the Exchequer', *London Review of Books*, **18** (20), October, 8–11.

Fudenberg, Drew and Jean Tirole (1993), *Game Theory*, London: MIT Press.

Gale, D. (1960), *Linear Economic Models*, New York: McGraw Hill.

Gamble A. and G. Kelly (1996), 'The politics of ownership', *New Left Review*, **220**, 62–98.

Ghoshal, S. and N. Nohria (1993), 'Horses for courses: organizational forms for multinational corporations', *Sloan Management Review*, Winter.

Goold, M. and A. Campbell (1987), *Strategies and Styles. The Role of the Center in Diversified Companies*. Oxford: Basil Blackwell.

Hahn, Frank (1990), *The Economics of Missing Markets Information and Games*, Oxford: Clarendon Press.

Hamel, Gary, and C.K. Prahalad (1994), *Competing For The Future*, Boston, MA: Harvard Business School Press.

Hammer, Michael and James Champy (1993), *Reengineering the Corporation*, New York: Harper Collins.

Hofstede G. (1980), *Culture's Consequences: International Differences in Work Related Values*, Beverley Hills, CA: Sage Publications.

Hofstede G. (1983), 'The cultural relativity of organizational practices and theories', *Journal of International Business Studies*, Fall.

Holmstrom, B. and J. Tirole (1989), 'The Theory of the Firm', in R. Schmalensee and R.D. Willig, *Handbook of Industrial Organization, Vol 1*, Handbooks of Economics No 10, Amsterdam: North-Holland, 61–133.

Hurwicz, L. (1972), 'On Informationally Decentralized Systems', in R. Radner and C.B. McGuire (eds), *Decision and Organization, a Volume in Honour of Jacob Marshak*, Amsterdam: North-Holland, 297–336.

Hutton, Will (1995), *The State We're In*, London: Jonathon Cape.

Kauffman, Stuart (1993), *The Origins of Order: Self Organization and Selection in Evolution*, New York: Oxford University Press.

Kauffman, Stuart (1995), *At Home in the Universe*, London: Penguin.

Kay, John and Aubrey Silberston (1995), 'Corporate governance', *National Institute Economic Review*, **153** (3).

Keynes, J.M. (1936), *The General Theory of Money Interest and Prices*, London: Macmillan.

Koopmans, T.C. (ed.), (1951), *Activity Analysis of Production and Allocation*, New York: McGraw Hill.

Kreps, David M. (1996), 'Corporate culture and economic theory', in Buckley and Michie, op. cit., 221–76.

Ledyard, J. (1978), 'Incomplete Information and Incentive Compatibility', *Journal of Economic Theory*, **18**, 171–89.

Ledyard, J. (1979), 'Incentive Compatibility in Allocation Information and Markets', in J. Eatwell, M. Milgate and P. Newman (eds), *The New Palgrave*, London: Macmillan.

Levi-Strauss, C. (1974), 'Structural Anthropology', trans. Jacobson, Claire and Grundfest, Brooke, Schoepf, New York: Basic Books.

Mandleson, P. and R. Liddle (1996), *The Blair Revolution: Can New Labour Deliver?* London.
Matthews, Robin (1994), 'The organizational matrix: core businesses and structure', British Academy of Management: proceedings, Lancaster University.
Matthews, R. (1995), 'A general theory of corporate structure', Western Decision Sciences Institute, Papers and Proceedings, A1. S. Khade and R.B. Brown (eds), Californian State University, Stanislaus.
Matthews, Robin (1996), 'Corporate structure as a cooperative game: theory and applications', Occasional paper, Kingston Business School Series.
Maynard Smith, J. (1982), *Evolution and the Theory of Games*, Cambridge: Cambridge University Press.
Minns, R. (1996), 'Who really owns big business?', *New Left Review*, **219**, 42–62.
Moulin, H. (1988), *Axioms of Cooperative Decision Making*, Cambridge: Cambridge University Press.
Myerson, Roger B. (1980), 'Conference structures and fair allocation rules', *International Journal of Game Theory* **9**.
Myerson, Roger B. (1991), *Game Theory: Analysis of Conflict*, , London: Harvard University Press.
Nozick, Robert, (1995), *The Nature of Rationality*, Chichester, UK: Princetown University Press.
Penrose, Edith (1959), *The Theory of the Growth of the Firm*, Basil Blackwell: London.
Radner, Roy (1982), *Information, Incentives and Economic Mechanisms: Essays in Honour of Leonid Hurwicz*, London: Blackwell.
Radner, Roy (1986), *Information, Incentives and Economic Mechanisms: Essays in Honour of Leonid Hurwicz*, Oxford: Blackwell.
Richardson, G.B. (1996), 'The Organization of Industry', in P.J. Buckley and J. Michie, *Firms Organizations and Markets*, Oxford: Oxford University Press.
Schelling, Thomas C. (1980), *The Strategy of Conflict*, London: Harvard University Press.
Simon, H.A., (1980), *Models of Bounded Rationality*, 2 Vols, Cambridge, MA: MIT Press.
Teece D.J. and G. Pisano (1994), 'The dynamic capabilities of firms: an introduction', *Industrial and Corporate Change*, **3** (3), 537–55..
von Neumann, J and O. Morgenstern (1944), *The Theory of Games and Economic Behaviour*, Princeton University Press.
Williamson, O.E. (1975), *Markets and Hierarchies: Analysis and Antitrust Implications*, New York: The Free Press.
Williamson, O.E. (1985), *The Economic Institutions of Capitalism: Firms, Markets, Relational Contracting*, New York: The Free Press.
Winter, S., (1964), 'Economic natural selection and the theory of the firm', *Yale Economic Essays*, **4**, 225–72.

PART II

Methodological Issues in Economic Policy

4. Problems of time-series econometrics

Paul Ormerod*

1 INTRODUCTION

The postwar period, and in particular the past 20-odd years, has seen a major programme of research involving the application of the techniques of time-series econometrics to macroeconomic data.

The journal *Applied Economics*, under the editorship of Maurice Peston, has become a prestigious outlet for the findings of such research. With its emphasis on empirical findings rather than on seemingly impressive but often dubious theoretical nuances, the journal attracts scholars from all over the world, writing on a wide range of topics.

Increasingly, however, the contents of the journal show how little of value has been contributed to knowledge by the use of time-series econometrics in applied macroeconomics. Maurice Peston himself drew my attention to a phenomenon in the output of *Applied Economics*. Following the publication of a carefully crafted article, several years later another one appears on the same, or very similar, topic, and the results of the latter are often substantially different from those of the former. As a former economic modeller and forecaster myself, a profession which involves confronting estimated equations with new data on a regular basis, I had been aware of this problem for a long time. Econometric equations estimated on time-series macroeconomic data are rarely stable for any length of time, and the error variance on genuine out-of-sample data is often substantially higher than would be expected theoretically on the basis of the in-sample performance of the equation.

The aim of this chapter, stimulated by Maurice's perception, is to offer an account of why time-series econometrics has yielded so little of value in macroeconomic research. Section 2 sets out some brief general remarks on the output of, and problems with, applied macroeconometric research. Section 3

* I first met both Maurice and Bernard when I was a young research officer at the National Institute of Economic and Social Research in the mid-1970s. Although neither of them held formal positions at NIESR, they actively encouraged young applied economists and their support was very valuable. In 1983 they arranged for me to be appointed as a Visiting Professor in their department. I found this very stimulating and held this position until 1991.

illustrates how problems arise for the techniques in a very simple two-equation system containing a mild degree of non-linearity. Section 4 shows how the application of techniques from the dynamic systems approach to time-series analysis offers a general explanation of the failure of the research programme in time-series econometrics.

2 APPLIED MACROECONOMIC RESEARCH: SOME GENERAL REMARKS

It is now 60 years since the publication of Keynes's *General Theory*. For the most part, the book eschews empirical analysis. But Keynes did venture to place an estimate on the multiplier, suggesting that in an open economy such as Britain its value was likely to be somewhere between 2 and 3. This figure was arrived at in a single paragraph using simple arithmetic, a key assumption being that foreign trade accounted for only 20 per cent of consumption. This was probably realistic for the 1930s, but taking account of the more open nature of the economy in the 1990s, similar arithmetic gives a figure of the order of 1.25 to 1.5. Such an estimate simply requires assumptions on the marginal propensities to consume and import, as well as on the marginal rate of taxation.

The concept of the multiplier has, rightly or wrongly, played a central role in government policy throughout the West ever since the war. An enormous amount of both intellectual effort and taxpayers' resources have gone into an attempt to estimate the size of the multiplier via the research programme in macroeconomic modelling. But the net result is wholly inconclusive. The only thing which it appears we might be able to say is that, once account is taken of potential feedbacks through the monetary sector, the multiplier is probably, though not completely conclusively, lower than the simple arithmetic of the above paragraph would suggest.

Church et al. (1993) describe the policy simulation properties of the six leading macroeconomic models in the UK. Even on the highly simplifying assumption that nominal interest rates are held fixed, a sustained increase in public expenditure after three years has a multiplier effect of between 0.29 and 0.75, depending upon which model we choose. But once allowance is made for interest rates to change, even the sign of the multiplier is inconclusive over this time horizon: some of the models suggest that it is negative, and others that it is positive.

These are models which are constructed using a common set of data from the UK national accounts, and using a common set of econometric techniques, namely those described by Mizon (1995) as the 'LSE methodology'. The models also share a common background of economic theory, being based upon the synthesis which became 'Keynesian' economics. The precise periods over which key equations are estimated do vary from model to model, but not usually by very much. So the failure to produce a consensus on the size of the multiplier is really quite a remarkable comment on the underlying econometric methodology.

The differences are not confined to different models of the same vintage. Following the initial article by Laury, Lewis and Ormerod (1978), a series of papers has reported comparisons of the policy simulation properties of the main UK macroeconomic models. The size of the multiplier in different vintages of the model maintained by any single one of the institutions varies, sometimes by substantial amounts.

A residual feeling persists amongst applied econometricians in the wider academic community that the existence of such problems with macro-models may reflect the time and resource pressures under which the modellers operate, for these models are used not just to investigate the properties of policies, but to carry out regular forecasts. But whilst constraints of this nature do exist, the standard of applied econometrics amongst UK macro-modellers has been very high over the past 20 years, which makes the failure to arrive at a consensus on even the most basic properties of the UK economy all the more worrying.

The problems of achieving well-established, settled results are by no means limited to the experiences of the macro-modellers. The consumption function, for example, has been studied intensively by the academic community for many years. It has not been possible, however, to obtain individual equations whose general specification and individual parameters have been stable over long periods of time. The addition of new data beyond the sample period almost invariably brings problems, no matter how carefully the equation has been tested in advance. Not only are the individual parameters in any particular specification of the consumption function not stable over time, but new terms have to be added, and old ones deleted in order to obtain a new equation which satisfies the battery of statistical tests demanded by the LSE methodology.

This methodology, described very clearly by Mizon (1995), places great emphasis on tests of validation of the specified equation. A range of different tests is used, but from the initial development of the methodology during the 1970s, particular stress has been laid upon tests of parameter stability. Typically, part of the available data is retained as a hold-out sample on which to test the null hypothesis of parameter stability.

Yet despite the importance of testing for stability in the methodology, and no matter how carefully an equation is constructed, when confronted with genuinely new data (as opposed to hold-out data used to test the specification) the error terms on the equation often become, quite rapidly, distinctly larger than statistical theory would indicate on the basis of the estimated equation. Chatfield (1995) suggests that this experience is rather general in time-series analysis.

Macro-modellers who forecast on a regular basis are the group most aware of this phenomenon. In macroeconomic forecasting, it is the main reason for the 'constant' or 'intercept' adjustments which are widely used, which Surrey and Ormerod (1977) were perhaps the first to document explicitly, and which Clements and Hendry (1995) have recently tried to put into a more rigorous theoretical setting.

Indeed, having been instrumental in introducing the emphasis on testing into econometric methodology, Hendry's own views on the question of parameter stability now appear to have changed, in the light of the overwhelming empirical evidence which has accumulated over the years. In Clements and Hendry (1995), he now argues that the assumptions of a constant, time-invariant, data generating process and of a unique model of the economy which coincides with this process are 'an inappropriate view of the world'.

There are several reasons why models frequently break down when confronted with genuinely new data, despite testing equations for stability. One reason is a misapplication of the testing procedure, which I suspect has a rather more corporeal existence than many care to admit. The fact that Tong (1990) cautions against it in the context of non-linear autoregressive modelling in general implies that it is more widespread than simply within the applied macroeconomics profession. This is the practice of using the whole of the available data set to build an equation, and then reporting a 'successful' parameter stability test obtained by re-estimating the equation over a subset of the same data.

More importantly, it is not completely obvious what is being tested in practice even when a hold-out sample is used correctly. Referees rarely accept articles with equations which fail parameter stability tests. As a result, researchers modify the specification of their equation to ensure that it *does* satisfy such tests (as well as other tests which are regarded as important). In a more subtle way than the crude misapplication of such tests described above, this undermines the whole validity of the testing procedure. The equation is designed so that it satisfies tests on a hold-out sample of data, which may not give a good indication of the ability of the equation to be generalized to other, unseen, data. The tests have become design criteria, rather than genuine statistical tests.

The ease with which computer technology enables equations to be re-specified further undermines the validity of reported test statistics, no matter how impressive they may seem. Chatfield (1995) describes this rather neatly as 'computer technology running ahead of developments in statistical theory'. In general, we simply do not know what a reported statistic for, say, a Lagrange multiplier test for white noise residuals means, when the equation has been respecified a large number of times in order to ensure that the null hypothesis is not rejected according to the statistic reported in the suite of tests in the software.

It is instructive to re-read one of the classic articles of applied econometrics, such as that by Phillips (1957). In those days, even carrying out a two or three variable regression was not a trivial task. The data in this article are analysed and discussed with great care before any regression is attempted. The statistical information on the regression reported in the paper, sparse though it is by modern standards, has real meaning because it is used exactly in accordance with the precepts of statistical theory. As a result, even four decades later, it is scarcely possible to improve upon Phillips's specification of the wage equation in pre-First World War Britain.

In contrast, computer technology and software have advanced so rapidly, that it is now possible for a graduate student to run 20 or 30 versions of an equation in a single day, and to obtain a wide range of test statistics computed for each variation of the specification. Statistical theory has not kept up.

In principle, of course, the above problems, if they were the only reason for equations breaking down, could be surmounted by returning to the standards of the early, classic articles in time-series econometrics. The idea of estimating a very limited number of versions of a fairly simple equation, and only doing so after careful analysis of the data, is one with which I have a great deal of sympathy.

But even following these precepts, there are good reasons to expect time-series macroeconometric equations not to be stable over time. Hendry (1996), for example, argues that 'considerable empirical evidence suggests that [the economy] is a dynamic, non-linear, high dimensional, and evolving entity, so studying it is difficult . . . [and] establishing any invariants of an economic system is not easy'. In this context, the words 'difficult' and 'not easy' might be thought to be considerable understatements.

It is to a discussion of two of these particular points that I now turn. For exposition, non-linearity and high dimensionality are discussed separately although, as Hendry points out, both are likely to exist in practice. Section 3 considers the potential implications for time-series econometrics of non-linearity in an extremely simple model. Section 4 presents evidence, using techniques of phase space reconstruction of attractors, which suggests that the economy certainly is a high dimensional system.

3 THE POTENTIAL IMPACT OF NON-LINEARITY: A SIMPLE ILLUSTRATION

Some of the potential consequences of non-linearity for time-series analysis, particularly with relatively short data series such as those encountered in macroeconomics, can be illustrated in the context of a simple two variable system. The system is not intended to be a realistic approximation to the economy, but does illustrate how non-linearity can lead to problems.

Consider the simple system of differential equations

$$\begin{aligned} dx/dt &= g(x,y) \\ dy/dt &= h(x,y) \end{aligned} \tag{4.1}$$

and suppose that there is a single equilibrium point (x^*, y^*), that is, at these values $dx/dt = g(x^*, y^*) = 0$ and similarly for y. Imagine that the system is at its equilibrium values, and it is then subjected to a large, exogenous shock. How useful is the data which is observed following the shock likely to be in enabling us to describe the system? Obviously, the answer to this question depends in part on the speed with which the system converges or returns towards (x^*, y^*), but assume for the purpose of exposition that this process is not very rapid.

It is helpful in considering the above question to introduce the idea of a vector field. A vector field is a function or rule that associates a vector with each point in the plane in exactly the same way that a function of one variable associates a value or number with each point on the line. The system of differential equations (4.1) is in fact equivalent to a vector field. The vector field associates the point with coordinates (x, y) in the plane with the vector $(dx/dt, dy/dt)$. Any system of differential equations can be expressed in this way. A solution of the equations $[x(t), y(t)]$ traces out an unbroken curve in the plane as t increases. It has the property that at each point (x, y) on the curve, the tangent to the curve is the value of the vector field at that point, that is, $(dx/dt, dy/dt)$.

A vector field can be plotted. Suppose that a vector field denoted by F is defined on some region of the plane, and choose a grid of points that covers the region. At each point v on the grid, the value of the vector field $F(v)$ is a vector. To plot the vector field, draw an arrow representing the vector $F(v)$ from the point v. (Depending on how you think of a vector, the arrow either represents or *is* the vector $F(v)$. The arrow points in the direction of the vector and its length is equal to the norm of $F(v)$.) The pattern of the vectors plotted in this way gives a good indication of the vector field.

Plotting the vector field of our example provides the answer to the question of the value of the data which are observed following a large exogenous shock. Providing that the system (4.1) is linear, even if the postulated shock takes the system far from its equilibrium at (x^*, y^*), the resulting data can be used to get accurate information on the nature of the functions g and h. This is precisely because a linear function is completely determined by its behaviour over any range of values no matter how large or small the values may be.

However, even a mild degree of non-linearity can create serious problems. For values of (x, y) which are close to equilibrium, a good linear approximation to the system can almost certainly be made. But at values which are far from equilibrium, movements in x and y over time can give quite misleading information about the nature of the system (4.1).

Figure 4.1 plots the vector field of an illustrative two-equation system with a single equilibrium point at (x^*, y^*) containing a mild degree of non-linearity. As is readily apparent, when moving between points which are far from equilibrium, the data give potentially contradictory information, on both the direction of change of one of the variables with respect to changes in the other, and the magnitude of the change for any given change in the other.

Suppose, for example, that the shock took the economy to the point marked u, or (x_1, y_1), and that we used observations between this point and v to estimate equations linking x and y. Unless we knew the true non-linear relationships in (4.1), as our data sample was extended over time to include observations up to point w, the approximate relationships which we estimated would be very likely to exhibit instability, for the direction and magnitude of the changes in, say, x as y changes, vary as the path between u and w is followed.

This stylized example is very simple. The system is postulated to be (very) low dimensional; it is assumed to be stable over time, and a single equilibrium

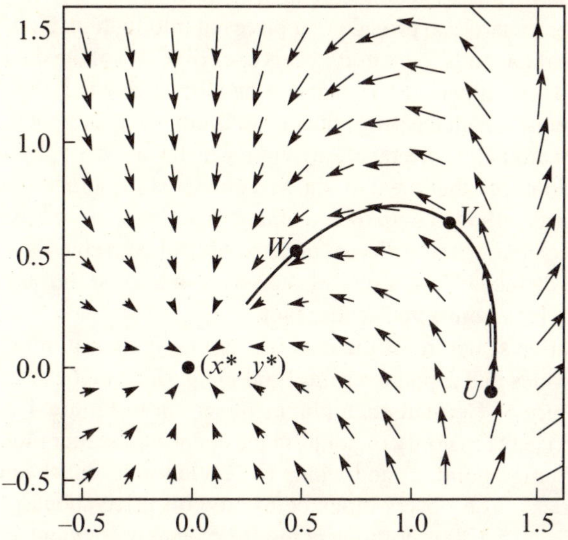

Figure 4.1 Vector field of illustrative non-linear system

solution is assumed. But even in this system, provided that a (mild) degree of non-linearity exists, time-series equations which are estimated with data sampled far from the equilibrium point are unlikely to be stable. Any sort of model which might be a reasonable approximation to the actual behaviour of the economy is bound to have a similar property.

The type of behaviour described above does seem to be an important element in the experience of Western economies in the past two decades or so. First, the evidence that macroeconomic data are mildly non-linear is growing rapidly (see, for example, Tiao and Tsay, 1994; Potter, 1995). Second, we also know that the Western economies do from time to time receive severe shocks, such as the oil price increases of 1973–74, which coincided with the breakdown of the postwar international monetary order. The further oil price increase of 1979–80 coincided, for the European economies, with a dramatic shift of emphasis in macro-policy towards the reduction of inflation and the attempts to create a reasonably stable system of exchange rates in Europe (the ERM).

By way of illustration, the impact of these shocks can be demonstrated for unemployment, and the inflation/unemployment relationship. The traditional way of presenting graphically the movement of a series such as unemployment over time is in fact a simple plot of the data against time. An alternative way, which may give valuable insights into the structure of the system which generates the data, is to use a connected scatter plot. In this case, a scatter plot is set out of unemployment in any particular year against unemployment in the previous year, and the resulting points connected in sequence.

To anticipate slightly, such charts can provide four pieces of information. First, they establish whether the data tends to exhibit cycles over time. If so, the data in a connected scatter plot will appear in the shape of an ellipse. Second, they show the average value around which the series fluctuates. Third, the charts show the magnitude of the cycles around the average. An ellipse which was very tightly drawn, for example, would imply that the data showed only small fluctuations over time. Fourth, the charts will also help to reveal any major shocks and the transitional periods between periods of different patterns of cyclical behaviour. These points can also be deduced from a plot of the series over time, but are shown much more clearly by a connected scatter plot.

The underlying qualitative structure of the data on unemployment in most Western European economies and Japan over the 1960–94 period can be seen in the connected scatter plot of German unemployment set out in Figure 4.2. Cyclical patterns characterize the majority of points in the connected scatter plot, but the position of the average point around which the cycle moves has been subject to two major shocks. The observations before the oil price shock of 1973–74 form a cycle around a very low average rate of unemployment in Germany. The economy was then shocked out of this particular cycle, and began to settle into a new cycle around an average of around 3.5 per cent unemployment.

But this point was short-lived, because of the impact of the 1980–82 shock, which again moved unemployment up rapidly before a further cycle emerged around a still higher level of unemployment.

The chart shows clearly that, whilst a simple relationship in some local time neighbourhoods may well be sufficient to give a good account of the movements of unemployment, over the period as a whole such local approximations will be quite inadequate. The series is clearly subject to major shocks, with years of transition between more settled patterns of behaviour.

Considering now the relationship between unemployment and inflation, the evidence suggests that, in terms of the relationship between inflation and unemployment, any constant rate of inflation is consistent with *any* constant rate of unemployment (within the range of postwar experience). For considerable periods, economies can behave as if the true underlying relationship were between inflation and the level of unemployment. Once settled on such a path, there is no tendency for inflation to accelerate or decelerate over time. But shocks to the system of sufficient size do not merely move the economy up and down a particular path. The whole path is shifted in (inflation, unemployment) space and there can be prolonged periods of transition.

Figure 4.3 shows a scatter plot of annual inflation and lagged unemployment in Belgium over the 1953–93 period, which is typical of the experiences of many

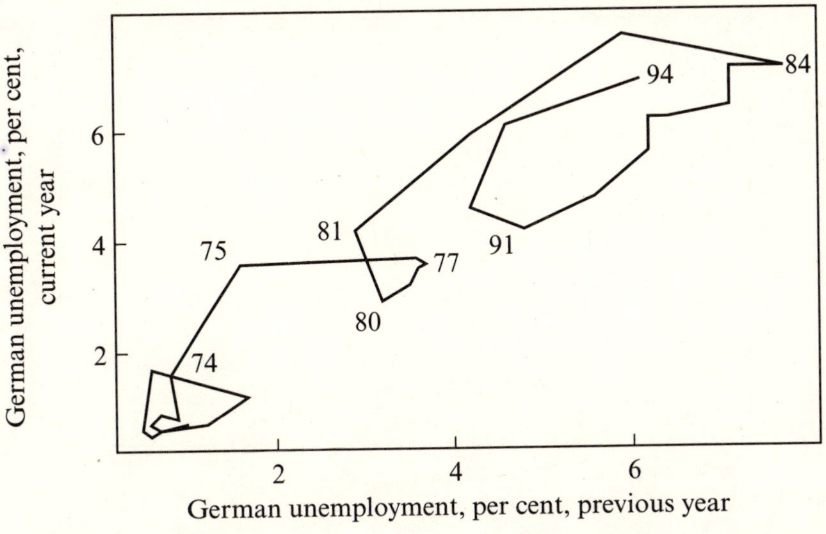

Figure 4.2 Connected scatter plot of German unemployment, 1961–94

European economies. The observations, marked with the date, are corralled into sets. A reasonably stable relationship between the two variables seems to have existed over the 1953–71 period. Since then, it is hard to identify any lengthy period when this has been the case. The years 1972 and 1973 are clearly a period of transition. The years 1974–80 appear to form a coherent sample, but there was then a long period of transition as the economy adjusted to the new emphasis on the control of inflation and the stronger version of the ERM. Arguably, a new relationship emerged from 1986 onwards, but the whole of the period since 1971 has clearly been subject to abrupt shifts.

Most econometricians are entranced by equations which are far more complicated than the simple linear approximations in local time neighbourhoods which are implied in Figure 4.3, for example. But, despite the apparent sophistication of the specifications, they certainly fare no better in practice than does this straightforward approach. And the value of data screening, which subsequent regression analysis merely confirms, is that it brings out very clearly that much of the macroeconomic data of the 1970s and early to mid-1980s, particularly for the European economies, can be thought of as arising from a system which was far from equilibrium. It is hardly surprising that equations, of whatever form, estimated using this data have a distinct tendency to exhibit parameter instability.

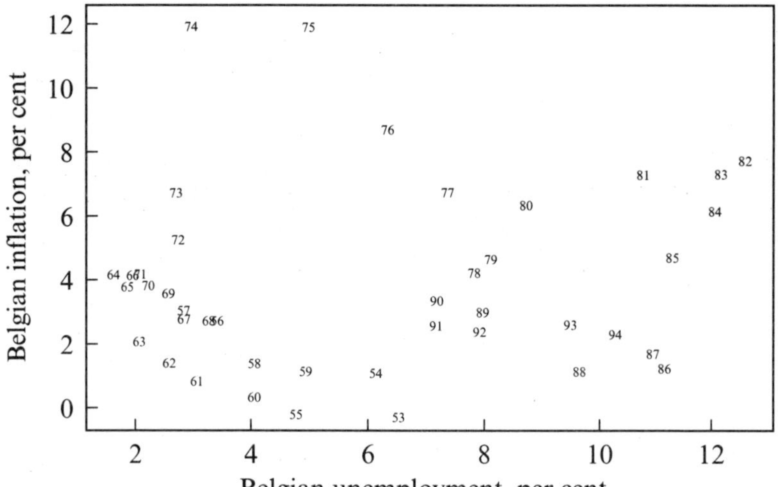

Figure 4.3 Unemployment and inflation in Belgium, 1953–94

4 PHASE SPACE RECONSTRUCTION AND THE CURSE OF DIMENSIONALITY

In this section, I consider the hypothesis that the economy is a high dimensional system. To many, this will seem self-evident. But the consequences of high dimensionality for time-series macroeconometrics are often disregarded. If there are many factors which in principle influence a particular variable, the selection of a subset of them to build a model over any given period of data will often lead to a model whose properties do not generalize well onto data from other periods, no matter how carefully the model is tested. To take an obvious example, an important explanatory factor may not be very much in evidence during the estimation period, but becomes so outside this period.

The idea that the business cycle is determined by too many factors to enable systematic, empirical mathematical modelling of it to be carried out is not new. Irving Fisher (1925) suggested 70 years ago that it was not possible to generalize from the experience of past business cycles to those in the future because, in modern terminology, the dimension of the problem is too high relative to the available number of observations. He argued that movements over time in the volume of output were 'a composite of numerous elementary fluctuations, both cyclical and non-cyclical', and quoted approvingly from his contemporary Moore who wrote that '[business] cycles differ widely in duration, in intensity, in the sequence of their phases and in the relative prominence of their various phenomena'.

In such circumstances even though deterministic structure exists and hence in principle could be modelled mathematically, in practice given the limited amount of data available it could well be virtually impossible to distinguish data generated by such a system from data which was genuinely random. This latter point was in fact argued by Slutsky (1937), who postulated that economic data was generated by a series of random shocks, and that transformations of random data based upon the principle of moving summation could generate data which looked very similar to genuine time-series macroeconomic data on output.

In the *General Theory*, Keynes stated that 'any actual instance of the Trade Cycle . . . is highly complex', and this scepticism about systematic modelling was made more explicit in his later criticism of Tinbergen's initial work on econometrics (Keynes, 1939).

Recent developments in non-linear signal processing theory enable us to examine the hypothesis that the macro economy is a very high dimensional system. This can be done using the technique of singular spectrum analysis (SSA) which is described rigorously by Broomhead and King (1986) and Vautard and Ghil (1989). It is important for economists and econometricians to realize that SSA is not concerned in any way with the task of actually building a model, whether uni- or multivariate, of any particular data series. Rather, its aim is to identify the degree of structure or consistent pattern in the data. It can also be interpreted as giving some measure of the noise or random component in a series.

In other words, the technique can be thought of as providing information on issues which are logically prior to any attempt to build a model of any particular data series. First, SSA indicates the extent to which there is any systematic structure in the data. Another way of thinking of this is to say that the technique shows the degree of randomness of the data, or how much signal exists relative to noise. Second, to the extent that structure does exist it gives an indication of the number of dimensions which are required in order to characterize this structure.

We should make clear what is meant by the word 'structure' in this context, given that econometricians use a word such as 'structural' in their own particular way. A hypothetical example might help to clarify the use of the word. Suppose that the price of wheat is determined by an exogenous variable such as the number of sunspots, along with a random error term whose variance is small compared to the variance of the wheat price. Sunspots are chosen as the illustrative explanatory factor because they are known to follow a well-determined, quasi-periodic pattern over time. Statisticians such as Tong (1990) and his collaborators have obtained good, univariate representations of the data using threshold autoregression and bilinear models, which give excellent genuinely *ex ante* predictions. In the context of this paper, we say that the sunspot data has structure.

By assumption, the price of wheat in this example also has structure. Even if we do not know that it is determined by the number of sunspots, we could obtain, with sufficient ingenuity, a well-determined univariate model of the price, which we could use for accurate prediction. A clever econometrician might also discover that the price is determined by sunspots, and could build what econometricians might term a 'structural' model by regressing the wheat price on sunspots.

But if the sunspot data itself were random, then, again by assumption, so too would be the wheat price data. Even though a good 'structural' model could be built of the price, the data, being a random series, would lack structure (more precisely, there would only be a very small probability of it having any structure).

SSA identifies characteristics of a series by finding the dominant patterns or structure in smaller sections or windows of the data. For example, for a series $X(t)$ where t runs from 1 to N, we choose a number m which is small by comparison with N and define vectors x_t in m-dimensional space by taking the m consecutive observations centred on t, that is

$$x_t = (X(t-(m-1)/2), \ldots, X(t-1), X(t), X(t+1), \ldots, X(t+(m-1)/2).$$

These vectors are called *m*-histories and *m* is chosen so that the length of time spanned by the observations in the embedded vector is long enough to include any structure in the data. We will also refer to the series of vectors x_t as the *embedded series* derived from *X*(*t*) and call *m* the *embedding dimension*.

The embedded series x_t forms a cloud of points in Euclidean space. In general any regularity or consistency in the series *X*(*t*) will give the embedded series some discernible structure. For example if the series is predominantly periodic, the embedded series will be largely confined to two dimensions rather than extending in all of the dimensions of Euclidean space. In this case the embedded series is essentially the same as a scatter plot of the series against the lagged value of the series. On the other hand if the original series is genuinely random and entirely lacking in structure then the embedded series will be a relatively symmetric ball without any significant pattern.

The regularity or structure present in a data series is measured by taking the embedded series to be approximately an ellipsoid and calculating its principal axes or directions in Euclidean space and calculating the (root mean square) projection of the vectors x_t on to those principal directions. This amounts to finding the eigenvectors and eigenvalues of a matrix of covariance coefficients of the series *X*(*t*). The eigenvalues of this matrix, which are typically arranged in decreasing order, are usually referred to as the singular spectrum of the series. This phrase is by no means ideal, for the technique of singular spectrum analysis relies on both the eigenvalues and eigenvectors of this matrix.

The eigenvectors and eigenvalues obtained in this way from the embedded series of *m*-histories indicate, respectively, the characteristic patterns in the data that exist over a period of time covered by *m* observations and the relative significance or strength of those patterns.

The characteristics of the data are shown by the eigenvectors associated with the larger eigenvalues. The eigenvectors represent the principal directions of the cloud of points formed by the embedded series. They therefore indicate the pattern or regularity that exists in the data on the timescale covered by the choice of embedding dimension. In the example of a predominantly periodic series, the two eigenvectors corresponding to the dominant eigenvalues would show smooth fluctuations of the same periodicity as the original series. The remaining eigenvectors would be irregular and lacking in structure since they represent the small inconsistent deviations from periodic behaviour.

It must be emphasized that SSA, unlike many other techniques in the dynamic systems literature such as the calculation of correlation dimension or Lyapunov exponents, can be used successfully with short, noisy data series. For example, Michael Campbell and I simulated 200 observations from the Lorenz equations, clothed with a mild amount of dynamic noise. As we report in Campbell and Ormerod (1997), SSA is able to identify the underlying structure in this noisy, chaotic system (although, obviously, as the amount of dynamic noise is increased, this comes to dominate the underlying equations so that structure becomes much weaker).

It is again important to stress that the evidence of the existence of structure in a noisy Lorenz system is quite separate from the task of actually building a model to try to capture this structure. Even if structure exists, it may prove to be very difficult to build a good model. But the existence of structure tells us that, in principle, one *can* be built.

With Michael Campbell, I have applied the technique of singular spectrum analysis to a range of output and expenditure series in a number of Western economies, some of the results being reported in Campbell and Ormerod (1997). The significance of the pattern of the eigenvalues obtained was assessed by a bootstrapping exercise. From each of the original series, a random draw with replacement was carried out to generate a new data series of the same length. By construction, there is only a small probability that this series has any discernible structure. The singular spectrum of this artificial data was calculated, and the procedure repeated 500 times.

The results are striking. For the European economic series which we have examined, the results are virtually indistinguishable from those of a random data series. By way of illustration, Figures 4.4a and 4.4b plot the singular spectrums of postwar data of quarterly growth rates of real GNP in the US and real GDP in the UK respectively, along with, in each case, the singular spectrum of an entirely random series with the same number of observations. American data seems to have a small amount of underlying structure, but the series is still heavily dominated by noise.

In other words, the results are entirely consistent with what we might term the Fisher hypothesis. They are those which would be obtained if the business cycle were determined by a large number of factors, which 'differed widely in duration, in intensity, in the sequence of their phases and in the relative prominence of their various phenomena'.

In such circumstances, it is hardly surprising that the project of trying to understand the short- and medium-term behaviour of modern capitalist economies by the application of ever more sophisticated techniques of time-series econometrics has yielded so few positive results. Indeed, the lack of structure is such a deep property of the data that, in the current state of scientific knowledge, it will not be possible to do any better by the use of such techniques.

We need to return to basic principles. Careful prior screening and understanding of the data are essential in order to formulate a relatively simple specification of a model to be estimated. Any such model is at best an approximation, valid only in a particular local time neighbourhood, and post-sample failure is a fact of life. A role also exists for international cross-sectional estimation of data series over a substantial number of years to embrace more than one business cycle, but here again parsimonious specifications are to be preferred.

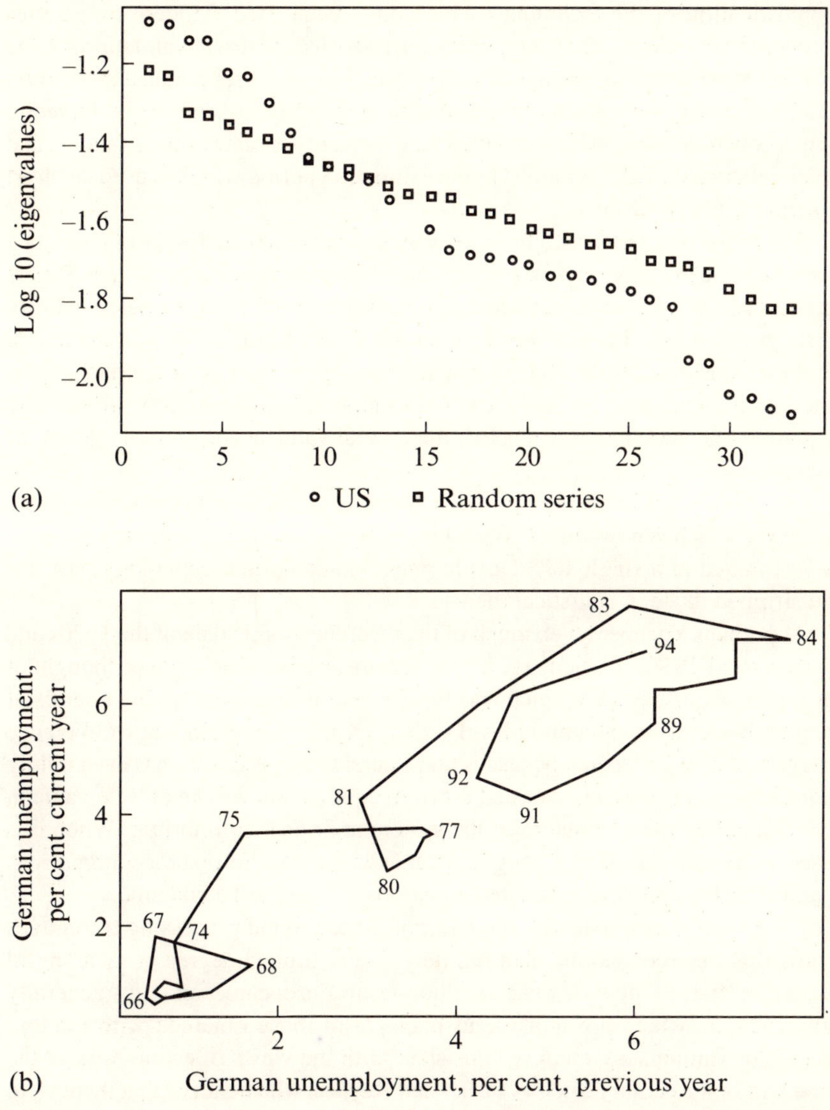

Figure 4.4 Singular spectrum of quarterly real US GNP growth and of a random series

5 CONCLUSION

The aim of this paper is to offer an account of why time-series econometrics has yielded so little of value in macroeconomic research, despite the increasing sophistication of the techniques which have been used. Modern time-series econometrics places great emphasis on statistical tests of validation of the specification of the equation, not least of which are tests for parameter stability. But, seemingly paradoxically, parameter instability appears to be endemic when equations are confronted with data which are genuinely out of sample, and even relatively small variations in the estimation period which is used can lead to quite different results.

Part of the problem arises from the way in which statistical tests of equations have become in many ways design criteria rather than formal tests as such. Papers are rarely sent to journals containing equations which fail parameter stability tests, for example. In other words, the models are modified in order to ensure that they pass such tests. But statistical theory gives little or no guidance as to the actual power of a test statistic which is reported after n modifications of an equation to ensure that it lies below the critical value at conventional levels of significance.

This problem is intensified by the very power and ease of use of econometric software which is now widely available. Many versions of an equation can now be estimated in a single day. Developments in computer technology have far outstripped those of statistical theory.

At perhaps a deeper level, much of the macroeconomic data of the 1970s and early to mid-1980s, particularly for the European economies, can be thought of as arising from a system which was far from equilibrium, following a series of major shocks to such economies. Further, an increasing amount of evidence suggests that macroeconomic data is non-linear. In a system which is even mildly non-linear, data which is sampled far from equilibrium will be of little value in understanding the true nature of the system at or near equilibrium. When it is used in samples of limited length, such as is the case in macroeconometrics, parameter instability of estimated equations is likely to be endemic.

Even more fundamentally, modern non-linear signal processing techniques show that macroeconomic data has only a very limited degree of meaningful structure. Indeed, applying such techniques to European economies generally gives results which are indistinguishable from those obtained with random data. The findings are entirely consistent with the views of economists of the first half of the century, such as Fisher and Keynes, who believed that there were far too many factors which influenced the business cycle, whose relative importance varied from one cycle to the next, for empirical modelling of macroeconomic data to be of any great value.

In short, the failure of the research programme of time-series econometric modelling of macroeconomic data is due not to deficiencies of economic or econometric theory which could in principle be remedied, but to inherent properties of the data.

REFERENCES

Broomhead, D.S. and G.P. King (1986), 'Extracting qualitative dynamics from experimental data', *Physica*, **20D**, 217–236.

Campbell, M. and P. Ormerod (1997), 'Predictability and economic time-series', in C. Heij, J.M. Schumacher, B. Hanzon and C. Praagman (eds), *System Dynamics in Economic and Financial Models*, John Wiley.

Chatfield, C. (1995), 'Model uncertainty, data mining and statistical inference', *Journal of the Royal Statistical Society A*, **158** (3).

Church, K.B. P.R. Mitchell, P.N. Smith and K.F. Wallis (1993), 'Comparative properties of models of the UK economy', *National Institute Economic Review*, **145**, August, 87–107.

Clements, M.P. and D. F.Hendry (1995), 'Macroeconomic forecasting and modelling', *Economic Journal*, **105**, (431), 1001–31.

Fisher, I. (1925), 'Our unstable dollar and the so-called business cycle', *Journal of the American Statistical Association*, June.

Hendry, D.F. (1996), 'Business Cycle Empirics', *Economic Journal*, **106** (438),

Keynes, J.M. (1939), *The General Theory of Employment, Interest and Money*, Macmillan.

Laury, J.S.E., G.R. Lewis and P.A. Ormerod (1978), 'Properties of macroeconomic models of the UK economy: a comparative survey', *National Institute Economic Review*, **83**, February.

Mizon, G.E. (1995), 'Progressive modelling of macroeconomic time series: the LSE methodology', European University Institute Working paper ECO 95/10, Florence.

Phillips, A.W. (1958), 'The relationship between unemployment and the rate of change of money wage rates in the United Kingdom, 1861–1957', *Econometrica*, **25**, 293–99.

Potter, S.M. (1995), 'A nonlinear approach to US GNP', *Journal of Applied Econometrics*, **10** (2), 109–26.

Slutsky, E. (1937), 'The summation of random causes as the source of cyclical processes', *Econometrica*, **5** (2), 105–46.

Surrey, M.J.C. and P. Ormerod (1977), 'Formal and informal aspects of forecasting with an econometric model', *National Institute Economic Review*, 81, August.

Tiao, G.C. and R.S. Tsay (1994), 'Some advances in non-linear and adaptive modelling in time-series analysis', *Journal of Forecasting*, **13** (2), 109–32.

Tong, H. (1990), *Non-linear Time Series*, Oxford University Press.

Vautard, R. and M. Ghil (1989), 'Singular spectrum analysis in nonlinear dynamics, with applications to paleoclimatic time series,' *Physica*, **35D**, 395–424.

5. Why firms invest less but adopt higher capital intensity as the capital stance tightens: the makings of an unemployment problem

Ciaran Driver

> Another side of the successful pursuit of full employment and stable growth is the reduction of the risk and uncertainty that accompanies private investment. Thus, investment itself may rise and become more stable, which in turn may diminish the need for a full employment policy. Of course the same point holds in reverse. A diminution in the commitment to full employment, for anti-inflation reasons, may reduce the average level of private investment and increase its variance. Maurice Peston (1979, p. 8)

INTRODUCTION

The views above are sidelined by academics and policy makers today. One reason for this is the scale of the unemployment problem in Europe which seems beyond the hand of government and which makes interventionist policies seem unrealistic. But the cultivation of 'realism', as George Orwell (1961, p. 376) once reminded us, 'does extraordinary damage to our sense of reality'. In recent years, a necessary corrective to policy has become, in time, a new orthodoxy. At its heart is the message that lean government and stable inflation will deliver enough growth and jobs. Although initially conceived as a concession to realism, the new mindframe no longer recognizes its own contingency. From this perspective, ideas such as those in the quotation above no longer need to be challenged but are instead ignored. It is, perhaps, one of the functions of a *Festschrift* to reclaim the reality appreciated by earlier writers in terms that will be acceptable to those who follow on.

THE PROBLEM STATED

This chapter endorses the view that economic instability arising from abandoning full-employment policies makes job creation more problematic. There are three theoretical links in this argument: that loosening the commitment to full employment creates risk; that risk depresses investment; and that investment is important for employment growth. Of these, I will concentrate on the second, where the theoretical arguments seem less well known.[1]

Risk Depresses Investment

The theoretical literature on investment under uncertainty is complex.[2] It is often suggested that there are two basic kinds of models which give conflicting directions of influence of risk on investment. Robert Pindyck (1993), for example, argues that the older-style models such as Hartman (1972) showed how risk would *increase* investment, due to assumptions which made the profit stream from a marginal unit of capital convex in the uncertainty variable (usually price). By contrast models of irreversible investment can produce the opposite effect – investment is postponed because a wait-and-see approach can avoid downside errors. While this sketch of the theory is not incorrect, it is incomplete. The older style models are much more varied than the characterization above and contain a number of important theories which suggest a downward bias to investment (Aiginger, 1987; Driver and Moreton, 1992). In the main, the differences between these models and the 'irreversibility' ones have less to do with irreversibility as such than with the way information arrives over time. In the older models, the uncertain variable (demand, price, cost, and so on) is revealed after capital has been committed. In the newer models, information arrives over time characterized by a Markov stochastic process (Dixit and Pindyck, 1994).[3] Under *realistic* conditions, both sets of models tend to show that risk depresses investment and the older-type models give fairly robust indications of a downward bias to the capital stock as well.

The large variety of the models on offer compels us to narrow down the available set. Here I consider three main models of the first type, introducing them with a review of the so-called Newsboy model of capital input (Model 0).[4] The cases considered are:

Models discussed in the text

	Capacity	Price	Demand	Technology
Model 0	*ex ante*	fixed*	$D = aD_0(p)$	fixed
Model 1	*ex ante*	*ex-ante**	$D = aD_0(p)$	fixed
Model 2	*ex ante*	flexible	$D = aD_0(p)$	fixed
Model 3	*ex ante*	fixed*	$D = aD_0(p)$	putty-clay

*as a ratio of cost

All of these models are of the type where the uncertainty – represented by the stochastic parameter **a** is resolved once capital has been installed; monopoly is assumed throughout.[5] The first model is the familiar Newsboy model and may be set out as follows.

Model 0

The following symbols apply:–

p = output price;
y = capacity;
c = capacity cost per unit of production;
$D_0(p)$ = demand under certainty;
$\mathbf{a}$ = a stochastic multiplicative shift parameter.

Letting marginal cost with respect to y equal expected marginal revenue, with an absolute capacity constraint at $y = \mathbf{a}D_0$,

$$c = p.\text{prob}[\mathbf{a}D_0(p) > y]$$

$$1\text{–}c/p = \text{prob}[\mathbf{a}D_0(p) < y] = \text{prob}[\mathbf{a} < y/D_0(p)] = F(Z)$$

where Z – the ratio of capacity to mean demand – is termed the 'capacity stance'. Note that $Z > 1$ implies that the firm plans to hold excess capacity. For a symmetrical distribution of $\mathbf{a}$, $F(1) = 1/2$. It then follows that:

$$p > 2c \Rightarrow Z > 1$$

The intuitive result of the Newsboy model is that, for a symmetric distribution, more capacity (newspapers) will be held as a cushion against demand, the higher the price–cost ratio. If the price does not exceed twice the cost, the seller will plan to run out of capacity because the penalty for holding an unused unit (c) will more than outweigh the gain from holding a marginal unit ($p - c$). Furthermore the higher the variance of demand, the more extreme is the deviation of the capacity stance Z from unity. For example, with $Z < 1$, the higher the risk, the fewer units the seller will hold for any given unit profit.[6]

Model 1

Model 1 relaxes the assumption of fixed price in favour of an *ex ante* price–cost margin (Driver et al., 1993). Both capacity and price are set at the decision point and demand is revealed after commitment, with price remaining a constant multiple of unit fixed cost which is regarded as the only significant cost. The *ex ante* price–cost margin may be justified on the grounds that, in practice, price behaviour appears dominated by considerations of cost-based pricing *and* coordination failure (Hall et al., 1996). We again assume multiplicative uncertainty which is probably realistic in that demand, conditional on price is assumed to vary within a constant multiple of its mean.

The maximand of Model 1 is expected profit before commitment which may be set out as a sum of the expected profit conditional on not being capital rationed ($a < Z$) and expected profit conditional on maximum capacity ($a \geq Z$).

$$\int_0^Z \pi(a, p; \varepsilon, c) f(a) da + \pi(Z, p; \varepsilon, c)[1 - F(a)]$$

This needs to be differentiated with respect to Z and p and the results equated with zero. The model requires a specification of the stochastic parameter **a** before it can be solved. The simplest case to consider where there is an analytical solution is the uniform distribution for **a** with supports [0,2]. Here there is a solution for the ratio of optimal capacity (and price) to their respective certainty levels, as follows (Driver et al., 1993).

$$p^* / p_c = (e + 1) / e$$

$$Y^* / Y_c = 4e^e / (e+1)^{e+1}$$

The biases obtaining under uncertainty – as compared with the certainty case (**a** = 1) – are shown in Figure 5.1, against a range of demand elasticities. Capacity (as a ratio of certainty capacity) is shown on the left axis along with optimal price as a ratio of certainty price. The bias is up for price and down for capacity. It is apparent that the more market power a monopoly has, the higher the upward price bias and the less the downward bias to capacity. This is not surprising as the Newsboy condition in Model 0 above is one of the first order conditions for the solution of the model. Put differently, a higher unit profit will tend to cause the firm to plan to hold excess capacity and this will counter the downward effect on capacity of the higher price. In sum, the most severe downward effect on capacity will be felt by firms with low market power. In this model, when the price elasticity of demand is in some middling range of 2–3, firms will tend to put in place only 50–60 per cent of the capacity they would under certainty.[7] Results are also available for the log-normal distribution, these being generally similar to those for the uniform case. Here it is possible to show that the magnitude of the downward investment bias increases with increasing risk, that is, increasing variance of **a**.

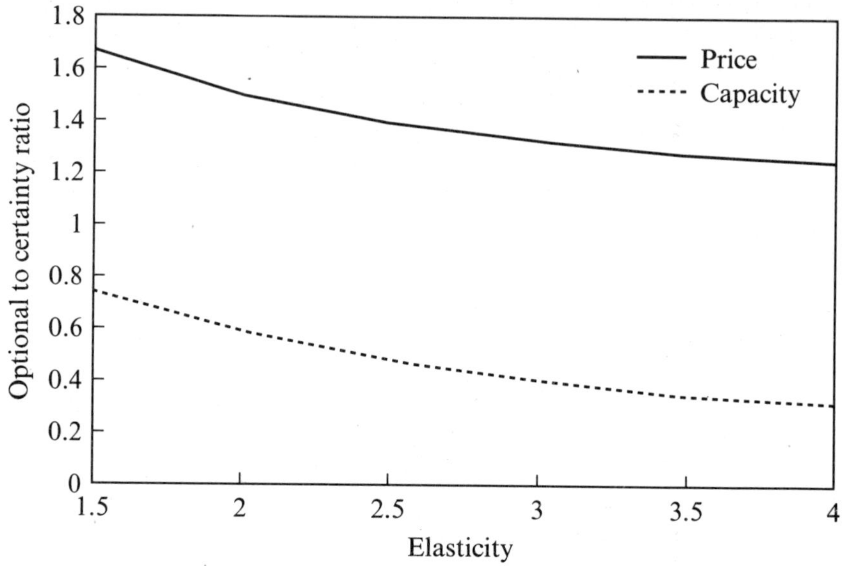

Figure 5.1 *Optimal to certainty ratios for price and capacity in Model 1*

Model 2

Model 1 may be regarded as somewhat extreme in its assumption of an *ex ante* price, unchanged in the face of demand realizations. Model 2 relaxes this assumption by allowing the firm to vary prices fully after commitment. Long-run marginal cost is the sum of unit fixed costs and unit variable cost and price can fall as far as the profit-maximizing level permits. Again, the maximand may be set out as the expected level of profits (Driver et al., 1996) as in Model 1. The difference in this case is that p is flexible *ex post* and the maximization of expected profit is carried out with respect to Z only, though with $Z = Y/p^{\varepsilon}$. In this model, there is no analytical solution, even for the uniform distribution case. Simulation results show that the bias to investment will be downward as long as the absolute elasticity is not too low and as long as the ratio of variable to fixed costs per unit is not too high. For comparison with Model 1, we may set the variable to fixed unit cost ratio at, say, unity, and examine the magnitude of the bias at different elasticities. The full and dashed curves in Figure 5.2 show the respective biases in the flexible and *ex ante* price cases. It is clear that the downward capacity bias is much lower for the case of a fully flexible *ex post* price. Even with this extreme assumption, the bias is significant at higher values of absolute price elasticity because with less market power, the incentive is less for the firm to risk carrying excess capacity.

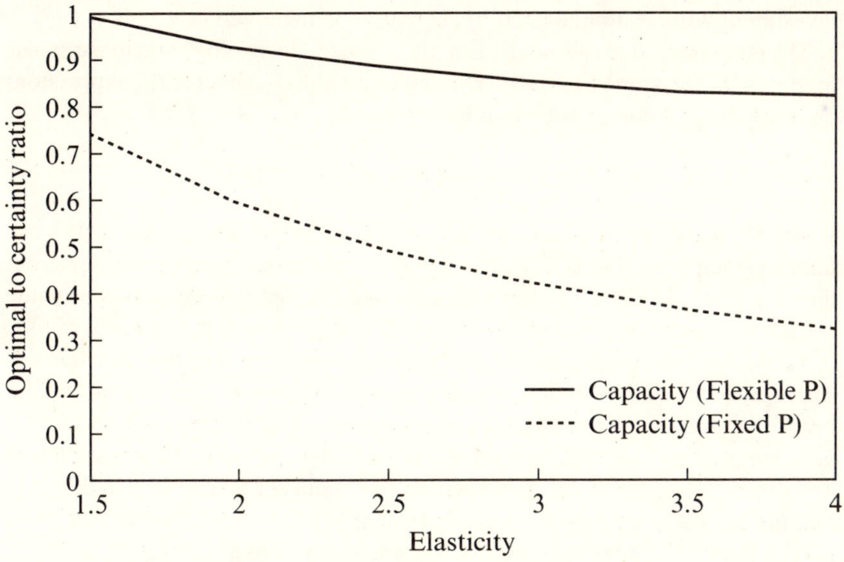

Figure 5.2 *Comparison of optimal to certainty ratios for capacity in Models 1 and 2*

When the ratio of variable costs to fixed costs is less than unity, the tendency towards a downward bias becomes larger in the flexible price case and for sufficiently small variable cost an upward bias becomes impossible at any elasticity.

Model 3

So far we have considered capacity as a composite variable. Model 3 offers new insights into investment under uncertainty in that it allows an *ex ante* choice of both capacity and technology. The capital–labour ratio at full capacity is set at the outset in a putty-clay (CES–Leontief) representation, with the choice of this ratio depending on the expected relative cost of a labour intensive or capital intensive mode (Lambert and Mulkay, 1990). The maximand is, as before, a discontinuous expression for expected profit, but here this is subject to a fixed price p where the choice variables are Z and the capital-to-labour ratio at full capacity.

The result on capacity is, as expected, a variant on the Newsboy principle in that capacity will be lower than under certainty if the unit profit at full capacity utilization is lower than some critical value. Once again a higher variance of demand leads to an enhancement of the bias, for example a tendency to lower investment will be strengthened by increased demand variance.

The main interest in this model is in the choice of technology and in particular in any bias occasioned by risk. The optimal capital–labour ratio expression, omitting the technology time trends, is given by:

$$\ln(K^*/L^*) = \text{constant} + b.\ \ln[\ (w/c)\ E(DUC)]$$

where K^* is the optimal capacity; b is the elasticity of substitution; w/c is the relative price ratio; and $E(DUC)$ is the expected degree of capacity utilization, that is, the ratio of expected production (or sales) to optimal capacity; this value can never exceed unity and will be strictly less than unity in the presence of risk.

The magnitude of the bias to the capital–labour ratio depends on $E(DUC)$. The sign of the bias is always negative so that the capital–labour ratio will be lower in the presence of risk than under certainty. The intuitive reason for this direction of bias is that labour can be varied down *ex post* whereas capital is irreversible. Because of this, firms will want to hold excess capacity in the most flexible form so that only the capital element has to be paid for when demand is such that there is excess capacity (Lambert and Mulkay, 1990).

While the Lambert and Mulkay result demonstrates an unambiguous bias towards labour intensity arising from risk, it is not clear from their work how the bias varies with Z, since $E(DUC)$ and Z are endogenous. At the certainty Z of unity $E(DUC)$ under risk is less than unity but it can rise back towards unity as Z falls.

To see this, recall the definition of the capital stance, Z:

$$Z = [\text{optimal capacity/certainty demand}]$$
$$E(DUC) = [1/Z].[\text{expected production/expected demand}]$$ [8]

The right hand square bracketed term (< 1) will vary with Z in a way that is dependent on the distribution for expected demand. For example, with **a** distributed uniform with supports [0,2] as before, we may show that

$$E(DUC) = (1/Z)(Z - Z^2/4) = 1 - Z/4;\ 0 \le Z \le 2$$

Thus, the bias in favour of labour intensity increases with Z. Intuitively, as the capital stance loosens, the extra amount of spare capacity carried requires the technology to be more labour intensive. This means that factors that tend to reduce Z, such as enhanced competition or lower profitability, will also lessen the labour intensive bias of production. The same effect is observed also in other distributions where Z tends to decrease with higher risk below threshold levels of unit profit. Put differently, enhanced risk will tend indirectly to reduce labour intensity by causing a tightening of the capacity stance Z.[9]

The magnitude of this tendential lessening of a bias towards labour intensity needs to be assessed empirically. It is generally accepted that OECD manufacturing sectors have experienced a rise in both competition and risk from the 1970s on. If, as the theory above predicts, this has led to both a tightening of the capacity stance *and* a lessening of a labour-intensive bias, the effects could be quite severe (Driver, 1996b).

The appropriate policy response may involve an encouragement of capacity creation rather than capital deepening. Obviously this is highly contentious since it contrasts with the usual argument that productivity-enhancing investment is what is important for growth. From a new growth perspective any investment that results in spillover or external benefits may produce a downward bias to investment and some evidence asserts that this spillover is strongest for efficiency investment. But whatever the outcome of this empirical research, the arguments outlined above suggest that capital broadening is of paramount concern. If the tendency to a tighter capacity stance is not countered, the result will be higher inflation and higher induced unemployment.

CONCLUSIONS

I hope to have shown in this chapter how heightened risk causes firms to adopt a more conservative approach to the amount of capacity needed to service a given estimated demand level. In addition I have also built on the work of Lambert and Mulkay (1990) to show how a longstanding bias towards labour intensity has tended to be eroded by increased competition. I have not developed formally the argument that these tendencies have contributed to the high levels of unemployment currently afflicting European economies – mainly via the effect of capital shortage on inflation and restrictive macroeconomic policy. Nevertheless, the drift of the argument is clear and so too are the general policy steps required. More capacity rather than more capital intensity should be the watchword. Is anyone listening? We could do worse than remember another maxim from Maurice's work quoted at the outset. 'A problem of economic policy is solvable when politicians can be persuaded to solve it' (Peston, 1979, p. 11). But we might also add that the politicians need economists to persuade them away from the cultivation of 'realism'.

NOTES

1. For a discussion of the first of these links, see Driver (1996a). Most commentators would probably disagree with the extraordinary view of Lord Weinstock that instability was particularly severe in the 1950s and 1960s rather than in subsequent decades – see his interview in the *Financial Times* 31 December 1996. The third link is addressed in Driver and Shepherd (1997).

2. I focus in this piece on business risk since this appears to correspond to the concerns of managerial decision makers.
3. The relative merit of these characterizations will depend on the problem analysed. The reassessment of the older-type models is important because it is unclear that the predictions of the newer models are robust. Furthermore, investment in new markets and technology may be better characterized by information arrival at the time of product launch.
4. The models discussed here are formal profit maximizing models. For a broader treatment, see Driver and Moreton (1992, Chapter 5).
5. Model 1 has been extended to oligopoly, where the results are preserved (Driver and Goffinet, 1998).
6. This result is for a symmetrical distribution but can easily be generalized.
7. This severe bias is partly explainable by the large variance of demand implied by the uniform distribution. However, using a log-normal distribution with lower variances we also obtain large biases (Driver et al., 1993).
8. Note that expected demand is the same as certainty demand by construction. Note also that expected production and sales are equal because production is defined as the minimum of demand and capacity.
9. Of course the direct effects of increased risk will be in the opposite direction.

REFERENCES

Aiginger, K. (1987), *Production and Decision Theory under Uncertainty*, Oxford: Basil Blackwell.

Dixit, A. and R. Pindyck (1994), *Investment under Uncertainty*, Princeton, NJ: Princeton University Press.

Driver, C. (1996a), 'Stagnation as a problem of transition: arguments and proposals', *Cambridge Journal of Economics*, **20**, 553–64.

Driver, C. (1996b), 'Tightening the reins: the capacity stance of UK manufacturing firms 1976–95', in J. Michie and J. Grieve Smith (eds), *Creating Industrial Capacity*, Oxford, OUP, 75–9.

Driver, C. and F. Goffinet (1998), 'Investment under demand uncertainty, ex-ante pricing and oligopoly', *Review of Industrial Organisation*, **13**, 409–23.

Driver, C, and D. Moreton (1992), *Investment, Expectations and Uncertainty*, Oxford: Basil Blackwell.

Driver, C. and D. Shepherd (1997), 'Supply constraints and the price–cost relationship', SWP 9707/E ,Imperial College Management School.

Driver, C., P. Lambert and S. Vial (1993), 'Risky production under ex-ante prices and monopoly', *Bulletin of Economic Research*, January, 59–68.

Driver, C., S. Abubacker, and G. Argiris (1996), 'Capacity choice under monopoly, flexible price and demand uncertainty', *Southern Economic Journal*, **63** (2), 526–32.

Hall, S., M. Walsh and T. Yates (1996), 'How do UK companies set prices?', *Bank of England Quarterly Bulletin*, May, 180–92.

Hartman, R. (1972), 'The effect of price and cost uncertainty on investment', *Journal of Economic Theory*, **5** (2), 258–66.

Lambert, J.-P. and B. Mulkay (1990), 'Investment in a disequilibrium model or does profitability really matter?', in J.J. Gabszewicz, J.F. Richard and L.A. Wolsey (eds), *Economic Decision Making: Games, Econometrics and Optimisation*, Amsterdam: North Holland.

Nickell, S. (1978), *The Investment Decision of Firms*, Oxford: OUP.

Orwell, G. (1961), 'Second thoughts on James Burnham', *Collected Essays*, London: Mercury Books.

Peston, M. (1979), 'When is a problem of economic policy solvable?', *Thames Papers in Political Economy*, Autumn.

Pindyck, R.S. 'Irreversibility, uncertainty and investment', *Journal of Economic Literature*, **XXIX** (3), 1110–48.

6. Do shocks matter?

Rod Cross*

Standard economic analysis assumes that shocks, in the sense of temporary disturbances, have only temporary effects. This proposition has several components: that shocks lead actual economic outcomes to deviate from equilibrium values; that equilibrium values remain unchanged by what happens when away from equilibrium; and that equilibrium points or paths are strong attractors, so that there is an actual return to equilibrium values as the shocks abate. Thus economic equilibria are characterized by *homeostasis* in the sense that they are taken to be self-maintaining or self-adjusting (see Arrow, 1988 for this terminology).

The present essay argues that in many circumstances the assumption of *homeostatic* equilibria is implausible, it being more plausible to postulate that shocks change economic equilibria. In such a world shocks matter, in that they are capable of changing the economic equilibria towards which actual economic outcomes are attracted.

This chapter is organized as follows. Section 1 outlines where the conventional wisdom that shocks do not matter, or do not matter much, came from, focusing on the metaphors used by the early neoclassical economists. Section 2 looks at the reservations expressed by Marshall on this issue. Section 3 outlines some micro foundations. in which economic agents respond discontinuously to shocks, for a model in which shocks matter. Section 4 then applies such foundations to firms' decisions as to whether to enter markets and employ labour, or quit markets and make labour redundant.

1 NEOCLASSICAL ANALYSIS

Contemporary mainstream economic analysis is usually seen as having its roots in the neoclassical 'revolution' initiated in the 1870s: Jevons, Menger,

* I am grateful to Bernard Corry and Maurice Peston for their encouragement, stimulus and friendship since I worked at Queen Mary College in the mid-1970s. My most vivid memories of Bernard and Maurice relate to 1974/5 when I was a temporary lecturer at the then QMC. The department was based in the ex dog biscuit factory in Bow Road. Bernard and Maurice managed to instil an atmosphere in which economics was taken seriously both in terms of rigorous analysis and political economy. But socially, the atmosphere was more that of a miners' welfare club.

Walras, Edgeworth, Marshall, Pareto and Fisher are some of the more prominent economists associated with this 'revolution'. In turn, as Mirowski (1989) has reminded us, virtually all of the early neoclassical economists were quite explicit in using mechanics as the metaphor source for their economic analysis. Fisher, for example, in his PhD thesis, constructed a hydrostatic model in which economic equilibrium is brought about by water 'finding its own level' in a system where consumers and producers are represented by cisterns interconnected by a series of levers. As Fisher described this neoclassical restructuring of economic analysis,

> scarcely a writer on economics omits to make some comparison between economics and mechanics . . . one speaks of a 'rough correspondence' between the play of 'economic forces' and mechanical equilibrium . . . another compares uniformity of prices to the level-seeking of water . . . another (Jevons) compares his law of exchange to that of the lever . . . another (Edgeworth) figures this economic 'system' as that of connected lakes of various levels . . . another compares society to a plastic mass such that a 'pressure' in one region is dissipated in all directions . . . in fact the economist borrows much of his vocabulary from mechanics . . . instances are: equilibrium, stability elasticity, expansion inflation, contraction, flow, efflux, force pressure, resistance, reaction, distribution (price), levels, movement, friction. (Fisher 1892/1995. p. 24)

Metaphors serve to carry over meaning from some word or object to another to which the meaning is not literally applicable, in this case from mechanical to economic systems. The question then is whether this metaphorical borrowing from mechanics made an important difference to the structure of economic analysis. Klamer and Leonard's distinction (1994) between *pedagogic*, *heuristic* and *constitutive* metaphors is interesting in this respect. If the mechanical metaphors had been used for purely illustrative or pedagogic purposes, the 'so what' reaction (Solow, 1988) would have been relevant. However, it is reasonably clear that the mechanical metaphors also involved the transference of an analytical structure to economics which propelled heuristic or problem-solving along a particular path, and played a constitutive role in saying how economic systems are structured.

The reason why the mechanical metaphors made an important difference to neoclassical analysis was that systems obeying Newton's laws of motion also conform to principles of conservation, symmetry and reversibility. Conservation principles apply to energy, momentum and so on: 'a conservation law means that there is a number you can calculate at one moment, then as nature undergoes its multitude of changes, if you calculate this quantity again at a later time it will be the same as it was before . . . the number does not change' (Feynman, 1992, p. 59). Symmetry means that 'there are things we can do to the physical laws, or to our way of representing the physical laws, which make no difference and leave everything unchanged in its effects' (ibid., pp. 84–5). Reversibility means that the processes are reversible over time: 'if you have a lot of particles doing something, and then you suddenly reverse the speed. they will completely undo what they did before . . . if you watch the waves of the sea breaking, you can stand there and wait for the great moment when the foam collects together, rises up out of the sea, and falls back further out from the shore' (ibid., pp. 108–9).

Importing these principles into economic analysis by way of metaphors drawn from Newtonian mechanics, or from conservative fields of force, implies that economic equilibria will be homeostatic, and hence that shocks do not displace economic equilibria. The conservation principle implies that nothing is lost or gained if a temporary shock to supply or demand moves the actual economic outcome away from an equilibrium position, and the symmetry and reversibility principles ensure that there will be a return to the original equilibrium as the shock abates. Thus the drawing of metaphors from Newtonian mechanics was not purely illustrative and innocuous, but instead conditioned neoclassical analysis to have fixed point or path equilibria which are invariant with regard to out-of-equilibrium behaviour.

The influence of mechanical metaphors on standard economic analysis is not immediately apparent from contemporary texts or articles. This is partly because, from the 1930s onwards, neoclassical economics was reconstructed on a formal axiomatic basis. During this reconstruction phase the argumentation runs more in terms of mathematical analogies than mechanical or conservative field of force metaphors (Ingrao and Israel, 1990). In the Arrow–Debreu proof of the existence of a unique, general equilibrium solution for a competitive economy the mathematical methods used are those appropriate to systems in which the conservation, symmetry and reversibility properties hold. Thus fixed-point theorems are used in existence proofs, ensuring that the equilibria found have the fixed-point characteristic; and the Liapunov methods of stability analysis employed do not allow the out-of-equilibrium behaviour of economic systems to affect the equilibrium configuration. This means that original mechanical metaphors continue to exert a posthumous influence:

> the energy metaphor, from field theory, is at the heart of the neoclassical conception of optimisation . . . with the Liapunov theory the mathematical structure of stability analysis was thus wholly reconciled with the intellectual structure of economic equilibrium theory – what I am suggesting here is thus consistent with the Mirowski thesis, for the rapid acceptance of Liapunov theory in economic dynamics is simply the 'long-awaited' linking of field theory's dynamics with field theory's statics. (Weintraub, 1991, p. 76)

2 A PILGRIMAGE

Although part of the movement that reshaped economic analysis on the basis of metaphors drawn from Newtonian mechanics, Marshall also displayed an awareness of the limitations of the metaphors. In particular, he argued that the conditions necessary for market equilibria to be homeostatic, and hence for shocks not to matter much, were unlikely to hold in actual economic systems. The present author is grateful to Milton Friedman (letter 2 November, 1990) for pointing out that Marshall expressed such concerns in the main text of the first edition of the *Principles*.

Marshall's view was that:

> the theory of stable equilibrium of normal demand and supply in its most abstract form assumes a certain rigidity in the conditions of demand and supply, which does not really exist . . . this theory. especially when aided by diagrams, helps to give a definiteness to our ideas . . . and in its elementary stages it does not diverge from the actual facts of life so far as to prevent its giving a fairly trustworthy picture of the chief methods of action of the strongest and most persistent group of economic forces . . . it is only when pushed to its more remote and intricate logical consequences, especially those connected with multiple positions of equilibrium. that it slips away from the conditions of real life, and soon ceases to be of much service in dealing with practical problems . . . the chief cause of this divergence is the fact that, if the normal production of a commodity increases and afterwards again diminishes to its old amount, the demand price and the supply price are not likely to return, as the pure theory assumes that they will, to their old positions for that amount. (Marshall, 1890, pp. 425–6)

Marshall invoked both demand and supply-side reasons why market equilibria might not be homeostatic in the face of shocks to demand or supply which lead to changes in consumption or production. On the demand side stress was placed on the endogeneity of habits or preferences with regard to actual consumption: 'habits which have grown up around the use of a commodity while its price is low are not quickly abandoned when its price rises again' (Marshall, 1890, p. 426). Thus if an expansionary supply shock leads to a lower price and higher consumption this is likely to engender new habits and learning-by-consuming which will see an outward shift in the relevant portion of the demand schedule: 'the schedule of demand prices which holds for the forward movement of the production of a commodity will seldom hold for the return movement but will in general require to be raised' (ibid., p. 426). The example used to illustrate this violation of homeostasis is that 'the price of cotton during the American war showed that the consumers were bidding for the reduced supply a price higher than that for which an equal amount could have been sold if its previous low price had not brought it into common use to meet a great variety of wants, many of which indeed it had itself created' (ibid., p. 426). Thus a temporary supply shock can have a permanent effect on a market equilibrium in that it can engender a shift in the demand schedule.

As far as the supply side is concerned a shock to demand, by stimulating a change in production, is likely to change the supply conditions that will prevail once the shock to demand abates:

> the supply structure may have fairly represented the actual fall in the supply price of the thing which takes place when the supply is being increased . . . but if the demand should fall off, or if for any other reason the supply should have to be diminished, the supply price would not move back by the course by which it had come, but would take a lower course . . . the schedule of supply prices which had held for the forward movement would not hold for the backward movement, but would have to be replaced by a lower schedule . . . this is true whether the production of the commodity obeys the law of Diminishing or Increasing Return . . . but it is of special importance in the latter case because the fact that the production does obey this law proves that its increase leads to great improvements in organization. (Marshall, 1890, pp. 426–7)

This means that shocks to demand, although temporary, are likely to stimulate endogenous changes in the conditions of production through learning-by-doing and the like which will remain, and therefore occasion a new equilibrium position, when demand conditions return to the *status quo ante*. Thus equilibria are not homeostatic: 'when conditions of a branch of manufacture are such that the supply price would fall very rapidly. if there should be any great increase in the scale of production. then a passing disturbance by which the demand for the commodity was increased might cause a very great fall in the stable equilibrium price. a very much larger amount than before being henceforward produced for sale at a very much lower price' (ibid., p. 427).

In subsequent editions of the *Principles* Marshall expressed unease with the 'relatively large place given to mechanical analogies' and remarked that 'the Mecca of the economist lies in economic biology' (Marshall, 1920, p. xii). The homeostatic limitations of neoclassical supply and demand analysis were seen as 'partly due to the imperfections of our analytical methods, and may conceivably be much diminished in a later age by the gradual improvement of our scientific machinery – we should have made a great advance if we could represent the normal demand price and supply price as functions both of the amount normally produced and of the time at which that amount became normal' (Marshall 1920, p. 667). With the introduction of such analytical methods bygones, in the form of past shocks to demand or supply, would not just be bygones but would be part of the set of forces shaping market equilibria.

In terms of the behaviour of economic systems as a whole. it is interesting that Keynes chose 'Is the economic system self-adjusting?' as the sub-title for his contribution to a radio debate held in 1934. Keynes pointed out that

> the strength of the self-adjusting school depends on its having behind it almost the whole body of organised economic thinking and doctrine of the last hundred years . . . it is the product of acute minds and has persuaded and convinced the great majority of the intelligent and disinterested persons who have studied it . . . it has vast prestige and a more far-reaching influence than is obvious . . . for it lies behind the education and the habitual modes of thought, not only of economists, but of bankers and businessmen and civil servants and politicians of all parties. (Keynes, 1934, p. 488)

By 'self-adjusting' Keynes clearly meant, in the terminology of the present essay, homeostatic. Keynes himself answered his own question in the negative. arguing that economic systems were not self-adjusting in the sense that they did not tend to return to some unchanged 'full employment' equilibrium after deflationary shocks such as those experienced in the run-up to the UK return to gold in 1925. The articulation of why this was not the case occupied a central position in Keynes's *General Theory*, and remains central to contemporary economic controversies such as the real costs of European Economic and Monetary Union.

3 DISCONTINUOUS ADJUSTMENT

Marshall was exercised by the effects of the changes in consumption and output occasioned by shocks to the preference and production sets that pin down demand and supply schedules. A further issue is that of how economic agents adjust their behaviour, including whether they adjust or not, in response to shocks. The standard analytical assumption is that adjustment costs are convex, and that there is some 'representative' economic agent who adjusts continuously, but partially, to shocks which lead to discrepancies between the desired and actual values of the variables under the control of the agent (see Arrow et al., 1958, for example). This analytical assumption complements the framework of homeostatic equilibria in which it is usually embedded, but does not correspond to much of the adjustment behaviour that is actually observed. Instead, many of the adjustments made by economic agents are done in discontinuous, lumpy doses; and economic agents are not homogeneous in their adjustment behaviour, but instead have different adjustment responses even when faced with a common shock. Such discontinuous adjustment by heterogeneous agents has been investigated in the recent literature (Bertola and Caballero, 1990; Caplin and Leahy, 1991, for example), and raises the possibility that economic equilibria will be shaped by the way agents respond to shocks.

The most obvious reason why many adjustments take place discontinuously is that adjustment costs are often fixed in relation to the size of the adjustment to be made, thus imparting increasing returns to adjustment processes. Further, adjustment costs are often sunk in the sense that they cannot be recovered should the agent want to reverse the adjustment. The most familiar fixed adjustment cost framework is that which gives rise to an (S, s) rule, where adjustment is only undertaken when the control variable reaches a critical value s, the lumpy adjustment dose of $(S - s)$ restoring the control variable to some upper critical value S (Arrow et al., 1951). Such a framework is only relevant to control variables that follow monotonic paths in the absence of adjustment behaviour. When the control variable moves upwards or downwards in the absence of adjustment behaviour two-way switching rules become relevant (Miller and Orr, 1966, for example).

This two-way switching framework is central to the analysis of investment behaviour, or of market entry and exit, in Dixit and Pindyck (1994). Firms are faced with fixed, sunk costs of investment or market entry which cannot be recovered, or recovered fully, should the investment project be abandoned or the firm exit the market, which are sometimes inextricably connected. In this set up it is plausible to postulate that each firm has an upper switching point a: if the expected net returns from the investment project or market entry are a or higher the firm will go ahead with the investment project. On the downside each firm will have a lower switching point b: if the expected net returns are b or lower the firm will abandon the investment project and/or exit the market.

This two-way switching or adjustment process is illustrated in Figure 6.1 with regard to market entry and exit. Each firm requires a market price p of $p \geq a$ to induce it to enter the market. In the absence of sunk costs a would also be the trigger for market exit, so the firm would quit the market if the price were to fall to $p < a$. Given the sunk costs incurred when market entry takes place, which cannot be recovered on market exit, the relevant exit trigger point is some price b, $b < a$, at and below which the revenues do not cover the recoverable costs of being in the market. Thus for $p \leq b$ the firm will be out of the market.

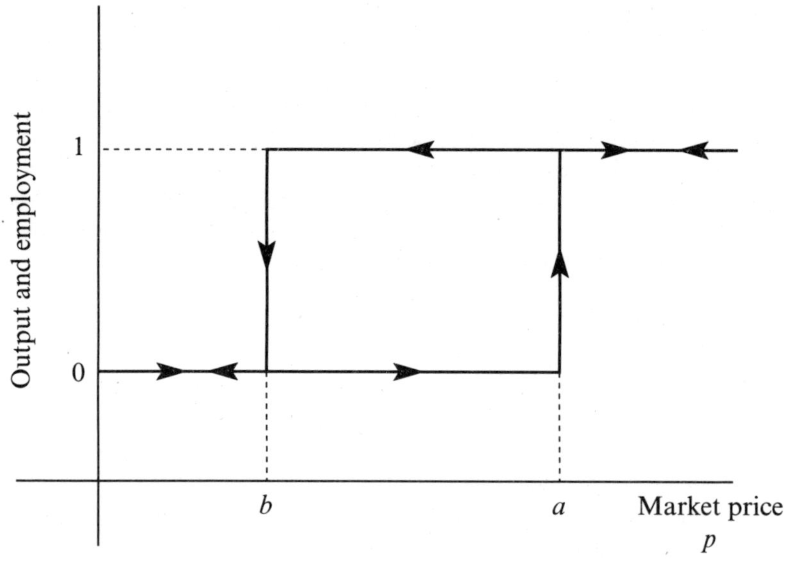

Figure 6.1 Switching points

Figure 6.1 illustrates the (a, b) switching points. For $p \geq a$ the firm will be in the market, which in this simplification means producing one unit of the good. For $p \leq b$ the firm will be out of the market, producing zero units of the good. This means that there is an intermediate range of prices, $b < p < a$, in which the firm can be in or out of the market. The firm will be in the market if this price range has been approached from above that is, if the firm was previously induced by a price $p \geq a$ to enter the market. If the intermediate range has been approached from below, however, the $b < p < a$ range will be associated with the firm not having entered the market. At an intuitive level it can be seen that there is a role for past shocks to prices in this set-up, it being necessary to know what the recent direction of price movements has been in order to know whether a firm will be active or not when present prices are in the $b < p < a$ range.

4 A SIMPLE MODEL

The preceding account has a firm responding discontinuously, with separate action and inaction thresholds, to shocks affecting the price of its output. To construct an account of the influence of discontinuous adjustment at the market level requires a specification of the adjustment behaviour of other firms. Here there are several reasons for expecting firms to be heterogeneous in the sense that they have different (a, b) switching points: 'different firms have different technologies or managerial abilities . . . historical accidents may leave different firms with stocks of capital that are differently situated relative to their action thresholds . . . then they will have different action thresholds' (Dixit and Pindyck, 1994, p. 421). In order to work out how the firms, and hence market supply, will respond to a series of shocks affecting the market price it will then be necessary to know the distribution of (a, b) switching points across firms.

The following exposition is based on a model analysed in Piscitelli et al. (1996). Let the market have M potential suppliers, and let the number of active firms be N. Each firm produces one unit of output and employs one unit of labour when in the market, and zero units of output and labour when out of the market. The market price is specified as:

$$p_t = x_t f(q_{t-1}) \tag{6.1}$$

where p is the market price, x is a stochastic shock to demand facing all firms, $f(q)$ is the deterministic component of the inverse demand function and $q \equiv N/M$, that is, the proportion of active firms (the set-up here is similar to that in Dixit and Pindyck, 1994).

The dynamics of (6.1) turn on how this period's market price p_t determines next period's proportion of active firms q_{t+1}. This can be written as:

$$q_{t+1} = \frac{1}{M}\sum_{i=1}^{M} F_{ab}\left[x_{t+1}f(q_t)\right] \tag{6.2}$$

where F_{ab} is an operator specifying the (a, b) switching points of the M potential firms which serves to map from the shocks affecting prices to output and employment. In a shockless economy, that is where x is a constant, it can be shown that every initial condition converges to a fixed point or to a two-period solution in which q swings between two points (see Piscitelli et al., 1996, p. 3).

The interesting case is what happens in an economy with shocks. Consider the sequence of shocks that generates the price fluctuations illustrated in Figure 6.2. As the price rises to p_1 firms with $a \leq p_1$ enter the market, produce output and employ labour; as the price falls to p_2 firms with $b \geq p_2$ leave the market and cease to produce output or employ labour; and so on for p_3, p_4, p_5 … . The resulting division between active and inactive firms is illustrated in Figure 6.3, which uses the Mayergoyz (1991) half-plane diagram in which each firm is represented by its F_{ab} operator, that is by its (a, b) switching points. The (a_0, b_0)

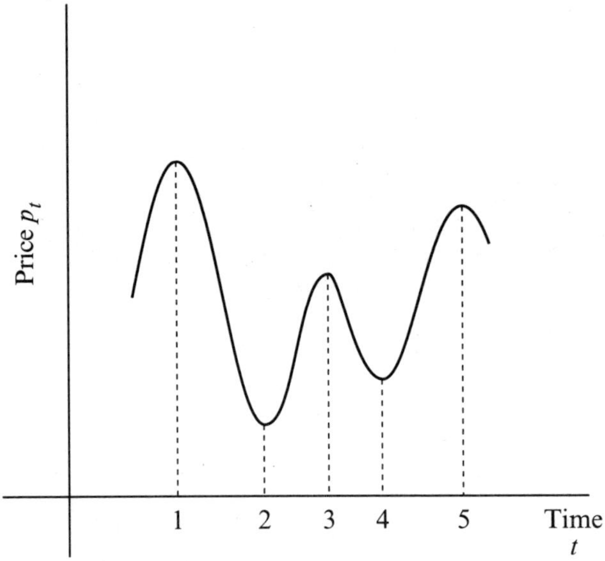

Figure 6.2 A sequence of shocks

vertex of the right-angled triangle for points above the $a = b$ line is determined by initial conditions, the simplest of which is that the price was initially so low that all the firms were out of the market. Figure 6.3 can be used to illustrate how the shocks that generate the price fluctuations illustrated in Figure 6.2 affect the balance between active and inactive firms.

As the price rises to p_1 a horizontal line drawn at this price serves to partition the firms between N_1 active firms below the p_1 line and $(M - N_1)$ inactive firms above this line. The subsequent p_2, p_3 and p_4 shocks to prices then serve to trace a staircase partition in period 4 between N_4 and $(M - N_4)$, the coordinates being (p_1, p_2), (p_3, p_2) and (p_3, p_4). This illustrates a first key property of how such systems respond to shocks: *only the extremum values of the shocks matter*. The second key property is that the system has an erasable. selective memory. This can be seen by considering the effects of the rise in price to p_5. This dominates the previous local maximum at p_3, but not the maximum at p_1 which remains intact as the global maximum. This serves to wipe the effects of the dominated local extremum at p_3 from the memory bank, which removes the

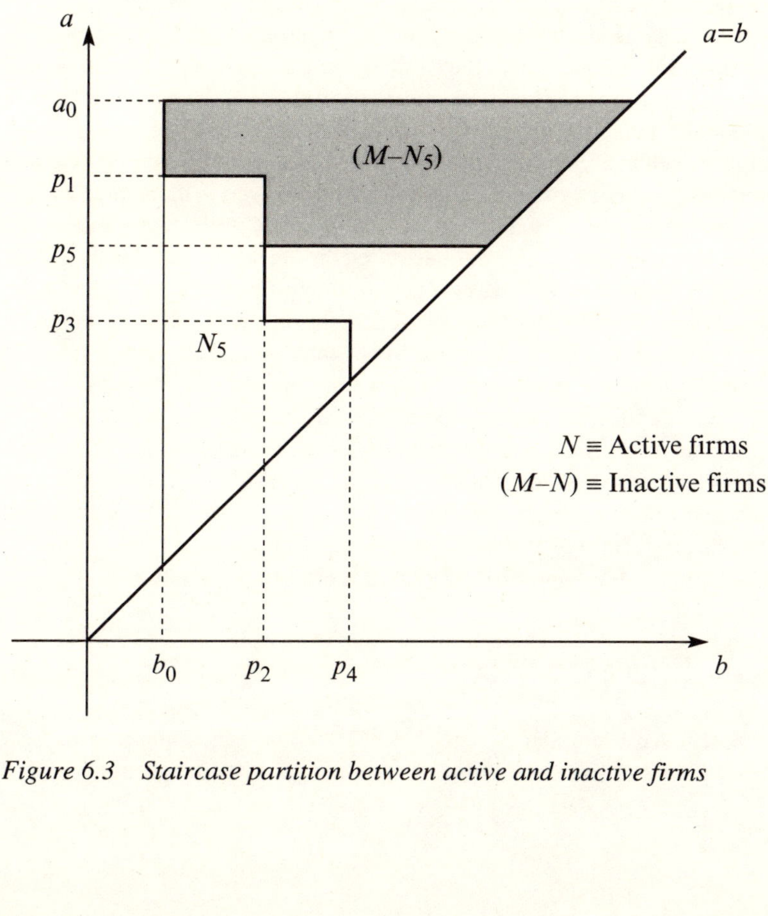

Figure 6.3 Staircase partition between active and inactive firms

coordinates associated purely with p_3, that is (p_3, p_2) and (p_3, p_4) from the memory of the system. The effect is to create a new staircase partition between N_5 and $(M - N_5)$, which is illustrated in Figure 6.3 by the unshaded and shaded areas respectively. Thus there is a selective, erasable memory of shocks: *only the non-dominated extremum values of the shocks remain in the memory bank.*

Given that in the above model active firms produce one unit of output and employ one unit of labour, the rate of inactivity of firms $(M - N)/M$ also provides a proxy for the rate of unemployment. Moving from $(M - N)/M$ to the aggregate rate of unemployment requires further analytical steps, including the interaction with supply-side influences on unemployment and the aggregation over the rest of the markets in the economic system under consideration (see Cross et al., 1996). A sketch of some of the implications for the aggregate equilibrium rate of unemployment, however, can be provided.

Consider the effects of contractionary monetary policies, in the form of the higher interest rates used to back the UK return to gold in 1925, or the UK's membership of the Exchange Rate Mechanism (ERM) of the European Monetary System 1990–92, for example. The higher exchange rates engendered by such policies served to reduce the domestic currency prices of UK exports. With homeostatic equilibrium analysis, as in the natural rate of unemployment hypothesis, such nominal shocks would not affect the equilibrium rate of unemployment, actual unemployment falling back to an unchanged natural rate as the price level or rate of inflation falls. In the above model, however, the output and unemployment lost at the higher exchange rate will not be restored by some magic of conservation and reversibility even if the real exchange rate were to revert to the *status quo ante* once the monetary shock abates: at least some firms will remain out of the market as a result of their propensities acquired during the contractionary shock, and the employment rate will be lower and the unemployment rate higher in the new equilibrium. Expansionary shocks, such as those arising from UK monetary and fiscal policies in 1987–88, or the lower interest and exchange rates on departure from the ERM in 1992, in turn are capable of generating lower unemployment equilibria, though the effects are not symmetric. Thus firms induced to enter markets and employ labour during such shocks will not all abandon the markets and cease to employ labour once the shocks abate. Thus abandoning the conservation, symmetry and reversibility properties associated with homeostasis produces a picture of economic equilibria in which shocks matter (see Amable et al., 1995 and Cross, 1995 for more detailed analysis).

5 CONCLUDING REMARKS

This chapter has attempted to establish that the standard analysis of how temporary shocks affect economic systems is heavily conditioned by the homeostasis metaphor, which serves to import conservation, symmetry and reversibility properties to the analysis. In this framework shocks can only have temporary effects, leaving the underlying economic equilibria unchanged. If this analysis is seen as implausible or inconsistent with the evidence regarding, for example, the tendency of output and employment to remain buoyant/depressed in the wake of expansionary/contractionary shocks a different metaphor is required. Changing the metaphor to one of heterostasis creates an analytical framework in which such concerns can be accommodated. one in which shocks matter in the sense that they help shape economic equilibria.

REFERENCES

Amable, B., J. Henry, F. Lordon and R. Topol (1995), 'Hysteresis revisited: a methodological approach', in R. Cross (ed.), *The Natural Rate of Unemployment: Reflections on 25 Years of the Hypothesis*, Cambridge, UK: Cambridge University Press.

Arrow, K.J. (1988), 'Workshop on the economy as an evolving complex system', in P.W. Anderson, K.J. Arrow and D. Pines (eds), *The Economy as an Evolving Complex System*, Addison-Wesley, Massachusetts.

Arrow, K.J., T. Harris and T. Marschak (1951), 'Optimal inventory policy', *Econometrica*, **19**, 205–72.

Arrow, K.J., S. Karlin and G. Scarf (1958), *Studies in the Mathematical Theory of Inventory and Production*, Stanford, CA: Stanford University Press.

Bertola, G. and R.J. Caballero (1990), 'Kinked adjustment costs and aggregate dynamics', in O.J. Blanchard and S. Fischer (eds), *NBER Macroeconomics Annual 1990*, Cambridge, MA: MIT Press.

Caplin, A.S. and J. Leahy (1991), 'State-dependent pricing and the dynamics of money and output', *Quarterly Journal of Economics*, **105**, 708.

Cross, R. (1995), 'Is the natural rate hypothesis consistent with hysteresis?', in R. Cross (ed.), *The Natural Rate of Unemployment: Reflections on 25 Years of the Hypothesis*, Cambridge, UK: Cambridge University Press.

Cross, R., J. Darby and J. Ireland (1996), 'Hysteresis and ranges or intervals for equilibrium unemployment', Robert Schuman Centre Discussion Paper, European University Institute Florence.

Dixit, A. and R. Pindyck (1994), *Investment under Uncertainty*, Princeton, NJ: Princeton University Press.

Feynman, R. P. (1992), *The Character of Physical Law*, London: Penguin Books.

Fisher, I. (1892/1925), *Mathematical Investigations in the Theory of Value and Prices*, New Haven, CT: Yale University Press.

Ingrao, B. and G. Israel (1990), *The Invisible Hand: Economic Equilibrium in the History of Science*, Cambridge, MA: MIT Press.

Keynes, J.M. (1934), 'Poverty in plenty: is the economic system self-adjusting?', *The Listener*, 2I November.

Klamer, A. and T.C. Leonard (1994), 'So what's an economic metaphor?', in P. Mirowski (ed.), *Natural Images in Economic Thought*, New York: Cambridge University Press.

Marshall, A. (1890), *The Principles of Economics*, 1st edition, 8th edition 1920, London: Macmillan.

Mayergoyz, I.D. (1991), *Mathematical Models of Hysteresis*, Berlin: Springer-Verlag.

Miller, M.H. and D. Orr (1966), 'A model of the demand for money by firms', *Quarterly Journal of Economics*, **80** (3), 413–35.

Mirowski, P. (1989), *More Heat than Light*, New York: Cambridge University Press.

Piscitelli, L., M. Grinfield, H. Lamba and R. Cross (1996), 'On entry and exit in response to aggregate shocks', mimeo, University of Strathclyde, Scotland, forthcoming *Applied Economics Letters*.

Solow, R.M. (1988), 'Comments from inside economics', in A. Klamer, D.M. McCloskey and R.M. Solow (eds), *The Consequences of Economic Rhetoric*, New York: Cambridge University Press.

Weintraub, E.R. (1991), *Stabilising Dynamics: Constructing Economic Knowledge*, New York: Cambridge University Press.

PART III

Policy Issues

7. Household production, human capital and optimal linear income taxation

Patricia Apps and Ray Rees

1 INTRODUCTION

The question of how to tax married couples has long been a central issue in public finance. In the traditional literature the problem was posed in terms of whether a progressive income tax should be based on the individual incomes of the partners or on their combined income. This could be seen as the problem of the choice of tax unit: the individual versus the household. With the increasing participation rates of women in the labour force the issue has gained substantially in importance in the last few decades. The starting point of this paper[1] is the view that the theoretical literature on optimal income taxation is insufficiently well-developed to provide a satisfactory treatment of this issue, essentially because of the way in which the household is modelled. We propose some alternative models and discuss their implications in the context of the theory of the optimal linear income tax.

The traditional textbook approach sees the problem as one of balancing three conflicting goals:

1. *horizontal equity*, defined as the equal treatment of couples with the same combined income;
2. *marriage neutrality*, the avoidance of a tax penalty on marriage;
3. *progressivity*, which we here interpret to mean that the proportion of a person's income that is paid in tax increases with the amount of that income.

So, for example, under a progressive individual tax system, a household with two earners with incomes of £15 000 and £5000 respectively could pay less tax than one with a single earner making £20 000 and the other partner not working, though obviously this possibility disappears if there is a simple proportional tax. This appears to violate horizontal equity. But switching to a joint taxation system under which each household would pay the same amount of tax could violate marriage neutrality. Moreover, under a joint taxation or 'income splitting' system such as that in the US and Germany the marginal rate faced by the secondary earner is the same as that faced by the primary earner, despite possibly large differences in their incomes, and the tax paid by the secondary earner would exceed that paid by a single person with the same income. This then reinforces what may be regarded as an already significant degree of discrimination against women's participation in the labour force.

Note that nothing so far has been said about the incentive effects of taxation. If we accept what appears to be the empirical evidence that the labour supply elasticities of working wives is significantly higher than that of their husbands,[2] standard Ramsey-type arguments would suggest that secondary earners should in fact face *lower* marginal tax rates. For example Boskin and Sheshinski (1983) and Feldstein and Feenberg (1996) argue for a system of individual taxation under which primary and secondary earners would be subject to separate, progressive tax schedules, with that for the latter having lower rates at each income level. Though possibly a step in the right direction, we would argue that a limitation of these studies is the complete neglect of distributional issues, which in turn is due to the limitations of their underlying model of the household.

The model used in the public finance literature is one in which the household is assumed to have a standard utility function defined on a single consumption good and two types of leisure, which it maximizes subject to a pooled income constraint. This clearly runs counter to the principle of methodological individualism underlying neoclassical economics, both positive and normative, according to which the individual is the basic unit of analysis. From this principle it follows that the household should be considered as a collection of individuals with their own utility functions, and the analysis should be concerned with the impact of tax parameters on the utilities of the individuals *as mediated through the household resource allocation process*. The household *per se* cannot have a utility. Its significance is rather that it is a unit within which production and consumption are organized in a way which creates interdependencies among individuals, and the effects of external parameter changes, such as changes in tax rates., on individual utilities are determined by the joint decisions of the household members.

Given this view, the problem is how to model this kind of household. The approach adopted in Apps and Rees (1988) is simply to think of the household as a small economy.[3] Goods are produced and consumed within the household, and labour time of one or both household members is exchanged for goods on the market. Only these market exchanges are subject to taxation: production and exchange within the household are untaxed. Naturally, then, this produces distortions, of which overspecialization by a household member in domestic production is one example. As we shall see, formal models embodying this approach are easy to work with, given that we are allowed an assumption which could serve as a characterization of rational behaviour in this context: *whatever the process by which the household reaches its decisions, the resulting resource allocation is Pareto efficient.* The household is rational enough to exhaust all possibilities of costless welfare improvement for its members. As we know, this says nothing about the equity of the achieved utility distribution in the household.

As compared to the standard 'household utility function' approach therefore we make two extensions: the first, to two individuals; the second, to replacement of the usual dichotomy between time spent at 'work' and 'leisure', by the idea that time is divided between market work, domestic production and, if its inclusion would be of interest in a model, pure leisure defined as the direct consumption of one's own time. A second principle of neoclassical economics, that of modelling parsimony, suggests then the question: why bother? Clearly there is a gain in descriptive realism, but that in itself is not considered to be, worth very much. Do we gain in terms of insight, understanding, policy relevance and so on?[4]

As we shall see below, the extension to two individuals is required if we want to consider explicitly the issue of welfare distribution within the household and its relationship to taxation. The household utility function approach is adequate for making the point about efficiency but cannot deal with equity issues *within* as opposed to *across* households. But why should we be concerned about the effect of taxation on the welfare of individual 1 in household h relative to that, of individual 2 in household j, $h \neq j$, and not on the relative welfares of two individuals in the same household?

The relevance of the extension to include domestic production is much less obvious. It could be argued that what really matters is the substitution between time spent at market work and remaining time. It doesn't matter what we call the latter, as long as its use generates utility. We could argue that extension of the household model to two individuals *without* also incorporating domestic production[5] leads to a very unsatisfactory theory of the household. Consider for example a household in which one member supplies no labour to the market. Her consumption of leisure is total, her consumption of the market goods is entirely a result of a transfer from the working spouse. This is descriptively speaking a model of specialization in consumption roles and of parasitic dependency matched by extreme altruism. That may be perhaps how men have liked to view themselves and their wives. It contrasts unfavourably, however, with a model in which this kind of time allocation would be seen as the outcome of specialization in domestic production and corresponding exchange of domestic for market goods, which is at the same time more interesting, more true to life, and less derogatory to the partner specializing in household production.

This argument however does not meet the point raised. Does it matter, in terms of the analytical results, *what* we call time not spent at market work? In fact we show in this paper that it does, for reasons essentially related to human capital and the across-household welfare distribution. Take for example Sheshinski's (1972) classic analysis of optimal linear income taxation of individuals who divide their time between work and leisure. There is a distribution of wage rates across individuals which reflects their productive capacity or human capital. For each, however, one unit of time not spent working produces one unit of the consumption good leisure: despite their human capital differences all individuals are equally productive at 'producing' leisure. This implicit assumption and its possible generalization only really become evident when we explicitly incorporate domestic production. For example, the assumption that, because of their human capital, individuals who are highly productive in market work are also highly productive in household production, has important implications for the optimal linear income tax. The point is that the total consumption a household can enjoy is determined not only by its money income from market work, but also by its capacity to produce domestic output. A household in which only one partner works in the market may be much better off than one with a higher money income resulting from both partners working in the market, because of the greater consumption of domestic output the former can enjoy. This also implies that the idea of horizontal equity based on *money income* discussed at the beginning of this paper is likely to be totally misleading in an economy with household production. The precise nature of the correlation between the two productivities is of course an empirical matter. Our point here is that the extension of the model to incorporate domestic production makes us aware of the issue and allows us to explore the implications of alternative assumptions.

The points made in this introduction are explored more formally in the rest of the paper. We first retain the assumption of one-person households and show the implications of introducing household production in the simplest possible context. We then present some models of two-person households without domestic production.[6] We hope that in this way the relative contributions of the two types of generalization will be clear.

2 ONE-PERSON HOUSEHOLDS WITH PRODUCTION

Take the simplest model, in which a household consumes two goods, x and y, with x a bought-in market good with price 1 and y the domestically produced good. The household produces y according to the strictly increasing and concave function $f(t)$, with t the time input into domestic production, and $f(.)$ has the inverse $\phi(y)$. The household wants to maximize its utility $u(x, y)$ subject to this production constraint and its budget and time constraints

$$x - \beta w l = \alpha \tag{7.1}$$

$$l + t = T \tag{7.2}$$

$$l \geq 0, t \geq 0 \tag{7.3}$$

where l is market labour supply, w is the market wage, β is 1 minus the marginal tax rate and α is the lump sum payment to each household under the linear tax regime. We can eliminate the time constraint and give ourselves a problem in x, y by writing the budget constraint as

$$x - \beta w[T - \phi(y)] - \alpha = 0. \tag{7.4}$$

Figure 7.1 shows the compensated and uncompensated effects of a reduction in the marginal tax rate (increase in β), and they are exactly as we would expect from the usual analysis in the labour supply space. A rise in the after-tax wage has a substitution effect that increases consumption of the market good and reduces that of the domestic good, which must be associated with a reduction in time spent in domestic production and an increase in market labour supply. If both goods are however normal the income effect could cause

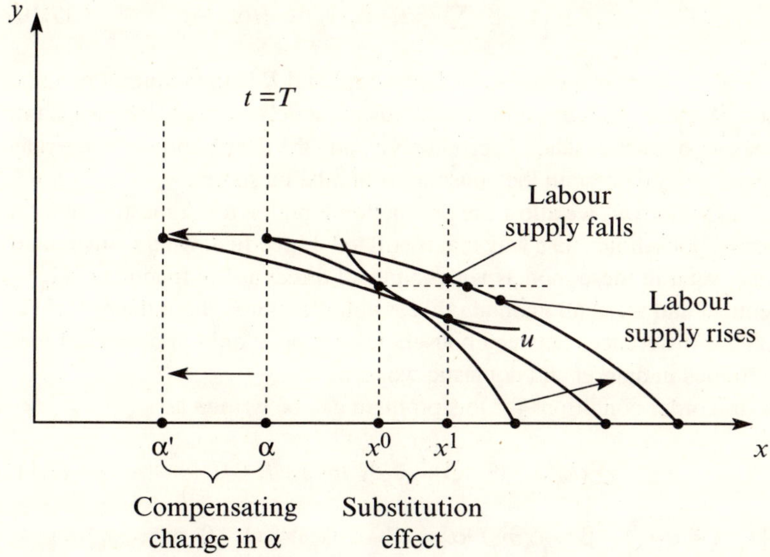

Figure 7.1 Effects of a reduction in the marginal tax rate

consumption of the domestic good to rise overall, thus reducing market labour supply and giving a backward-bending labour supply curve.

For later reference it is useful to record that the usual comparative statics gives

$$\partial v/\partial\beta = w\lambda[T - \phi(y)] \tag{7.5}$$

$$\partial v/\partial\alpha = \lambda \tag{7.6}$$

$$\partial x/\partial\beta = ws_x + w[T - \phi(y)]\partial x/\partial\alpha \tag{7.7}$$

$$\partial y/\partial\beta = ws_y + w[T - \phi(y)]\partial y/\partial\alpha \tag{7.8}$$

where s_i is the compensated demand derivative, $i = x, y$ and $v(\beta w, \alpha)$ is the indirect utility function.

Now consider the optimal linear income tax problem. We assume the planner wants to maximize the utilitarian social welfare function (this is easily generalized)

$$W = \sum v^h(\beta w_h, \alpha) \tag{7.9}$$

subject to the budget constraint

$$R \leq (1 - \beta) \sum w_h[T - \phi_h(y_h)] - H\alpha \tag{7.10}$$

where $h = 1, \ldots, H$ is the household subscript and R is the required revenue, assumed constant. As is usual in these kinds of models we regard the wage rate as a measure of the household's productivity and the distribution of wage rates is exogenously given, with the households numbered so that $w_h \leq w_{h+1}$, $h = 1, \ldots, H - 1$. Moreover, we allow the production function for domestic output to vary across households, in a way that is still to be specified. On the other hand, as is also usual in these models we assume all direct utility functions $u(x_h, y_h)$ are identical and we shall maintain this assumption throughout the rest of this paper. Thus differences between households can arise only in respect of their productivities in market and domestic work.

The first order conditions for this problem can be written as

$$\sum[\lambda_h/\mu - (1 - \beta)w_h\phi_h'\partial y_h/\partial\alpha] - H = 0 \tag{7.11}$$

$$\sum\{[\lambda_h/\mu - 1 - (1 - \beta)w_h\phi_h'\partial y_h/\partial\alpha]w_h[T - \phi_h(y_h)] - (1 - \beta)w\phi' w_h s_{yh}\} = 0 \tag{7.12}$$

where μ is the Lagrange multiplier attached to the revenue constraint and use has been made of the Slutsky equations in the second condition. We can define

$$\sigma_h = \lambda_h/\mu - (1-\beta)w_h\phi_h'\partial y_h/\partial\alpha \tag{7.13}$$

as the net social marginal utility of income to household h, so that the first condition becomes

$$\sigma \equiv \sum\sigma_h/H = 1. \tag{7.14}$$

We also define the household's compensated labour supply elasticity as

$$\varepsilon_h \equiv \beta w_h\phi_h' s_{yh}/[T-\phi_h(y_h)] \tag{7.15}$$

and so we can finally write the second condition as

$$\frac{1-\beta}{\beta} = -\frac{\sum_h w_h[T-\phi_h(y_h)](\sigma_h-\sigma)/H}{\sum_h w_h l_h \varepsilon_h/H} \tag{7.16}$$

where in the denominator of the last term we have simply used the fact that $l_h = T - \phi_h(y_h)$.

This condition has the usual interpretation of showing how the marginal tax rate depends on the trade-off between efficiency, as expressed by the compensated elasticities in the denominator, and income distribution, as expressed by what is essentially a covariance between household gross wage income and the net social marginal utility of household income. For example if high wage incomes are associated with low σs and conversely then this covariance will be negative,[7] implying a positive marginal tax rate (since of course the compensated elasticities in the denominator are always positive), which is higher the greater the inverse correlation between wage income and social marginal utility of income. Clearly the introduction of household production makes no real difference to the efficiency term, and so in what follows this will he taken as given and denoted by E. The point of interest is the interpretation of the distributional term in the presence of household production.

In the standard model in which time is divided between market work and 'leisure', in effect households are assumed to have identical productivities in domestic production regardless of the differences in human capital that give rise to differences in wage rates. That is, the good 'leisure' is produced as a linear function of time and one unit of time produces one unit of leisure for all households. The advantage of the explicit introduction of household production is that it allows the consequences of varying this assumption to be analysed. First we consider the opposite extreme: suppose all households have the same productivity in market work, and therefore the same wage rate, but there is a given distribution of productivities in domestic production. We can model this by introducing the parameter $k_h > 0$, with $k_h \leq k_{h+1}$, $h = 1, \ldots, H-1$, and by writing the household production function as

$$y_h = f(k_h t_h) \tag{7.17}$$

implying

$$t_h = \phi(y_h)/k_h. \tag{7.18}$$

In words, domestic output is the same function of efficiency units $k_h t_h$ across households. The expression for the optimal marginal tax rate (recalling that the wage rate is now constant across households) becomes

$$\frac{1-\beta}{\beta} = \frac{w\sum\left[\phi(y_h)/k_h\right](\sigma_h - \sigma)/H}{E}. \tag{7.19}$$

The question now is: how is time allocated to domestic labour supply t_h and net marginal social utility of household income σ_h likely to be correlated across households? It is intuitively clear, and straightforward to prove, that this correlation will be negative. The argument goes as follows: with the wage rate constant, the higher is k_h, *ceteris paribus*, the greater is the marginal productivity of time in domestic production and, since the household chooses t_h by equating marginal product with the wage, we have that t_h increases with k_h. In other words market labour supply decreases with increasing (marginal) productivity in domestic production. On the other hand household utility increases with increasing k_h since the production boundary of the household is shifting outward, and this reduces the social marginal utility of income for the household. This implies a negative covariance between t_h and σ_h and therefore a negative marginal tax rate, implying in turn that the lump sum α must also be negative.

This apparently perverse result has a straightforward interpretation: increasing wage income $w_h l_h$ is associated with decreasing household welfare and so the redistribution has to be away from households with lower wage incomes and toward those with higher wage incomes. This redistribution can only be achieved in the linear tax system by taking a lump sum from all households and then paying households a given proportion of their wage income, so that the better-off households, those with lower wage incomes, end up as net payers and the worse-off households, with higher wage incomes, are net beneficiaries.

This case then, though in a sense extreme, is no more so than the standard labour supply model, and demonstrates in a stark way the danger of assuming that household wage income is a reliable indicator of household welfare in the presence of domestic production.

Both the standard case and that just considered assume that there is no correlation between productivity in market work, as measured by the wage, and productivity in domestic work, as measured by k_h. This is of course an extreme assumption. Let us consider the opposite extreme and assume they are perfectly correlated, which we can represent by setting $w_h = k_h$. Now from the first order conditions for the household's problem we have the condition

$$\frac{u_y}{u_x} = \frac{\beta w_h \phi'(y_h)}{k_h}. \tag{7.20}$$

Clearly, therefore, since the expression is identical for all households each chooses the same y-value and $\phi(y_h)$ is the same across households. The expression for the optimal marginal tax rate then becomes

$$\frac{1-\beta}{\beta} = -\frac{\sum w_h T(\sigma_h - \sigma)/H}{E}. \tag{7.21}$$

This shows that the relevant covariance is that between household full income and net marginal social utility of income and we can expect this to be negative, with higher wage rates associated with lower σ_h. Thus the marginal tax rate will again be positive.

3 TWO-EARNER HOUSEHOLDS

The first issue in approaching the analysis of taxation of two-person households is that of the basic modelling approach: how should such a household be modelled? The usual answer in the literature,[8] as we discussed in the introduction, is to treat the household as if it were a single individual possessing a standard utility function defined on a consumption good x and two types of leisure, y_1 and y_2. The household's maximization problem is then written

$$\max u = u(x, y_1, y_2) \tag{7.22}$$

$$\text{subject to } x = \beta \sum w_i l_i + \alpha \tag{7.23}$$

$$l_i + y_i = T \tag{7.24}$$

$$l_i \geq 0, y_i \geq 0, i = 1, 2 \tag{7.25}$$

y_i now denotes i's pure leisure, the remaining notation is as before. In particular α and β are the parameters of a linear tax system. Note that neither differentiates between individuals. Thus in effect we have a tax system in which the lump sum is paid to the household while incomes are added together to determine the household tax liability, so that both household members face the same marginal tax rate. This then reflects the situation under 'joint filing' or 'income splitting' as for example prevails in the USA and Germany. The equilibrium of the household is then perfectly straightforward: optimal labour supply or equivalently leisure consumption of each type is found by equating the marginal rate of substitution between the consumption good and a leisure consumption to the respective after-tax wage rate. It is straightforward to derive the Slutsky equations and partials of the indirect utility function:

$$\frac{\partial x}{\partial \beta} = \sum_i \left(w_i s_i + w_i l_i \frac{\partial x}{\partial \alpha} \right) \tag{7.26}$$

$$\frac{\partial l_i}{\partial \beta} = \sum_j \left(w_j s_{ij} + w_j l_j \frac{\partial l_i}{\partial \alpha} \right), i, j = 1, 2 \tag{7.27}$$

$$\frac{\partial v}{\partial \beta} = \lambda \sum_i w_i l_i \tag{7.28}$$

$$\frac{\partial v}{\partial \alpha} = \lambda \tag{7.29}$$

where v is the indirect utility function, s_i is the compensated demand derivative of x with respect to i's after-tax wage, and s_{ij} is the compensated demand derivative of i's labour supply with respect to after-tax wage j. The summations arise because both wage incomes are subject to the same marginal tax rate.

We formulate the optimal tax problem by introducing the subscript $h = 1, \ldots, H$ for households and again assuming a utilitarian social welfare function, so that the problem becomes

$$\max W = \sum_h v^h(\beta w_{1h}, \beta w_{2h}, \alpha) \tag{7.30}$$

$$\text{subject to } R \leq (1-\beta)\sum_h \sum_i w_{ih} l_{ih} - H\alpha. \tag{7.31}$$

The first-order conditions can be written

$$\sum_h \left[\frac{\lambda_h}{\mu} + (1-\beta)\sum_i w_{ih}\frac{\partial l_{ih}}{\partial \alpha}\right] - H = 0 \tag{7.32}$$

$$\sum_h \left\{\frac{\partial v^h}{\partial \beta} + \mu\left[(1-\beta)\sum_i w_{ih}\frac{\partial l_{ih}}{\partial \beta} - \sum_i w_{ih} l_{ih}\right]\right\} = 0. \tag{7.33}$$

We can again define

$$\sigma_h \equiv \frac{\lambda_h}{\mu} + (1-\beta)\sum_i w_{ih}\frac{\partial l_{ih}}{\partial \alpha} \tag{7.34}$$

as the net marginal social utility of income to household h, and note that

$$\sigma \equiv \sum_h \sigma_h / H = 1. \tag{7.35}$$

Using this and the results given earlier we can express the condition for the optimal marginal rate as

$$\frac{(1-\beta)}{\beta} = -\frac{\sum_h I_h(\sigma_h - \sigma)/H}{\sum_h \sum_i w_{ih} l_{ih} \sum_j \varepsilon_{ijh}/H} \tag{7.36}$$

where $I_h \equiv \Sigma_i w_{ih} l_{ih}$ is total household gross wage income and

$$\varepsilon_{ijh} \equiv \frac{\beta w_{jh} s_{ijh}}{l_{ih}} \tag{7.37}$$

is the compensated elasticity of i's labour supply with respect to j's after-tax wage in household h, for $i, j = 1, 2$.

The first thing we can note about this optimal tax condition is that the distributional term in the numerator is essentially as it was in the case of one-person households. There is a single net marginal social utility of income for a household and the deviation of this from the average is weighted by the total household wage income. Thus the household, rather than the individual, is the basic 'welfare unit'. The formulation of the household utility function therefore makes it impossible to discuss the issue of the effect of the distribution of welfare *within* the household on the optimal marginal tax rate. As we shall see below, it is as if the household carries out the optimal – from the point of view of the 'social planner' – income redistribution between its members and so all the planner has to be concerned with is the income distribution *across* households.

The essential contribution of the modelling approach is reflected in the denominator. A variation in the marginal tax rate has two substitution effects for each individual: the effect of the change in his/her own net of tax wage, and the effect of the change in the partner's net of tax wage, on his/her labour supply. The sole effect of the formation of households captured by this model is the interdependence it creates between wage rates and labour supplies of the individual household members. As compared to the model where households consist of one individual, we have here a set of cross-substitution terms, which summarize the effect of joint decision-taking within households over the labour supply of their members. Each own-elasticity of labour supply is adjusted by a cross-elasticity reflecting the influence of the wage rate of the partner. This implies, for example, that for households in which only one partner supplies labour to the market, the existence of the other has no effect on the structure of taxation. It also implies that where the cross-elasticities are negative, perhaps empirically the most plausible sign, the efficiency term in the denominator will be smaller than where they did not exist, and so the marginal tax rate will *ceteris paribus* be larger and the tax system more progressive. Note, however, that the model itself says nothing about what these signs should be: in general these goods may be Hicksian complements or substitutes, it is simply a matter of what the household preferences happen to be. A possible further advantage of a household production approach therefore is that it may give some insight into what underlies these cross-elasticities, since presumably the substitutability or complementarity of the time the household members devote to domestic production, that is, the characteristics of the underlying household production process, in fact determine these cross-effects.[9]

The model can also be used to explore a further possibility. Since the primary and secondary earners in the household are readily distinguishable, it is possible to consider a tax system in which they would pay different marginal rates. It is easy to show that in general this would be optimal. This question has been analysed by Boskin and Sheshinski (1983) (hereafter B–S), whose analysis seems to suggest that it is much less easy to show clearly how the optimal individual marginal tax rates will depend on the parameters of the problem. Here we present an appealing new result which gives clear insights into this issue and moreover is not dependent on the special assumptions which B–S have to make to be able to make a clear interpretation of their results.

Thus suppose now that we have a lump sum α paid to each household, but that there are two marginal rate schedules according to which the individuals are paid, β_1 and β_2. We can then define the optimal tax problem as follows:

$$\max W = \sum_h v^h(\beta_1 w_{1h}, \beta_2 w_{2h}, \alpha) \tag{7.38}$$

$$\text{subject to } R \leq \sum_h \sum_i (1-\beta_i) w_{ih} l_{ih} - H\alpha. \tag{7.39}$$

The relevant derivatives from the household comparative statics are now

$$\frac{\partial l_j}{\partial \beta_i} = w_i s_{ji} + w_i l_i \frac{\partial l_j}{\partial \alpha}, i, j = 1, 2 \tag{7.40}$$

$$\frac{\partial v}{\partial \beta_i} = \lambda w_i l_i, i = 1, 2 \tag{7.41}$$

(ignoring the h subscript), and the first-order conditions for the optimal tax problem are now

$$\sum_h \left[\frac{\lambda_h}{\mu} + \sum_i (1-\beta_i) w_{ih} \frac{\partial l_{ih}}{\partial \alpha} \right] - H = 0 \tag{7.42}$$

$$\sum_h \left\{ \frac{\partial v^h}{\partial \beta_i} + \mu \left[\sum_j (1-\beta_j) w_{jh} \frac{\partial l_{jh}}{\partial \beta_i} - w_{ih} l_{ih} \right] \right\} = 0, i = 1, 2. \tag{7.43}$$

We now define

$$\sigma_h \equiv \frac{\lambda_h}{\mu} + \sum_i (1-\beta_i) w_{ih} \frac{\partial l_{ih}}{\partial \alpha} \tag{7.44}$$

as the net marginal social utility of income to household h, and note that

$$\sigma \equiv \sum_h \sigma_h / H = 1. \tag{7.45}$$

Using the Slutsky equations and substituting from the first condition into the other two gives the two conditions

$$\sum_h w_{ih} l_{ih}(\sigma_h - \sigma) + \frac{1-\beta_i}{\beta_i}\sum_h w_{ih} l_{ih}\varepsilon_{iih} + \frac{1-\beta_j}{\beta_i}\sum_h w_{jh} l_{jh}\varepsilon_{jih} = 0, i, j = 1, 2, i \neq j \tag{7.46}$$

where as before

$$\varepsilon_{jih} \equiv \frac{\beta_i w_{ih} s_{jih}}{l_{jh}} \tag{7.47}$$

is the compensated elasticity of j's labour supply with respect to i's after-tax wage in household h, for $i, j = 1, 2$. Denote the optimal values of the marginal tax rates by β^*_i and insert them into the first-order conditions. Writing C_i for the first (covariance) term in these conditions, E_i for the first weighted sum of elasticities and E_{ji} for the second, where of course all values are taken at the optimal point, we can write the conditions as the linear system, which holds identically at the optimal point:

$$\begin{bmatrix} C_1 - E_1 & -E_{21} \\ -E_{12} & C_2 - E_2 \end{bmatrix}\begin{bmatrix} \beta_1^* \\ \beta_2^* \end{bmatrix} = \begin{bmatrix} -(E_{11} + E_{21}) \\ -(E_{12} + E_{22}) \end{bmatrix}. \tag{7.48}$$

Assume now, as is usual, that the covariance terms are negative. If, as is also reasonable, the own elasticities are positive and at least as large as the cross-elasticities, the determinant of the left hand matrix will certainly be positive. Solving for β^*_1, β^*_2 gives on that assumption

$$\beta_2^* \gtrless \beta_1^* as \frac{-C_1}{E_1 + E_{21}} \gtrless \frac{-C_2}{E_2 + E_{12}}. \tag{7.49}$$

The first thing this tells us is that on reasonable assumptions secondary earners (working wives) should be taxed at a lower marginal rate than their husbands. If we make the assumption of 'assortative mating', which in this case can be interpreted to mean that wives' gross wage income is perfectly correlated with that of their husbands, and join this with the fact that wives' income is just a fraction of that of their husbands, then we certainly have $-C_2 < -C_1$. Secondly if we use the stylized fact that labour supply elasticities of working women are higher than those of working men, and assume this is not offset by the cross-elasticities term, then $E_2 + E_{12} > E_1 + E_{21}$. Note that this is in line with the intuition we would have from the 'Ramsey rule', that higher elasticities imply lower tax rates.

A further nice point of interpretation is that if the cross-elasticity terms were all zero, the term $-C_i/E_i$ is precisely that which gives the optimal linear tax term $(1-\beta_i)/\beta_i$ in an economy consisting only of type *i* individuals, given also the values σ_h. If, in such an economy, secondary earners would have a lower marginal tax rate, then so they should in the actual economy provided the cross-elasticities do not matter 'too much'.

The final point is of course that only under very special and circumstantial conditions would the optimal marginal tax rates turn out to be equal in this model and so generically we should have separate or individual taxation, even when intra-household distributional issues are left out of account, as they are in this model.

We asserted earlier that a severe limitation of this 'household utility function' model is that it rules out any discussion of the *intra-household* welfare distribution, or alternatively that it implicitly assumes that the welfare distribution chosen by the household corresponds to that which would be chosen by the planner. We now want to explore this issue. To do this we formulate a model which is a special case of that in Apps and Rees (1988). The household consists of two individuals each with his/her own utility function, and they pool the incomes they receive from their market labour supply. The key assumption, which can be regarded as a natural extension of individual rationality in this context, is that they choose a Pareto efficient allocation of resources. As well as having appeal on rationality grounds, this assumption allows a very simple and familiar formulation of the household's decision problem. They solve

$$\max u^1(x_1, y_1) \tag{7.50}$$

$$\text{subject to } u^2(x_2, y_2) \geq u_2^0 \tag{7.51}$$

$$\sum_i x_i = \beta \sum_i w_i l_i + \alpha \tag{7.52}$$

$$y_i + l_i = T, i = 1, 2. \tag{7.53}$$

The idea is that each partner has a minimum reservation utility that they require in order to remain in the household, but for simplicity we assume that the actual allocation is always in the interior of the set of allocations defined by these reservation utilities. The actual distribution of utilities within this set is determined in a way not specified here: it could be by bargaining, by patriarchal or matriarchal dictatorship, or whatever. It is at this stage that such aspects of personal relationships as caring and consideration for each other enter the process, the utility functions themselves just represent preference orderings over own consumptions of goods and leisure. The parameter u_2^0 summarizes the distributional outcome, and must be regarded as in general a function of the after tax wage rates βw_i and the lump sum α.

The model is straightforward to solve and yields demand functions for the consumption good and labour supply functions. Rather than analysing the comparative statics of this model in the 'primal space', however, it is more useful to apply a little duality, in the form of the Second Theorem of Welfare Economics (STWE). In this context this theorem says that the household resource allocation that solves the above problem can be generated *as if* there was first a lump sum redistribution within the household, giving i the lump sum income α_i, where $\Sigma_i \alpha_i = \alpha$, and then i solves

$$\max u^i (x_i, T - l_i) \tag{7.54}$$

$$\text{subject to } x_i - \beta w_i l_i = \alpha_i. \tag{7.55}$$

This problem yields the labour supply functions $l_i (\beta w_i, \alpha_i)$ and the indirect utility functions $v^i(\beta w_i, \alpha_i)$. One important point to note is that solution of this problem will give each individual a marginal utility of income $\partial v^i/\partial \alpha_i = \lambda_i$ and, even where utility functions are identical, there is nothing to say that these must be equal to each other and to a common household marginal utility of income – contrast this with the case of the household utility function model above. A second point to note is that j's wage rate affects i's labour supply only through the effect on the household distribution of income for $i,j = 1, 2, i \neq j$. The comparative statics of this problem gives

$$\frac{\partial v^i}{\partial \beta} = \lambda_i \left(w_i l_i + \frac{\partial \alpha_i}{\partial \beta} \right) \tag{7.56}$$

$$\frac{\partial l_i}{\partial \beta} = w_i s_i + \frac{\partial l_i}{\partial \alpha_i}\left(w_i l_i + \frac{\partial \alpha_i}{\partial \beta} \right) \tag{7.57}$$

$$\frac{\partial l_i}{\partial \alpha} = \frac{\partial l_i}{\partial \alpha_i}\frac{\partial \alpha_i}{\partial \alpha} = \lambda_i \frac{\partial \alpha_i}{\partial \alpha}. \tag{7.58}$$

In each case we see that the standard derivative is augmented by a term which gives the effect of the parameter change on the household income distribution. Implicitly we always regard α_i as a function $\alpha_i(\alpha, \beta)$, with

$$\sum_i \frac{\partial \alpha_i}{\partial \alpha} = 1, \ \sum_i \frac{\partial \alpha_i}{\partial \beta} = 0 \tag{7.59}$$

This says simply that the implicit distribution of income within the household depends in general on the tax parameters.

Turning now to the optimal tax analysis, we have the problem

$$\max \sum_h \sum_i v^{ih}(\alpha, \beta) \tag{7.60}$$

$$\text{subject to } R \leq (1-\beta)\sum_h \sum_i w_{ih} l_{ih} - H\alpha. \tag{7.61}$$

The first order conditions are

$$\sum_h \sum_i \left[\frac{\partial v^{ih}}{\partial \alpha} + \mu(1-\beta) w_{ih} \frac{\partial l_{ih}}{\partial \alpha} \right] - \mu H = 0 \tag{7.62}$$

$$\sum_h \sum_i \left\{ \frac{\partial v^{ih}}{\partial \beta} + \mu \left[(1-\beta) w_{ih} \frac{\partial l_{ih}}{\partial \beta} - w_{ih} l_{ih} \right] \right\} = 0. \tag{7.63}$$

Proceeding as before we define

$$\sigma_{ih} \equiv \frac{\lambda_{ih}}{\mu} + (1-\beta) w_{ih} \frac{\partial l_{ih}}{\partial \alpha_{ih}} \tag{7.64}$$

This is the net social marginal utility of income of individual i in household h. We then define

$$\sigma \equiv \sum_h \sum_i \sigma_{ih} \frac{\partial \alpha_{ih}}{\partial \alpha} / H = 1 \tag{7.65}$$

as the first condition. Note that since $\Sigma_i(\partial\alpha_{ih}/\partial\alpha) = 1$, we can think of a net social marginal utility of income of household h, σ_h, as a convex combination of the two individual values, where the weights depend on exactly how an increment in the lump sum would be distributed between the individuals, that is, on the household 'sharing rule'. The optimal lump sum then sets the average of these across households equal to unity.

Turning to the second condition and using the Slutsky equations as well as the final version of the first condition gives the result

$$\frac{1-\beta}{\beta} = -\frac{\sum_h \sum_i \left[w_{ih} l_{ih} (\sigma_{ih} - \sigma) - \sigma_{ih} \left(\frac{\partial \alpha_i}{\partial \beta} \right) \right] / H}{\sum_h \sum_i w_{ih} l_{ih} \varepsilon_{ih} / H}. \tag{7.66}$$

The efficiency term in the denominator could be affected in either direction by the inclusion of 'working wives'. Taking both the stylized facts that their labour incomes are lower but their compensated elasticities are higher, while little *a priori* seems to be known about how these vary together across households, the overall sum of income weighted elasticities could rise or fall.

More interesting are the effects on the distributional term in the numerator. Suppose first that the distribution of income within the household is exactly such as to equalize marginal net social utilities of income, $\sigma_{ih} = \sigma_h$, all h. Then the numerator becomes simply $\Sigma_h I_h(\sigma_h - \sigma)/H$, where I_h is total household wage income, and we can in effect ignore the two-person nature of the household (recall $\Sigma_i(\partial\alpha_i/\partial\beta) = 0$). We could therefore say that since the standard literature does just that, it is implicitly assuming that the household income distribution has already been optimized from the point of view of the 'planner'.

Next assume that the distribution of the lump sum between household members is independent of their net wage rates, that is, of β. Then the second term in the numerator vanishes and we are left just with the first. The two-person nature of households is nonetheless important: if the negative covariance between wage income and net marginal social utility of income is larger in absolute value for women than for men then this will tend to make the tax system more progressive than in the case where only men are considered.

Finally, the second term in the numerator has an interesting interpretation. It can be rewritten as

$$\sum_h (\sigma_{1h} - \sigma_{2h}) \frac{\partial \alpha_{1h}}{\partial \beta}. \tag{7.67}$$

In a household in which the individual with the lower marginal net social utility of income receives a higher share of the lump sum as a result of a reduction in the marginal tax rate (increase in β), this will be negative, otherwise it is positive. In the former case this tends to augment the negative value of the first covariance term, thus increasing the absolute value of the denominator and hence making the tax system more progressive. This of course implies that the lump sum can be higher, which will tend to benefit the individual with the higher net social marginal utility of income (given the reasonable assumption that both parties gain when the lump sum increases).

4 CONCLUSIONS

It is our contention that the facts that households typically contain two adults, and that the alternative to market labour supply is not only pure leisure but also household production, have more than just descriptive relevance. They also have important implications for tax policy. We have shown this within the admittedly rather narrow confines of optimal linear tax theory, and in a piecewise way, extending the household model to take account of just one of these facts at a time. Generalizations, however, appear to be perfectly tractable.

NOTES

1. Since this paper involves both the economics of labour supply and public finance theory, it intersects with the interests of both Bernard and Maurice. RR can also recall a number of forthright discussions on the taxation of working wives in the Senior Common Room at QMC.
2. Though Heckman (1996) cites evidence to suggest that it is the participation decision rather than hours worked that is really sensitive to the net wage. Failure to distinguish between the two leads to overstatement of the labour supply elasticities of working women. This has important implications for the Boskin–Sheshinski argument discussed below.
3. The idea can already be found in Samuelson (1956).
4. This 'and so on' includes the very important issue of empirical estimation of labour supply functions and welfare rankings of households. For extensive discussion of the argument that including household production is very important for empirical study of these issues see Apps et al., (1996a, 1996b).
5. This is in fact what is done in Chiappori (1988, 1994).

6. For systematic treatment of two-person households with domestic production, though not applied to optimal linear tax theory, see Apps and Rees (1988, 1996 and 1997).
7. We assume here and in the rest of the paper that this is the case.
8. See for example Boskin and Sheshinski (1983).
9. For further development of this point see Apps and Rees (1997).

REFERENCES

Apps, P.F. and Ray Rees (1988), 'Taxation and the household', *Journal of Public Economics*, **35**, 353–69.

Apps, P.F. and Ray Rees (1996), 'Labour supply, household production and intra-family welfare distribution', *Journal of Public Economics*, **60**, 199–219.

Apps, P.F. and Ray Rees (1997), 'Collective labor supply and household production', *Journal of Political Economy*, forthcoming.

Apps, P.F., M. Killingsworth and Ray Rees (1996a), 'On the specification of labour supply and household production models', unpublished.

Apps, P.F., M. Killingsworth and Ray Rees (1996b), 'Human capital, household production and prices in models of family labour supply', unpublished.

Boskin, M.J. and E. Sheshinski (1983), 'Optimal tax treatment of the family', *Journal of Public Economics*, **20**, 281–97.

Chiappori, P.-A. (1988), 'Rational household labor supply', *Econometrica*, **56**, 64–89.

Chiappori, P.-A. (1992), 'Collective labor supply', *Journal of Political Economy*, **100**, 437–67.

Feldstein, M. and D.R. Feenberg, (1996), 'The taxation of two-earner families', in M. Feldstein and J.M. Poterba (eds), *Empirical Foundations of Household Taxation*, University of Chicago Press, Chicago and London.

Heckman, J.J. (1996), 'What has been learned about labor supply in the past twenty years?', *American Economic Review*, **83**, 116–21.

Samuelson, P.A. (1956), 'Social indifference curves', *Quarterly Journal of Economics*, **70**, 1–22.

Sheshinski, E. (1972), 'The optimal linear income tax', *Review of Economic Studies*, **39**, 297–302.

8. *Ex post* value regulation of pharmaceutical prices

Hugh Gravelle[1]

1 INTRODUCTION

Different countries have adopted a bewildering range of methods of regulating prices and profits in the pharmaceutical industry (Bloor et al., 1996). In this chapter I examine the welfare properties of an *ex post* average value (EPAV) regulation scheme in which a pharmaceutical firm's revenue varies with the social value of its product.[2] The scheme, which is a variation on the mechanism proposed by Loeb and Magat (1979), leads to efficient investment, consumption, promotion and production under certain market and technological conditions. I investigate what adjustments are necessary when these conditions are not satisfied and whether the adjustments vitiate the chief advantage of the scheme: its simplicity and transparency.

Figure 8.1 illustrates the mechanism, as originally proposed by Loeb and Magat. A monopoly profit maximizing firm faces the demand curve *D* and has marginal cost curve *MC*. The firm has fixed costs so that its average cost curve *AC* lies above *MC*. If the firm is unregulated and cannot price discriminate it will set a profit maximizing price p^m, produce output x^m and earn profit equal to the area π. If the demand curve measures consumers' marginal willingness to pay, the efficient outcome is at x^* where the sum of consumer surplus and firm profit, not just profit, is maximized.

One remedy would be to nationalize or regulate the firm, instruct it to set price equal to marginal cost and fund the resulting loss out of taxation. Problems with these solutions include reduced incentives for cost minimization and the deadweight distortionary losses stemming from the increase in taxation to cover losses.

Loeb and Magat (1979) suggest that the firm's price should not be regulated but that it should be paid a tax-financed subsidy equal to the consumer surplus generated by its chosen price. The firm's revenue is then equal to the amount paid by consumers plus their consumer surplus: total willingness to pay. Hence the firm will choose its price to maximize willingness to pay less cost or, equivalently, consumer surplus plus profit, and it will price at marginal cost. Since

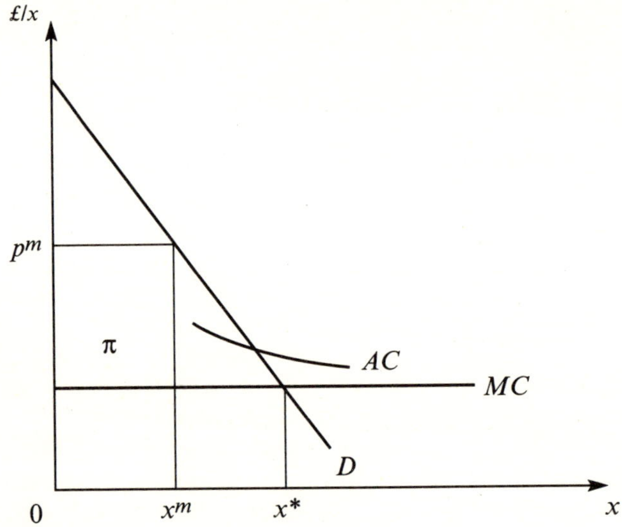

Figure 8.1 Monopoly pricing

the firm will be bearing all production costs it will have the right incentive to minimize costs at any level of output.

The difficulties with the Loeb–Magat scheme are that the regulator needs to know the demand curve, though not the cost function. The scheme still requires distorting tax finance and there are also distributional issues since the firms earn a reward equal to the social benefit from the industry. Loeb and Magat suggest that if the scheme is combined with a bidding competition in which firms offer payments for the right to run the industry under the scheme, the amount of subsidy which needs to be raised from distortionary taxation will be reduced, thereby also reducing distributional objections.

In the following sections we will investigate the scheme in the context of the pharmaceutical industry. The industry has a number of features which may affect the mechanism:

- the industry is R&D intensive, so that we need to examine incentives for investment in research and development of new products;
- the industry is also promotion intensive, so that we need to consider the impact of any scheme on the amount and type of information provided by firms to patients and doctors;
- demand curves may not reflect the social benefits from the product because doctors may not be perfect agents for their patients or because

patients with public or private health care insurance may not face the full price of the product;
- firms are multinational: they produce and sell in more than one country.

An alternative approach is to model the information asymmetry as less extreme and to investigate regulatory schemes based on the revelation principle which induce the firm to provide the regulator with its private information. Such schemes are usually complicated and assume sophisticated regulators who, in effect, have very precise information about their ignorance (Laffont and Tirole, 1993). As we will see the main information problems in the regulation of the pharmaceutical regulation arise from uncertainty about the benefits from new drugs and it is not obvious that information about these aspects are asymmetrically distributed. At the very least it seems of interest to consider whether there are simple schemes which can induce efficient investment.

2 THE EPAV RULE

2.1 Efficiency Conditions

Pharmaceutical price regulation schemes vary, depending on the objectives of the regulator, the set of policy instruments and information available to her and on the specification of demand, technology and uncertainty. We first consider a regulator whose objective is the maximization of the usual simple social welfare function: the unweighted sum of the expected surpluses accruing to individuals in the society in their role as consumers, taxpayers and owners of firms. Distributional and other objectives are introduced in Section 3.3.

Optimal regulation of a pharmaceutical firm requires optimal investment by the firm, optimal consumption of whatever drug results from the investment, optimal (least cost) cost production and optimal provision of information to patients and their doctors. For the moment we ignore information provision and consider a firm which can invest in R&D which may result in a new chemical entity (NCE) which may have therapeutic value (see Table 8.1).

The therapeutic value of the drug $B_s(x_s)$ depends on the amount consumed, x_s. The benefit function B_s may vary across states of the world s because of variations in its intrinsic qualities (proportion of cases of disease cured), the incidence of the condition treated and the value of health improvements. The state of the world is defined solely by reference to the therapeutic value function.

The firm makes an investment I in R&D and the probability of state s occurring is $f_s(I)$ which varies with the amount of investment. We assume that R&D is productive in the sense that increases in I increase the expected value of the NCE which results but at a decreasing rate:

$$\sum_s f_s'(I)B_s(x) > 0; \quad \sum_s f_s''(I)B_s(x) < 0.$$

Demand for the drug results from decisions by patients and doctors. The relationship between patients and doctors is one of imperfect agency (Arrow, 1963) and there is no reason to suppose that consumption will be efficient. We need not specify this decision-making process closely but assume that demand varies with the price charged to consumers p_s: $x_s = D_s(p_s)$, $D_{sp} < 0$.

Table 8.1 Notation

s	Payoff relevant state of the world defined by social value of drug
x_s	Quantity of drug consumed
α_s	Advertising by firm
$B_s(x_s, \alpha_s)$	Social benefit of drug in £
$B_{sx}(x_s, \alpha_s)$	Marginal social benefit of consumption
p_s	Price charged to consumers
$U_s(x_s, \alpha_s)$	Willingness to pay of consumers' agents
$c_s(x_s)$	Production cost of drug
$D_s(p_s, \alpha_s)$	Demand for drug
$c_s' > 0$	Marginal production cost
$v_s(x_s) = B_s - c_s$	Social value of drug in state s
r_s	Price paid to firm in state s
$R_s + R_0 = r_s x_s + R_0$	Reimbursement paid to firm
I	Investment in R&D by firm
$\pi_s = r_s x_s - c_s(x_s) + R_0$	Firm profit in state s
$f_s(I)$	Probability of state s
$V = Ev_s - I$	Expected social value of R&D investment
$\Pi = E\pi_s - I$	Expected profit from R&D investment
h	Welfare weight on firm profit
λ	Marginal deadweight loss from taxation

The firm's *ex post* profit in state s, gross of its R&D expenditure, is

$$\pi_s = r_s D_s - c_s(D_s) + R_0 = R_s - c_s(x_s) + R_0 \tag{8.1}$$

where $c_s(x_s)$ is the firm's production cost, r_s the price it receives for its product and R_0 a lump sum payment which does not vary with the state of the world. R_s is the non-lump sum payment to the firm which may vary with the state of the world and its actions.

The *ex post* welfare function of the regulator in state s is an unweighted sum of the therapeutic benefits to consumers less the price they pay, the budget surplus accruing to taxpayers and the profit of firms. Once a drug has been invented its social value is the difference between its therapeutic value and the cost of production

$$v_s(x_s) = B_s - c_s. \tag{8.2}$$

The *ex ante* social welfare function is expected social value net of investment costs:

$$V = \sum_s v_s(x_s) f_s(I) - I. \tag{8.3}$$

The first best choices of investment and consumption are defined by

$$V_I = \sum_s v_s(x_s) f_s'(I) - 1 = 0. \tag{8.4}$$

$$v_{sx}(x_s) = B_{sx}(x_s) - c_{sx}(x_s) = 0. \tag{8.5}$$

Note the interdependence of the consumption and investment decisions: the value of additional investment depends on the level of consumption in each state.

2.2 The EPAV Rule

Assume an NHS type of institutional framework where the firm provides the drug to consumers and is then reimbursed by the state. Any payment by consumers is made to the state. If the marginal reward to the firm from any decision is equal to the marginal social value of the decision the firm will be induced to act efficiently. This can be achieved by choosing R_s so that the state contingent element of the firm's profit is equal to the social value v_s of its activities: $\pi_s - R_0 = v_s$. Hence if the regulator sets the state contingent revenue so that

$$R_s = B_s(x_s) \tag{8.6}$$

or equivalently reimburses the firm at the price

$$r_s(x_s) = \frac{B_s(x_s)}{x_s} \tag{8.7}$$

its profit in state s is

$$\pi_s = R_s + R_0 - c_s(x_s) = B_s(x_s) - c_s(x_s) = v_s(x_s) + R_0$$

and the firm has the incentive to take socially optimal decisions on investment. Since it bears all its production costs it will also have the incentive to produce its output at least cost.

If the firm has the option of not investing, the lump sum payment R_0, which does not vary with the success of its R&D or any of its decisions, is constrained by the participation constraint that it must make a non-negative profit: $R_0 \geq I - \Sigma f_s(R_s - c_s)$. Since R_0 does not appear directly in the welfare function (8.3) and does not affect any of the firm's decisions the participation constraint will not be binding. We ignore the lump sum component of the regulation scheme until Section 3.3.

Efficient consumption is achieved by setting the price in each state so that

$$B_{sx}(D_s(p_s)) = c_{sx}(D_s(p_s)). \tag{8.8}$$

In general this will not imply that the price paid by patients is equal to marginal cost because the marginal social benefit from the drug need not be equal to the marginal private benefit.

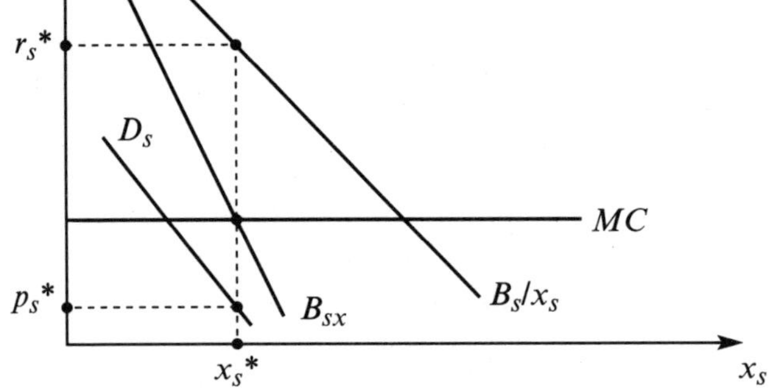

Figure 8.2 EPAV pricing

Figure 8.2 illustrates a case in which the marginal social benefit from the drug B_{sx} exceeds the marginal private benefit which is shown by the height of the demand curve D_s. The optimal consumer price is p^*_s which is less than marginal cost. The curve B_S/x_s plots the *ex post* average value and the optimal reimbursement price is r^*_s. The efficient per unit reimbursement paid to the firm for any drug is equal to the actual per unit therapeutic benefit its investment creates.

The optimal reimbursement rate is a declining function of consumption but always exceeds marginal therapeutic value since $B_{sx} < B_s/x_s$. When the optimal consumer price defined by (8.8) is set, we see that the price paid to the firm exceeds its marginal cost of production. Even when the level of consumption is not efficient the EPAV rule provides the correct incentives investment for the firm because it is paid the actual therapeutic value of whatever drug results from its R&D.

If the firm charged consumers directly for the drug, so that it could control consumption via the price, EPAV would also lead it to choose the efficient price. The firm would collect the revenue from consumers and then receive a top-up payment from the regulator such that its total state contingent revenue was $R_s = B_s$. Its profit is

$$B_s(D_s(p_s)) - c_s(D_s(p_s))$$

which is maximized by choice of p_s when

$$\{B_{sx}(D_s(p_s)) - c_{sx}(D_s(p_s))\}\, D_{sp}(p_s) = 0$$

so that the firm is led to set the optimal price satisfying (8.5) or (8.8) since $D_{sp} < 0$.

2.3 Incentives for Promotion

The firm may be able to affect the sales of its product by promotional activities. When the firm's promotional activities enhance the benefits from the drug (advertising is informative) we have $B_s = B_s(x_s, \alpha_s)$, $B_{s\alpha} > 0$ where α_s is the firm's expenditure on promotion in state s. The value of the drug in state s is now

$$v_s(x_s,\alpha_s) = B_s(x_s,\alpha_s) - c_s(x_s) - \alpha_s \tag{8.9}$$

and the efficient first best level of promotion α_s satisfies

$$B_{s\alpha} - 1 \leq 0, \quad \alpha_s \geq 0 \tag{8.10}$$

with complementary slackness. Consumption of the drug now also depends on promotion as well as on the price charged to consumers: $D_s(p_s, \alpha_s)$. Increases in promotion increase consumption ($D_{s\alpha} > 0$).

The EPAV reimbursement rule (8.7) ensures that the firm has efficient incentives to engage in informative promotion since under the rule its profit is equal to the social value of its product and it bears all the promotion expenses:

$$\pi_s = r_s D_s(p_s, \alpha_s) - c(D_s(p_s, \alpha_s)) - \alpha_s = B_s(x_s, \alpha_s) - c(D_s(p_s, \alpha_s)) - \alpha_s. \tag{8.11}$$

The firm will choose α_s to satisfy

$$(B_{sx} - c_{sx})D_{s\alpha} + B_{s\alpha} - 1 \leq 0, \alpha_s \geq 0 \tag{8.12}$$

with complementary slackness, so that if consumption is efficient and satisfies (8.5) the firm's choice of α_s will satisfy the first best condition (8.10). If consumption is inefficient ($B_{sx} \neq c_{sx}$) the firm's choice of advertising is second best efficient: it will take account both of the direct benefit from better information ($B_{s\alpha}$) and the indirect benefit from increasing or reducing consumption if it is too low ($B_{sx} > c_{sx}$) or too high ($B_{sx} < c_{sx}$).

Even when the firm could indulge in distorting or persuasive promotion which has no social value ($B_{s\alpha} = 0$) but does increase demand ($D_{s\alpha} > 0$) EPAV will still provide the firm with the right signals. The firm will only wish to indulge in persuasive advertising if consumption is less than the first best level. It is led to choose both the correct level and type of advertising.

It is essential for the above arguments that the reimbursement price r_s is equal to *actual* average therapeutic value, rather than to some fixed value. For example, even if the regulator could successfully forecast the output level and promotion activity which would result from a fixed average value price and set this price to equal the actual social value, the firm would not respond efficiently. To see this suppose that advertising is only informative and that there are no externalities in consumption so that the demand and marginal social benefit curves coincide. Let the regulator fix a reimbursement rate $r_s = r_s^0$ which does not vary with the quantity consumed. The firm's profit in state s is

$$r_s^0 D_s(p_s, \alpha_s) - c(D_s(p_s, \alpha_s)) - \alpha_s \tag{8.13}$$

and it chooses its promotion expenditure $\hat{\alpha}_s$ to satisfy

$$(r_s^0 - c_{sx})D_{s\alpha} - 1 = 0 \tag{8.14}$$

where $D_{s\alpha} = -B_{sx\alpha}/B_{sxx}$. Even when the regulator correctly forecasts the firm's promotional activity and sets $r_s^0 = B_s[x_s(p_s,\hat{\alpha}_s)]/[x_s(p_s,\hat{\alpha}_s)]$ the firm will not have the correct incentives since its marginal revenue from additional advertising is

$$\left(\frac{B_s}{x_s} - c_{sx}\right)\frac{-B_{sx\alpha}}{B_{sxx}} \neq B_{s\alpha} \tag{8.15}$$

2.4 Proportional Value Scheme

The firm would also choose an efficient price and promotion under a scheme in which its profit in a state was a fraction of the social value: $\pi_s = kv_s$, $k > 0$. This would imply

$$\hat{R}_s = kB_s + (1-k)c_s \tag{8.16}$$

so the firm received a weighted average of the therapeutic value and its costs. The proportional scheme has the appeal that when $k < 1$ the total payment to the firm is reduced since $kB_s + (1-k)c_s < B_s$ and the burden on taxpayers is reduced. The proportional scheme has greater information requirements than EPAV but its most obvious drawback is that it does not provide the correct incentives for R&D or for cost-reducing effort. Since the firm only gets a proportion of the social value of its invention it will be led to underinvest. Similarly if it gets only a fraction k of any cost reductions it will not minimize production costs if this requires unobservable effort.

2.5 Several Time Periods

The extension to many time periods is straightforward. The expected welfare function is a suitably discounted sum of costs and benefits and the firm's maximand is discounted expected profit. However, if its discount factor differs from the social discount factor the state contingent transfer must be adjusted to ensure that the firm's discounted profit in each period equalled the discounted social value of the drug. Efficient investment could still be achieved but the reimbursement rule would be more complicated and would require additional information.

For example, if the firm's constant one period ahead discount factor δ_f is proportional to the constant one period ahead social discount factor ($\delta_f = k\delta$) then the reimbursement in period t if state s occurs is $R_{st} = k^{-t}\,[B_{st} - (1-k^t)c_{st}]$.

2.6 Successive Innovations

The value of the drug B_s should be calculated as the additional value of the drug over the next best product currently available in each period. When a new drug is introduced, existing products for which it is a substitute will find their total and marginal benefit functions shifted downward. They will suffer both a loss in sales and a reduction in their reimbursement rates. They will, however, take this possibility into account when making their investment decisions and because the EPAV scheme equates revenue to social benefit of their product their investment decision will be socially optimal.

2.7 Information Requirements

Under EPAV the regulator must be able to estimate the benefit function in each state. This need only be done *ex post* at the end of each period: it is not necessary for the regulator to attempt to estimate *ex ante* the benefits from a drug in all future periods and states. The firm does have to estimate the benefits and costs in all future periods and states when taking its investment decision. Since this is precisely what is required for socially efficient investment, incentives for making good forecasts are correctly aligned.

When the setting of the consumer price is delegated to the firm the regulator does not need to know the firm's marginal cost. If for some reason the regulator wished to set the consumer price she could rely on the firm to truthfully report its marginal cost. The firm would realize that its report would affect the price set and therefore consumption. It would be motivated to offer a correct report because v_s is maximized when price is equal to marginal cost and its profit is increasing in v_s.

Even *ex post* the regulator's information requirements are not trivial but her task is made easier by having to make the estimates after consumption of the drug is known when they can be based on experience. The regulator does not need to know the firm's R&D technology, its production technology, or its level of investment.

Kremer (1996) has suggested a scheme which is very similar to EPAV. In his mechanism a firm which has discovered and patented a new product would be bought out of the patent by the government which could then either produce and sell the good at marginal cost or make the new technology available to any firm without charge. The price paid for the patent would be equal to the full social benefit of the good when consumed at a price equal to marginal cost. Even though Kremer suggests an ingenious auction mechanism to induce correct valuation of the patent to the firm (the stream of profits it would generate), the regulator would still need to know the benefit function in order to pay the firm the full social value of its invention.

3 DIFFICULTIES WITH THE EPAV SCHEME

3.1 Multiple Firms: R&D as Rent Seeking

The analysis so far has assumed that there is only one firm engaged in investment in R&D. But no set of property rights prevents firms from fishing in the pool of potential innovations. Exclusive rights are created by patents but these protect actual discoveries and do not limit access to the common pool of potential discoveries. With more than one firm the free access nature of R&D activity means that investment by firms may be inefficient even if the successful firm is paid the therapeutic value B_s of its discovery.

Suppose that there are only two states: either the drug is discovered or it is not. Consider a two firm example in which only one firm will discover the cure for some disease and the probability of the cure being discovered is $f(I_1,I_2), \partial f/\partial I_i > 0$. Assume that the probability that firm i makes the discovery, given that one is made, is $w_i = I_i/I$ where $I = I_1 + I_2$. The firm's expected profit (gross of investment) is $\pi^i = w_i f\ [R - c(x)]$ and it chooses its level of investment to satisfy (assuming it takes the other firm's investment as given)

$$\left(\frac{\partial w_i}{\partial I_i} f + w_i \frac{\partial f}{\partial I_i}\right)[R - c(x)] - 1 = 0. \tag{8.17}$$

The welfare function is now $f(B - c) - I_1 - I_2$ so that the condition for socially optimal investment by firm i is

$$\frac{\partial f}{\partial I_i}[B(x) - c(x)] - 1 = 0. \tag{8.18}$$

Setting $R = B$ will only lead to efficient investment by both firms when $\partial f/\partial I_1 = \partial f/\partial I_2 = f(I_1,I_2)/I$. There is no reason to suppose that the R&D technology would have such a special form.

The optimal reimbursement rate paid to firm i if it is successful is

$$R = \frac{[B(x) - c(x)]}{w_i} + c(x) > B(x). \tag{8.19}$$

The scheme induces the firm to invest efficiently. Its gross profit is $(B - c)/w$ so that it will choose an efficient price and promotion level. However it will not be led to choose an efficient level of cost reducing effort since it gets £$1/w_i > 1$ for every £1 reduction in cost: it will devote too much effort to cost reduction.

The regulator requires information about costs and firms' beliefs $w_i(I_1, I_2)$ about their chances of winning the R&D race. Note further that $R > B$. Thus consumers and taxpayers have a negative combined surplus from the optimal scheme if the lump sum component R_0 is zero. We return to this issue in Section 3.3.

3.2 Complementary Products

Some products are therapeutically complementary: a cocktail combining them may be more valuable than separate consumption. Take a very simple case in which two firms are investing in R&D and each may discover different drugs with f_i, $i = 1,2$. The event that a firm is successful is independent of the event that the other firm is successful. Assume that only the state in which both drugs are discovered is valuable: the drugs are useless if only one of them is used. The value of the drugs if both are invented is

$$B(z) - c_1(x_1) - c_2(x_s)$$

where $z = \min(x_1,x_2)$ because the drugs must be used in fixed proportions. The welfare function is $f^1 f^2(B - c_1 - c_2) - I_1 - I_2$.

If each firm faces the reimbursement scheme

$$R^i(x_1, x_2) = B(z) - c_j(x_j) < B(z) \tag{8.20}$$

it receives the social value of the drug cocktail and is motivated to invest the efficient amount. Its expected profit is $f^1 f^2(B_z - c_1 - c_2) - I_i$ and it chooses its investment to satisfy the efficiency condition $f^j \partial f/I_i\, (B - c_1 - c_2) = 1$.

The rationale is similar to that for the accident tax proposed by Vickrey (1968): when two or more parties can each affect the probability of some event they can be guided to make socially optimal decisions by making *all* of them bear the costs or receive the benefits of that event.

This version of the scheme requires cost information. The combined surplus of the consumers and taxpayers when both drugs are discovered is negative. The total payment to the firms is

$$2B - c_1 - c_2$$

so that the sum of consumer and taxpayer surpluses is $-(B - c_1 - c_2) < 0$.

3.3 Distributional Concerns

The EPAV scheme creates the right incentives for the firm because it pays it the social value of its decisions, so that the firm's objectives are identical to the welfare function. However, the firm gets all the surplus and the combined surplus of consumers and taxpayers is zero. Indeed in the circumstances of the previous two subsections the combined surplus of consumers and taxpayers may be negative. One answer is to use the lump sum part of the EPAV scheme. As we noted above a lump sum payment R_0 made irrespective of the state of the world does not affect the firm's incentives but does transfer some of the surplus back to the taxpayers. Thus the firm in effect buys the right to undertake R&D from the regulator, bears all the cost and keeps all the benefit. This is just another example of the standard principal–agent result: when the agent is risk neutral a first best allocation can be achieved by making the agent buy the productive opportunity from the principal.

The difficulty with the solution is that the regulator needs to know whether the lump sum exceeds the firm's expected gains: the participation constraint on the firm must not be violated. But this requires the regulator to know the R&D technology and to be able to forecast therapeutic benefits and production costs.

It might be possible in some instances to let potential investors bid for the right to invest. This would redistribute the surplus without the need for the regulator to be as well informed as the firms. Such a scheme would work only if the R&D was directed at a particular outcome (cure for a specific condition) and if it was certain that the R&D of other firms, engaged in the hunt for drugs aimed at other conditions, would not produce a cure for the condition. In effect the regulator would be selling the exclusive right to explore a piece of intellectual territory for valuable products. Unlike, say, selling the rights to explore for oil in particular areas, it not easy to define the territory.

Distributional concerns presumably arise because not all parties count equally in the welfare function. It is better to address the issue directly by reformulating the welfare function explicitly so that the implications of alternative value judgements are clearly spelled out, rather than by *ad hoc* adjustments to regulatory schemes derived from a welfare function in which only the total surplus, and not its distribution, matters.

One way of capturing distributional concerns is to give different weights to the surpluses of consumers, taxpayers and firm owners. As an example suppose that the weight on the surplus of firm owners is h so that the welfare function is now

$$V^h = E\,[B_s - h(c_s + I) - (1 - h)(R_s + R_0)] \tag{8.21}$$

where R_0 is the lump sum component of the regulatory scheme. In earlier sections we have implicitly assumed that $h = 1$ so that we have effectively been able to ignore R_0 because it had no effect on behaviour and was a pure transfer.

The firm's expected profit is $\Pi = E(R_s - c_s - I + R_0)$. Since R_0 does not vary with the firm's behaviour it can be induced to invest optimally by choosing R_s so that

$$\frac{\partial V^h}{\partial I} = \frac{\partial\left[B_s - h(c_s + I) - (1-h)R_s\right]}{\partial I}$$
$$= \frac{\partial \Pi}{\partial I} = \frac{\partial E\left[R_s - c_s - I\right]}{\partial I}. \tag{8.22}$$

Solving the equation, the optimal reimbursement is

$$R_s = \frac{B_s + (1-h)(c_s + I)}{2-h}. \tag{8.23}$$

Gross profit in each state is

$$\frac{B_s - c_s + (1-h)I}{2-h} \tag{8.24}$$

so that the firm will want to maximize the difference between therapeutic benefit and cost in each state. However, its incentives for cost reducing effort are too great for efficiency.

Since the marginal social value of the lump sum component is

$$\frac{\partial V^h}{\partial R_0} = -(1-h) < 0 \tag{8.25}$$

the regulator should reduce R_0 until the firm's participation constraint just binds.

If a zero weight is given to profit the reimbursement rate is

$$R_s = \frac{B_s + c_s + I}{2}. \tag{8.26}$$

Some manipulations show that this expression is greater or less than B_s if and only if $B_s - c_s - I$ is negative or positive. Since the expected value of $B_s - c_s - I$ is positive, the implication of being concerned only with the welfare of consumers and taxpayers is that the expected value of the reimbursement is smaller than if the welfare of owners counted equally. However in some states a higher reimbursement rate is required.

Suppose that the regulator bargains with the firm in each state about the level of the payment and, as in the previous paragraph, is concerned only about therapeutic benefits to consumers and the payment made by taxpayers. If the parties cannot reach agreement the regulator has zero payoff and the firm must bear its investment cost. The Nash bargaining solution which maximizes $(B_s - R_s)(R_s - c_s - I)$ is just (8.26). Thus a process of bargaining in each state where the firm anticipates the outcome of the bargain correctly would lead to a level of investment by the firm which maximized the expected payoff to consumers and taxpayers. The level of investment also maximizes the total surplus in the economy even though it is chosen by the firm and is not controlled directly by the bargain made since the Nash bargain gives the firm an expected profit of $E(B_s - C_s - I)/2$.

Compared with the case in which there are no distributional concerns the regulator's task is much more difficult: she requires information on the firm's costs in each state and on its investment. The firm will now have an incentive to mislead the regulator because its reimbursement depends directly on costs and investment.

3.4 Multinational Firms, Chauvinistic Regulators and Regulatory Coordination

The welfare function considered in the previous section is the difference between the expected value of the drug and the costs of production, promotion and R&D. It implicitly assumes that policy makers do not care about the nationality of the firm's owners or the consumers, or that they are all members of the same community. A more chauvinistic welfare function might attach lower weights to the profits accruing to foreign shareholders or the benefits accruing to foreign consumers. (See Peston et al., 1976, for a discussion of the implications of domestic and foreign consumers for public sector pricing.)

Consider a firm which produces a drug consumed at home and abroad and which is partly owned by foreigners. Denote the benefits accruing to home patients by B_{1s}, the amounts consumed by home and foreign patients by x_{1s}, x_{2s} respectively, and the non-lump sum and lump sum reimbursements in country i by R_{is} and R_{i0}. The *ex ante* welfare function for the home country is

$$V_1 = E\{[B_{1s}(x_{1s}) - (1-\theta)(R_{1s} + R_{10}) + \theta[R_{20} + R_{2s} - c_s(x_{1s}, x_{2s}) - I]\} \quad (8.27)$$

where θ is the proportion of the firm's profit which accrues to domestic owners of the firm.

The firm's expected profit is

$$\Pi = E\left[\sum_{i}(R_{i0} + R_{is}) - c_s - I\right] \tag{8.28}$$

and in order for the derivatives of (8.28) and (8.27) with respect to I to be equal we require that the reimbursement on home sales should be

$$R_{1s} = \frac{B_{1s} + (1-\theta)[c_s + I - R_{2s}]}{(2-\theta)}. \tag{8.29}$$

The lump sum component will be reduced until the firm's participation constraint binds since V_1 is decreasing in R_{10}. The regulatory scheme is similar to the case in which the welfare weight on the firm's surplus is less than on the surpluses of consumers and taxpayers. The reimbursement is increasing in the proportion of the firm's profit accruing at home, production costs and the level of investment, and falling in the level of foreign sales revenue. The regulator now needs substantially more information than in the case where a domestic firm sells solely to domestic patients.

Surprisingly, it is possible that the reimbursement rate could be larger or smaller than in the case where there are no foreign sales or foreign shareholders whose welfare is disregarded.

Suppose that the regulator in the other country had similarly chauvinistic objectives but took the home regulator's policies as given. At the regulatory Nash equilibrium (R_{10}, R_{1s}, R_{20}, R_{2s}) the firm would choose its investment to satisfy

$$\frac{\partial \Pi}{\partial I} = \frac{\partial V_1}{\partial I} = \frac{\partial V_2}{\partial I} = 0 \tag{8.30}$$

whereas total welfare in the two countries is maximized at

$$\frac{\partial \Pi}{\partial I} = \frac{\partial V_1}{\partial I} + \frac{\partial V_2}{\partial I} = 0. \tag{8.31}$$

The firm makes too small an investment in R&D and there are welfare gains from regulatory coordination which will increase with the number of countries in which the firm operates.

3.5 Distortionary Taxation

What might be called the first law of public finance is that there is no such thing as a lump sum tax: all taxes or subsidies alter the marginal rewards to actions and thus cause efficiency losses. To examine the implications of the deadweight loss from taxation, consider an NHS-like system in which revenue from consumers is paid to the government. We can write the welfare function as

$$V^{\lambda} = E[B_s - c_s - I - \lambda(R_0 + R_s - p_s x_s)] \tag{8.32}$$

where λ is the deadweight loss per £1 raised from taxation. The deadweight loss is assumed to be constant and independent of the value of the innovation. Since the regulatory scheme will make a small impact on net public sector revenues this seems reasonable.

The optimal price charged to consumers satisfies

$$\frac{\partial V^{\lambda}}{\partial p_s} = (B_{sx} - c_{sx})D_{sp} + \lambda(x_s + p_s D_{sp}) = 0. \tag{8.33}$$

Remembering that $B_{sx} = \gamma_s p_s$ because of imperfect agency we have

$$\frac{\gamma_s p_s - c_{sx}}{p_s} = -\lambda\left(1 + \frac{1}{e_s}\right) \tag{8.34}$$

where e_s is the elasticity of demand with respect to the consumer price. This is similar to the standard inverse elasticity rule except that price should be reduced if there are positive externalities in consumption ($\lambda_s > 1$).

We can induce optimal investment by the firm by choosing R_s so that the derivatives of V^{λ} and Π with respect to I are equal which implies

$$R_s = \frac{B_s + \lambda p_s x_s}{1 + \lambda}. \tag{8.35}$$

This also induces efficient behaviour in each state by the firm since once again the firm bears the marginal social benefits and costs. Consumer expenditure $p_s x_s$ is less than total benefit B_s, which implies that $R_s < B_s$. Deadweight costs of taxation lead to a smaller level of state contingent reimbursement for the firm. The optimal level of R_s is decreasing in the marginal deadweight cost λ. The greater the social cost of taxation the smaller the amount paid to the firm out of taxation. Note also that since there is a deadweight loss from taxation the lump sum component of the scheme should also be as small as possible.

4 CONCLUSIONS

The main objection to the NPAV mechanism is its informational requirements: even in its simplest form the regulator needs to know the therapeutic value of the drug. Some tentative steps have been taken to incorporating this kind of information directly in pharmaceutical regulation schemes (Drummond et al., 1993, 1996) but much more could be done. Without direct use of measures of therapeutic value firms will have only indirect and almost certainly inappropriate incentives. For example, in a market in which there is no regulation the signal of therapeutic value provided to the firm is its revenue. But this is not even a good measure of consumer willingness to pay, since it fails to capture consumer surplus. Imperfect agency will drive a further wedge between revenue and social value.

The difficulties of evaluating pharmaceutical innovations are clearly great but this information would be required for any mechanism which provides suitable rewards for innovation. For example, efficient direct regulation of or subsidy to investment in R&D requires not only information on therapeutic value but also information about the innovation technology.

NOTES

1. Support from the Department of Health to the NPCRDC is acknowledged. The views expressed are those of the author and not necessarily those of the Department of Health.
2. Maurice Peston has done much work on the regulation of pricing and investment of public sector firms. He maintains a current interest in the economics of the pharmaceutical industry through his role at the Office of Health Economics.

REFERENCES

Arrow, K.J. (1963), 'Uncertainty and the welfare economics of medical care', *American Economic Review*, **53**, 941–73.

Bloor, K., A. Maynard and N. Freemantle (1996), 'Lessons from international experience in controlling pharmaceutical expenditure III: regulating industry', *British Medical Journal*, **313**, 33–5.

Drummond, M. et al. (1993), 'Economic evaluation of pharmaceuticals: a European perspective', *PharmoEconomics*, **4**, 173–86.

Drummond, M., B. Jönsson and F. Rutten (1996), 'The role of economic evaluation in the pricing and reimbursement of medicines', mimeo, Centre for Health Economics, University of York.

Kremer, M. (1996), 'A mechanism for encouraging innovation', Harvard Institute for International Development Discussion Paper, no. 533, May.

Laffont, J.J. and J. Tirole (1993), *A Theory of Incentives in Procurement and Regulation*, Cambridge, MA: MIT Press.

Loeb, M. and W.A. Magat (1979), 'A decentralized method for utility regulation', **22** (2), 399–404.

Peston, M.H., E. Katz and H. Gravelle (1976), 'Public sector pricing with foreign demand', *Applied Economics*, **8**, 1–10.

Vickrey, W. (1968), 'Automobile accidents, tort law, externalities and insurance', *Journal of Law and Contemporary Problems*, **33**, 464–87.

9. Timing-of-payment conventions for consumer purchases[1]

Max Steuer*

THE PROBLEM

Game theorists sometimes wonder why people pay taxicabs at the end of journeys and leave tips in restaurants they are unlikely to visit again. Academic mythology has it that some experimentally minded economists tried not paying for a taxi taking them from the Jerusalem Airport to their hotel. The story goes that the driver responded by applying his central locking and driving them back to the airport. Sociologists find it difficult to understand the possible importance of the question why consumers pay and why producers deliver. Norms and conventions are so much a part of the thinking of other social sciences that it hardly seems worth making the enquiry. But they may be missing something in failing to appreciate the usefulness of modelling totally self-interested behaviour, free of moral restraints and uninhibited by culture. It can be insightful even though we know people are not like that. Both normative and positive considerations motivate the economists' investigation. There are, after all, different customs and conventions. We might want to explain why we observe what we do observe in particular situations. And we also might want to ask whether the convention is optimal in some well-defined sense, or whether it could be improved upon.

In this discussion I am going to confine myself to normal consumer transactions involving items considerably less expensive than a new car. I am also going to abstract from issues of consumer credit. For a wide class of these transactions payment for the item purchased normally occurs more or less simultaneously with the acquisition of the item. Of course payment by cheque or by plastic alters

* On joining the staff at LSE in 1959, I was more than pleased to be welcomed into the group of young economists which included Bernard Corry and Maurice Peston, and of course Richard Lipsey and Chris Archibald. A centre of our intellectual life was the weekly staff seminar in Methodology, Measurement and Testing. But my associations with Bernard and Maurice went way beyond that. They stretched from a kind of survival strategy, which included extra mural marking, to the most enlightening discussions of people and approaches which influence me today. All this, they offered, and friendship too. A measure of this on my side is my contribution here, in spite of a dogged reluctance to publish going back for many years.

the time at which money leaves one account and enters another. Yet we can characterize quite a range of transactions as roughly speaking involving a simultaneous exchange of money for goods or services.

While simultaneous exchange is common, it is also common for some transactions to involve payment before receiving the goods or services, and other transactions to involve payment typically after the goods or services are received. The conventions with respect to the three timings of payment – before, simultaneously, or after – are both fairly universal across countries and are quite rigid. In a fast food establishment you pay for your hamburger before you eat it. In a restaurant with service at the table you pay after you eat your meal. It is virtually certain that the offer to pay for a hamburger after eating it would be rejected by MacDonalds, as would the offer to pay for a theatre ticket after attending the show. In a bus you pay before. In a taxi you pay after. It may seem obvious why, but that does not mean it is not worth explaining. The explanation can have policy implications.

I contend that the timing conventions for consumer payment which we observe are not arbitrary, and that the conventions themselves add to welfare. The argument rests crucially on the assumption that enforcing the contract implicit in every transaction is costly. Whether it be the consumer who is stuck with a product which is less than transacted for, or a producer who fails to be paid, there are large costs to rectifying the situation. In some cases finding the defaulting seller or buyer may be difficult. It may be difficult to establish what was mutually assumed would be provided. If sellers and buyers assumptions as to the nature of the product differ, it can be difficult and costly to determine what view of the product or service should prevail. If there are no costs or uncertainty in effecting a transaction, the timing of payment would not be an issue. If the airline knew that you would show up and pay for the flight, it would be a matter of indifference whether you paid at the time of booking, or at a later time, including after the flight, apart from the costs of credit, and we are abstracting from these. Particularly when the amounts involved in the transaction are relatively small, enforcement costs are central to the existence and nature of timing-of-payment conventions.

EXAMPLES

Usually there is little uncertainty about the price. I give the man 30p and he gives me an *Evening Standard*. What little uncertainty surrounds that transaction has to do with whether the paper is complete and the latest edition. When there is uncertainty, for example what does 'Macon Rouge' actually mean on the wine list, it is about the product rather than the price. Simultaneous exchange of money for goods has the advantage of minimizing the expected costs of failure to pay and failure to deliver. If I give you the money first in exchange for later provision of the product, next week you may not deliver. But if you deliver now, I may not pay later. So there is a *prima facie* case for simultaneous delivery and payment. However, the potential advantages of simultaneous payment compared to paying before or after are overridden by other considerations in many transactions.

Typically, cases where simultaneous payment does not occur are cases where it is physically impossible. That is, the transaction itself has a significant time component. Many things take considerable amounts of time to consume, such as a meal at one end of the timescale, or an education at the other. The former is usually paid for after receiving the product, and the latter is normally paid for in advance. The question is why do conventions take the form they do?

The time we are referring to is, of course, producer time. It will take time to read a book, but the transfer of the book from the shop to the purchaser does not take a significant amount of time, and is usually subject to what we are calling simultaneous exchange. An interesting complication arises with respect to booking goods or services in advance. A booking is like an option. It is a promise to deliver at a future date. It also may be a promise to buy. A critical feature of a product or service that involves producer time to effect an exchange is that it cannot be stored and so sold to someone else. A booking for a potentially storable item is inherently different from one which cannot be stored. If I book a turkey for Christmas and fail to collect it, that turkey can be sold to someone else. If I book a hotel room, and do not take up the booking with the room going empty, that booking cannot be sold to someone else.

Consumer uncertainty about the good or service is another factor which influences the timing-of-payment convention. On a trip to the theatre or cinema, the goal is in some sense to purchase enjoyment. But the implicit contract on the part of the theatre is to supply the promised event, that is, a play by a particular author, performed by specified actors who are reasonably sober. Whether the theatre-goer enjoys the performance or not is up to him or her. The promise is simply to provide the show. When the audience for the *Rites of Spring* rioted at the premier in 1917, it was not because they did not like the ballet. It was because they felt it was not a ballet, and a ballet was what they had been promised. The riot was an exceptional event. Riots, and their two person equivalent, are costly to both buyers and sellers, so both sides will usually give in rather than have one, especially when the value of the transaction is not very great. If a transaction takes time to effect, there will be a period when either the buyer or the seller holds both the money and the product or service. This is an advantage, and one party or the other has to pay for it.

In a restaurant consumer uncertainty is of three kinds: what will be the quality; how much will be ordered; and how will the customer be treated. One may have a clear idea of what is an acceptable *coq au vin*, and a restaurant may have served many good ones, but the question remains, is this particular one acceptable? Natural justice and the regard accorded the customer both suggest that the consumer must decide. All three factors lead to payment after the meal. In a taxi, the main uncertainty is how much, both time and distance, will be consumed by the passenger, particularly as the journey is tailor-made. Identifying a reluctant payer is easy. And status leans towards payment after. On a bus the journey is well-defined, and tracking a non-payer can be difficult, so we pay in advance.

The symbolic status of consumers can be important in many transactions. It is rumoured that in the era when all gentlemen wore only bespoke suits, many tailors found it a very lengthy and difficult process to be paid.[2] We could ask why some tailors did not offer a lower price in return for payment on delivery? The answer is probably to be found in the insulting nature of the offer. Even hard-pressed gentlemen would not want to gain a lower price at such a heavy cost in terms of status. In the same way the restaurant is saying to the customer, you are a trustworthy person. They are also in effect saying that you will bear the cost of the odd untrustworthy customer. In principle they could offer a lower price in return for paying in advance. But this will not happen because for virtually all customers, the status is worth more than the potential price reduction. Fast food has no status, and the product is uniform. And so we pay in advance rather than pay the insurance premium to cover the occasional runner that would result from a payment-after convention.

In the case of domestic services like telephone, gas and electricity, there is no status involved, but there is uncertainty as to how much will be demanded in a given month or quarter. There is also likely to be a monopoly element and a creditable threat in cutting off the supply in the event of non payment. These both lead to payment after the event.

Two more important cases should be mentioned before attempting some generalization. The purchase of such services as the builder or the solicitor usually involves a sequence of work first, and then payment. Indeed, virtually all labour contracts involve work first, then payment. With the provision of skilled services and an inexperienced consumer, normal for consumers needing solicitors and builders, the information asymmetry is overwhelmingly on the side of the provider of the service. This leads to payment after the event. The other factor in such contracts, and labour contracts generally, is motivation. Both sides implicitly agree that payment after the event will reduce both the likelihood and intensity of dispute because the motivation to perform well is strengthened by the payment-after-the-work convention.

An interesting case is university education which is normally paid for in advance. Here is a case where payment precedes labour. The reason for this is that success depends on consumer effort more than producer effort. The producer relies on a reputation for providing a certain opportunity for learning. The promise is to provide that opportunity, not to provide the degree. The consumer wants the degree. A disappointed consumer has a strong incentive not to pay. The threat of withholding the degree cannot be made if no degree is forthcoming in any case. This leads to payment in advance. Institutions which in effect promise the degree are more inclined to accept payment after the event.

GENERALIZATION

If there is no producer time involved in the transaction, it is possible to have simultaneous exchange of goods or services for money. And where such exchanges are possible, they will usually be the dominant convention. Apparent exceptions usually involve consumer credit or purchase of items of unknown quality. Then there may be time to pay, or a money-back guarantee. The reason for the dominance of the simultaneous exchange is that neither party faces a cost of either securing delivery or in being paid. Without simultaneous exchange, these potential costs are there and will have to be met by the consumer as an additional cost in acquiring the good or service.

When producer time is involved in the transaction, we can have one or many payments, and these can be lagged either way around. Especially with unenforceable transactions, such as illegal drug transactions, game theorists have figured out that the way to effect the exchange is little-by-little, which in effect is falling back on simultaneous exchange with hardly any incentive to cheat. The issues which determine which way round the payment runs are whether the product or service can be sold to someone else if the potential consumer reneges, quality variability, quantity variability, motivation, information asymmetry, status signalling, and the presence or absence of a creditable collection threat.

If the consumer pays in advance, she or he pays less. If she or he pays after the event, she or he pays more. If quality uncertainty is the main issue, typified in the case of hiring a builder, the 'good' builder – and all builders must claim to be 'good' builders – will say, 'see my work, and then pay a bit more than I would have asked if you paid in advance'. The bit more covers, or more than covers, the risk of not being paid, and hence is worth it to the builder. The insurance to the consumer through seeing the work before paying, with the possibility of withholding payment if not satisfied, makes the larger payment worth it to the consumer. There is no information content in the offer to work first, as the convention requires all builders to make that offer. Payment after means buying the product with an insurance premium. The payment-after convention means that insurance is worth it to most consumers. Timing creates a surplus which can be divided between supplier and consumer.

When information is crucial, the payment-after convention cannot be invaded. The offer to charge less in return for payment in advance will be rejected by the consumer if it is not low enough, and in order for it to be low enough it would not be acceptable to the supplier. In other words, reversing the convention removes the surplus. When the product cannot be sold to someone else if the consumer reneges, by not showing up for the flight or the theatre, payment in advance creates a surplus. The consumer pays less, always to be preferred, and the certainty of payment is worth the lower price to the supplier. The amount more the supplier would have to charge for payment after the event would not be acceptable to consumers. The payment-in-advance convention in these cases is also uninvadeable.

POLICY

In addition to the conventions for the timing of payment, we also have legislation and proposed legislation. There has been much discussion in the United Kingdom about the alleged exploitation of relatively small suppliers by large buyers in interfirm transactions through delaying payment. The charge is that there is in some sense a use of an unfair balance of market power. The puzzle is why doesn't some supplier offer to charge less in return for a promise of prompt payment? The answer would appear to be that this promise is unenforceable because the supplier cannot afford to be in the bad books of the demanding firm. Essentially it is an issue of monopsony power.

The issue of the timing of consumer payments is usually different, but has also attracted, or is in the process of attracting, legislation. Article 8 of the European Community Directive 93/C308/02 states that no payment may be required of the consumer before delivery of the product or performance of the service. If the arguments made above are correct, applying this directive in many cases, namely all those cases where the convention is payment-in-advance, would result in a loss of surplus and be harmful to both consumers and producers who are currently splitting the surplus under the current convention. The alleged purpose of the proposed legislation is to protect consumers. What legislators may fail to see is that making things difficult for producers may be to the disadvantage of consumers as well, and will be so when a surplus generating convention is outlawed.

CONCLUSION

I believe that the analysis of convention outlined above makes a persuasive case for not legislating against existing conventions of timing of consumer payments.

At the very least, such legislation should be undertaken very cautiously and after careful analysis. But is the argument really persuasive? In my view it would be more so, but not much more so, if it were stated formally. PhD students should be required to present their arguments in a lemma-and-proof fashion. The reasons for this need not be spelt out here. However, it is unlikely that the extra rigour will add much because with proper assumptions the argument, and virtually any coherent argument, can readily be rescued. Almost any conclusion can be modelled, with appropriate assumptions. Rigour can be helpful in specifying the domain of applicability.

What is more interesting here than the question of rigour is the method of argument. In this paper it is little more than asserted that the conventions generate surpluses. Given that they do, they have good protection from invasion from alternative conventions. This means that they are fairly stable and they add to welfare. The big question is an empirical one. Are there really surpluses resulting from conventions in the ways suggested? Even if there were surpluses at some time, maybe circumstances have changed in some markets, but the conventions still persist. Deducing the existence of surplus from the existence of convention is worse than supporting the existence of surplus with casual argument, or with rigorous argument for that matter, but not much worse. As is common in economics, we rely on plausible intuition rather than evidence in defence of the surpluses because we are reasonably sure we are right and because the argument conforms to economic convention. While evidence would be wonderful to have, it is not at all clear how to obtain it, and in any event it would most probably be heavily dependent on maintained hypotheses very close to those it purports to test.

NOTES

1. I am indebted to Christine Allen for pointing me in the direction of this problem, to Ralph Turvey for encouraging me to solve it, and to Rafael Repullo for assuring me that the result need not be presented in the modern manner.
2. I am indebted to John Sutton for this example.

PART IV

Economic Policy, Transition and Development

10. China's overseas investment[1]

David Wall*

INTRODUCTION

Developing countries in pursuit of economic growth are generally seen to be in need of capital inflows. Among the policies it is suggested they adopt are those which will make their economies attractive to foreign investors, both direct and portfolio investors. By 1978 the Chinese government had accepted that its centrally planned command economy was not matching the desirable growth performance of other Asian developing countries. In an effort to catch up with its neighbours it began to introduce market-based policies. 'Open door' policies designed to attract foreign capital were among the first market-based policy reforms. In response to those policy reforms foreign capital did begin to flow in, in increasingly large quantities, mainly in the form of foreign direct investment. It is now the recipient of one of the largest inflows of foreign direct investment (FDI) in the world; it is, on average, second only to the USA. This contrasts sharply with the pre-reform situation in which foreign investment was prohibited.

The dramatic impact of the figures for capital inflows, which reached US$48.4 billion in 1995 (of which 27.7 billion was foreign direct investment) has, however, diverted attention away from other aspects of the Chinese economy's integration into the international capital markets.[2] This is particularly true of its emergence as a *lender* of capital. According to the International Monetary Fund (IMF) China now ranks as the eighth most important supplier of capital on world markets, accounting for 2 per cent of the total global flow.[3] In its study of world capital markets the IMF even concluded that 'it certainly is not inconceivable that fast growth and saving surges in countries like . . . China . . . could offset or even dominate saving declines in countries like Japan or France'.[4] This reference by the IMF to the growing importance of China as an important supplier of capital on world markets, and an article about the shifting

* Bernard and Maurice both encouraged me to stay on in university, Bernard saying that it was the only profession where you could decide for yourself when to get up in the morning and Maurice arguing that it was the best platform from which to try to change economic policy.

balance of economic power in the world economy in the *Financial Times*,[5] which quoted it, passed without comment.

The IMF ranking of countries by order of importance as suppliers of capital to world markets was based on each country's average net current account balance for the years 1989–93 compared to the average for all countries.[6] This is a crude measure and hides a good deal of volatility in the underlying data; for example, in two of the five years the current account was in deficit. Table 10.1 shows that over the five years covered by the IMF the net outflow of capital measured in this way was 14.45 billion dollars. Adding the 7.66 billion in 1994 and 1.62 billion in 1995 gives a total for the seven years of about 24 billion.

Table 10.1 International revenue and expenditure 1989–95, main items (billion US$)

	1989	1990	1991	1992	1993	1994	1995
Current account balance	–4.32	12.00	13.27	6.40	–12.90	7.66	1.62
Exports	43.22	51.52	58.92	65.59	75.66	102.56	128.10
Imports	–48.84	–42.35	50.18	–64.39	–86.31	–95.27	–110.10
Capital account balance	3.44	3.26	8.03	–0.25	23.47	32.64	38.67
Long-term capital inflows	11.99	11.61	12.86	27.64	50.35	60.79	66.07
Long-term capital outflows	–7.03	–5.16	–5.19	–26.97	–22.94	–25.03	–27.82
Errors and omissions	0.33	–3.13	–6.79	–8.27	–9.80	–9.77	–17.81
Changes in reserves	–0.55	–12.12	–14.51	2.12	–1.77	–30.52	–22.48

Note: Increases in reserves are shown as negative numbers.

Source: State Statistical Bureau, *Chinese Statistical Yearbook 1993, 1994, 1995* and *1996*, Beijing: State Statistical Publishing House, 1993, 1994, 1995 and 1996. The 1995 volume inadvertently substitutes the 1990 data for that of 1992.

Table 10.1 shows, however, that the gross outflow of long-term capital from China has been much larger than might be suggested by looking at the net current balance alone. Gross outflows of long-term capital totalled more than US$67 billion for the five years covered by the IMF. US$53 billion was added to the total in 1994 and 1995. In other words, China has indeed emerged as a major provider of capital on world markets. In 1995 roughly 64 per cent of gross outflows, almost two-thirds of the total, was accounted for by repayments of loans (and a small number of loans made by China). Another 40 per cent is also accounted for by errors and omissions. China's registered outflows of foreign exchange to finance overseas investment, US$2.0 1995; accounted for a further 7 per cent (down from approximately 20 per cent in 1993). Outflows for portfolio investment were US$380 million in 1994 and 79 million in 1995. Over the seven years covered by the balance of payments data, total overseas investment, direct and portfolio, by mainland Chinese entities was more than US$18 billion.

One commentator (Lardy, 1995, p. 1073) has suggested that 'contrary to what one might believe from observing the flood of foreign capital into China, on a net basis, such inflows have not contributed to domestic capital formation in China'. However, while it is true that after allowance is made for China's conservative reserves policy and overly restrictive import policy the *net*[7] flow of capital into China is small relative to the size of its economy, it is not true that inward foreign investment has 'not contributed to domestic capital formation'. Behind the accounting identity is the real economy: the investment financed by the inflows of foreign capital would not have occurred in the absence of those inflows. The outflows are not causally related to the inflows. The outflows would have occurred anyway and been financed out of reserves or covered by a policy-generated trade surplus, or if either of these options was not acceptable to the government it could have taken steps to restrict outflows; there is no evidence to suggest that the government's policy towards outflows is determined by the size of inflows.

Analysis of the real economy requires the use of gross data rather than the net data which are relevant for balance of payments accounting purposes. And similarly, while in accounting terms the net outflow of long-term capital may have been negative, in 1994 such outflows were equal to about a quarter of export income, or more than a quarter of China's total outstanding foreign debt at that time. Taking the approved and registered autonomous outflows alone, that is, direct overseas investment and overseas portfolio investment (and ignoring capital flight), in 1994 these flows represented roughly 72 per cent of new loans received from multilateral agencies that year (down from 174 per cent in 1993). Given the effort the government of China makes to obtain new loans from abroad the question can be asked as to why it also allows, even approves and encourages, overseas investment by Chinese enterprises, most of which are public sector enterprises.[8]

Not all of the outflow of long term capital from China is approved or encouraged by the government. Much takes the form of illegal transfers abroad, or capital flight. This is reflected in the large errors and omissions item in the balance of payments. This has increased annually in recent years: in the period covered by Table 10.1 it increased from the US$0.33 billion in 1989 to US$17.81 billion in 1995. All countries suffer to some degree from capital flight. China is no exception. The present paper is concerned only with officially approved and registered.

Even if we restrict our attention to officially approved outflows of direct and portfolio capital China is still a major player in world capital markets. Table 10.2 provides some comparative data on outward direct investment for a selection of countries for 1992 (comparable data on portfolio investment were not available and 1992 was the latest year for which comparative data on direct investment were available at the time of writing). At US$4 billion the outflow from China was far larger than that for any other developing country for which data are available (and is likely to be larger than the outflow from any developing country for which data were not available) and larger than the outflows from Canada and Australia (where net repatriation of direct overseas investment took place). It is more than 20 per cent of the figure for the United Kingdom. Table 10.2 also shows direct investment abroad as a percentage of inward direct investment for the countries covered – again China stands out with a much higher ratio (36 per cent) than the other developing countries (for which the unweighted average was 9 per cent). As can be seen from Table 10.3, however, 1992 was an exceptional year. The ratio of outflows to inflows of direct investment capital fell in 1993 to 15.99 per cent and again in 1994 to 5.92 per cent; over the six years the average ratio was 21 per cent, still well above the average for developing countries.

Table 10.2 Selected balance of payments data, 1992 (millions of US dollars)

	Current account balance	Direct investment abroad	Direct investment in country	Outward investment as a % of inward investment	Net errors and omissions
China	6 401	–4 000	11 156	35.86	–8 211
Brazil	6 275	–146	1 454	10.04	–1 132
Korea	–4 529	–1 047	4 469	23.43	1 099
Pakistan	–1 869	12	335	–3.58	121
Singapore	3 748	–748	6 730	11.11	–3 208
Thailand	–1	–136	2 116	6.43	–204
Australia	–10 945	81	5 299	–1.53	–3 824
Canada	–22 060	–3 650	4 637	78.71	–5 327
Turkey	–942	–65	844	7.70	–1 222
UK	–19 098	–19 341	16 738	115.55	6 667

Note: A positive number for investment abroad indicates a net repatriation of outward foreign direct investment; this is also reflected in the minus sign for the ratio of outward to inward foreign direct investment.

Source: *Balance of Payments Statistics Yearbook, 1994*, International Monetary Fund, Washington, DC, 1996.

Table 10.3 Inward and outward foreign direct investment, 1989–95 (billions of US$)

	1989	1990	1991	1992	1993	1994	1995
Foreign direct investments in China	3.39	3.48	4.37	11.16	27.52	33.79	37.74
Direct investment outside China	–0.78	–0.83	–0.91	–4.00	–4.40	–2.00	–2.00
Outflows as a percentage of inflows	23.00	23.85	20.82	35.84	15.99	5.92	5.30

Source: Appendix Table 10.4A. The difference with Table 10.2 is due to rounding.

Table 10.2 shows that, in 1992 at least, only Canada and the UK had roughly matched two way direct investment flows. The final column in the table shows that China's errors and omissions are greater than any of the countries covered in the sample. While this can to some extent be put down to the size effect of China's large economy, the relative significance of approved outflows of direct and portfolio capital from China, in terms of inflows of such capital or current account balance, is striking and worthy of further analysis.

The focus of this paper is on overseas investment from mainland China which goes beyond the territories of Hong Kong and Macao. The 'foreign' investment by Chinese companies, approved and unapproved, in those territories is a special case. The approved investments can be seen as part of the process of integrating the economic activities of the territories with the mainland economy – an assertion of both power and dependency. The unapproved flows reflect the ease of transferring resources to the physically and culturally contiguous territories. The size of the flows are analysed in more detail in Sung (1995), Ni (1994) and On (1996). MOFTEC (Ministry of Foreign Trade and Economic Cooperation) approvals for investment in Hong Kong stood at US$326 million at the end of 1994. In contrast, Ni suggests that by early 1994 'a conservative estimate puts total capital assets and investment by mainland entities in Hong Kong at more than US$30 billion'. This is substantially more than the Government of China's official estimate of US$5.16 by the end of 1992.[9] Even if the assets of the financial institutions such as the Bank of China are netted out Sung's 'conservative estimate' of the value of Chinese investments in the 16 leading mainland controlled Hong Kong listed companies puts the total at US$11 billion at the end of 1993 and, including all other non-financial companies, US$20 billion by the end of 1994. An analysis of the nature and role of Chinese investment in Hong Kong and Macao is beyond the scope of the present study; the interested reader is referred to the studies listed above.

In this paper the limited data which are available on the nature of government approved outward foreign non-trade investment are analysed in more detail in order to see what types of overseas investment activity by Chinese enterprises are considered, by implication, to be in the national interest. The following section examines aggregate, national level, data on the geographical and sectoral pattern of China's overseas non-trade investment (and such limited data as are available on trade enterprises). The subsequent section examines the geographic and sectoral allocation of the investment on an enterprise level basis, categorizing it according to the apparent motives for such investments. The data used in this paper mostly relate to non-trade activities. This category is used by Ministry of Foreign Trade and Economic Co-operation (MOFTEC) in its publications to include manufacturing enterprises, resources development projects such as mining and forestry companies, and contract projects, especially construction projects.[10]

THE AGGREGATE DATA

Chinese overseas investment is spread across the globe, with Chinese owned companies or joint ventures operating in 135 countries. However, Appendix Table 10.5A, which provides data up to 1994, shows a picture of strong concentration of Chinese investment in relatively few of these countries (even allowing for the substantial under-reporting of the figures for Hong Kong, see below). More than 86 per cent of it was concentrated in the 25 countries listed in the table. The top three countries alone, Canada, the USA and Australia, accounted for well over half (58 per cent) of the total. If the correct figures for Hong Kong were to be taken into account, the concentration effect would be seen to be even stronger than these data suggest.

The average share of Chinese investment in the enterprises varies greatly from country to country, from almost 100 per cent in Chile to the low of 19.0 per cent in Italy. The ratio was 50 per cent or more in only nine of the top 25 countries over the whole period covered. The average for all 25 countries, weighted by the value of investments in each country, was less than half, standing at 45 per cent. In the five countries of major concentration the share was greater than one half on average over the period since 1978 for Canada, the USA and Hong Kong, and below half in the cases of Australia (26.5 per cent) and Russia (just below half at 49.8 per cent). In the case of Australia the average of 26.5 per cent was one of the lowest ratios for all countries China has invested in, although the total investments of the firms in which China has a share is larger in Australia than in any other country, by a wide margin. The largest total commitment of funds by the Chinese side is in Canada, standing at US$370 million by the end of 1994.

The total sum invested by China in Canada is not only greater than that in any other country but at US$4.9 million the average value of the Chinese investment in each project is also the largest of any country invested in. By the end of 1994 China had invested in 75 non-trade enterprises in Canada, compared to the 86 in Australia, 218 in the USA, the reported 139 in Hong Kong and 225 in Russia. In Russia, however, the average investment was only 426 thousand dollars while the average in Australia was almost US$3.8 million and those in the USA and Hong Kong were US$1.5 million and just less than US$1 million respectively. China had only five investments in Chile but the average investment in them was US$4.3 million. The two investments in Bermuda had an average investment of US$2.5 million. Among the other countries in the top 25 only Turkey (1.7) had investments from China with an average value of more than US$1 million. The average for the top 25 countries was US$1.2 million – a figure heavily weighted by the figures for the top four in which the average investment by the Chinese was almost US$4 million each, compared to the average of US$616 thousand in the other 21 countries.

The picture which emerges from this analysis of the geographical distribution of China's overseas non-trade investment is one of a wide dispersal throughout the world with a strong concentration on a small number of countries in which the investments are on average large. The standard pattern in the other countries is one of a large number of small companies – known in China as 'Mom and Pop' or 'Husband and Wife' overseas investments.

Data for 'trade' investments, which is a catch-all category for all service activities, are not available on the same level of disaggregation as for non-trade investments. Appendix Table 10.6A presents such aggregate data as were available on the geographical distribution of trade investments at the end of 1993, with comparable data on non-trade investments. The table shows that China's overseas trade investments are also globally dispersed, although the pattern is different. China's (reported) trade investments are heavily concentrated in Hong Kong (and to a much lesser extent in Macao): 62 per cent are located in Hong Kong (and Macao) as against less than 8 per cent of non-trade investments. In all other areas of the world non-trade investments outnumber trade investments, except in Western Europe where there are about two-thirds more trade than non-trade enterprises and North America where there are roughly the same numbers of each.

The data indicates that China has invested in around twice as many overseas trade enterprises as it has in non-trade enterprises. This is largely explained by the large number of Chinese investments in trade enterprises in Hong Kong (and Macao). Appendix Table 10.6A shows that of the total 4479 overseas enterprises reported as having Chinese investment in 1993, 1648 of them, or 38 per cent, were trade enterprises located in Hong Kong (and Macao). It also shows that 62 per cent of all reported overseas trade investments were located in Hong Kong (and Macao) in 1993 compared to the 8 per cent of all non-trade overseas investments located in those territories, reflecting a strong concentration of trade investments in Hong Kong (and Macao).

Appendix Table 10.7A provides a more detailed breakdown of the sectoral distribution of China's outward foreign direct investment. The first three categories are those which China describes as non-trade categories, the rest are grouped together as trade categories. The table shows that the sectoral pattern of investment in Hong Kong is significantly different from that in other locations. In Hong Kong there is a strong relative concentration in the categories technology and trade, catering and tourism, finance and insurance, and consultancy. The two largest categories in Hong Kong, technology and trade, and catering and tourism, accounted for 75 per cent of all Chinese investments in Hong Kong (and Macao) but only for 19 per cent of the number of investments made elsewhere.

Leaving Hong Kong (and Macao) aside, most of China's overseas investments are in the first two categories: production ventures, mainly manufacturing, accounts for 30 per cent and contract projects (turnkey engineering and construction projects) for 24 per cent. The pattern in which production projects are the largest number of projects (in countries and regions other than Hong Kong and Macao) is only broken by Eastern Europe and the CIS where contract projects account for the largest number of investments (38 per cent). In the two regions where most of China's outflows of capital go (again, other than Hong Kong and Macao), the Americas (mainly the USA and Canada) and South Pacific (mainly Australia), production projects account for the largest number of projects, although the bias towards production projects is greater in the South Pacific (40 per cent of all projects) than it is in the Americas (29 per cent). And although the number of resource development projects in the South Pacific (30) is smaller than it is elsewhere its relative significance there is the greatest: 15 per cent compared to the average of 5 per cent.

Only one Chinese investment in the category, catering and tourism, is listed for the South Pacific, despite the presence of many Chinese restaurants in that area. This draws attention to the fact that investments by ethnic Chinese resident abroad, in companies registered abroad and which do not involve funds brought out of China are not listed as Chinese invested companies by the Chinese government.

MICRO-DATA: OVERSEAS INVESTMENT ACTIVITIES OF CHINESE FIRMS

The objectives of the Chinese government in supporting legal outflows of foreign direct investment are fourfold: the acquisition of proprietary technology;

the control of raw material supplies; the growth of foreign exchange earnings through export sales; the generation of foreign exchange income through contracts for turnkey projects and construction contracts; and the diversification of business interests. It is possible to find examples of all four types of foreign direct investment among overseas enterprises invested in by Chinese firms. Prominent examples of the four types are identified and discussed below. Although each case is placed in one category the distinction is not always clear-cut as an investment may be meeting several objectives, for example, the purchase of a mine will also provide access to mining technology.

Access to Technology

The best-known example of a Chinese firm investing abroad in order to gain access to proprietary technology is the investment made in the USA by the China Bicycles Corporation of Shenzhen. The company, in which the International Finance Corporation of the World Bank Group has a 15 per cent equity stake, bought an American bicycle company in order to gain access to the technology for producing the high specification models in demand in the USA and Europe. The company transferred the technology back to its Shenzhen plant which now has a highly successful export market. The existing technology of bicycle production in China is geared to low income markets. At least one Chinese company (see below) has transferred this technology abroad, via investments in other developing countries, in order to gain market access. Another example is the purchase in 1988 by the Shougang (Capital) Iron and Steel Corporation of Beijing of 70 per cent of the equity of the Californian company Masta Engineering and Design Inc. in order to obtain access to the US company's high technology design capability in steel rolling and casting equipment. Some of China's investment in Hong Kong is also motivated by the desire to acquire modern technology. For example, in January 1994 the Shenzhen Electronic Group formed a joint venture with Hong Kong partners to invest HK$230 million to develop a plant to manufacture special use integrated circuits with the express intention of acquiring new technology.[11]

Control over Raw Material Supplies

Gaining some security over access to raw materials is more often cited as the reason for Chinese enterprises' desire to invest overseas. There are many examples, including some of the largest of China's overseas ventures. In Australia, the China Metallurgical Import and Export Corporation has invested A$120 million, giving it a 40 per cent equity stake in an iron ore mining company. CITIC Australia has paid A$100 million for a 10 per cent stake in an aluminium smelter. Also in Australia, the Anshan Iron and Steel Complex is investing 40 per cent of the cost of developing the Kolynobbing and Cockatoo iron ore mining projects.[12]

The Baogang Iron and Steel Corporation of Shanghai has also invested abroad to gain assured access to iron ore supplies, although few details of the investments are available. The company is reported to have invested in six joint ventures in Australia, Brazil and South Africa covering both iron ore mining and steel marketing. Between 1990 and 1994 the company shipped 10.45 million tons of mineral back to China, saving an estimated 40 million RMB in fees and charges. Going the other way, the company has used its joint venture subsidiaries to act as marketing agents for its steel products and by 1993 had exported 1.77 million tons of steel, earning US$692 million. In 1993 the Shougang (Capital) Iron and Steel Corporation invested US$312 million to buy the Hierro Peru iron producer from the government of Peru in order to ensure raw materials supply for its plants in China – although the purchase also includes a steel plant and metals manufacturing plants in Peru. Shougang is deploying 30 ships to ferry iron and coal between China and Peru.[13]

One of the most successful Chinese overseas investments is that by CITIC's Canadian subsidiary in pulp and papers products and processed wood. The initial investment in 1986 was a 50/50 joint venture with the Canadian Baler and Basester Corporations in the Saijal paper pulp factory in British Columbia. CITIC financed its investment with a C$62 million mortgage loan from the Royal Bank of Canada. The 8–10 year loan was paid off out of profits in two and a half years. CITIC's head office in Beijing gave its Canadian subsidiary a guarantee that it would purchase the entire production if necessary. Rising world demand made this guarantee redundant and in addition to China the factory exports its products to Latin America, Australia, South East Asia, South Korea and Taiwan. The initial production capacity of 180 000 tons was expanded to 420 000 tons in 1992 after a further investment of C$700 million in 1991 aimed at modernizing the technology used in the plant. The investment was financed by twelve year loans from the Royal Bank of Canada and the National Westminster Bank of the UK. This investment is also a good example of Chinese enterprises' growing sophistication in raising capital for overseas investment on international capital markets. Earlier, in 1988, the company had used its retained profits to participate with Swedish and Hong Kong partners in a C$40 million joint venture in a wood processing plant producing 310 000 cubic metres of wood annually (Wang, 1995, p. 14).

Also in the area of wood products, the China Foreign Trade Transportation General Corporation (CFTTGC) paid US$87 million, at auction in 1990, for the exploitation rights for 30 years over 20 000 hectares of New Zealand forest. By the beginning of 1995 the company CFTTGC established to manage its investment, the Wenita Forestry Co. Ltd, was extracting at an annual rate more than 300 000 cubic metres for export back to China, and also to Japan, the USA and Korea. Since they purchased the exploitation rights the price of the wood per cubic metre rose from US$70 to US$100 by the beginning of 1995. This investment was part of a diversification policy of the company, which is well on the way to becoming an multinational conglomerate.[14] Another natural resource area where Chinese enterprises have been very active in setting overseas subsidiaries is fishing. Two Chinese companies have taken the lead in investing overseas to ensure supplies of fish for the rapidly growing Chinese market. The leader is China Ocean Fishing Corporation (COFC) which over the ten years from 1985 to 1995 established more than 50 wholly-owned, joint ventures and cooperative subsidiaries in almost 20 countries. These include the USA, Iran, Mauritius, Argentina and several countries in West Africa. It operates a fleet of more than 800 ships of various types and employs 15 000 sailors and land-based workers abroad. Its catch, of several hundred thousand tons per year, is all sent back to China (Wang, 1995, p. 12). Although COFC is now the largest Chinese multinational fishing corporation it was not the first Chinese company to break into this business, The first was the China Aquatic Product General Corporation (CAPGC) which started operations in 1985, shortly before COFC, with the purchase of deep-sea vessels which were stationed off West Africa. The subsidiaries established by CAPGC in West African countries have been shipping an annual average of 250 000 tons of fish back to China and are now also engaged in the production of fishing machines and boats.

Developing Overseas Markets

Many Chinese companies have invested abroad to develop overseas markets. These include small companies finding market niches for 'Chinese' products, such as the district enterprise from Nanjing which has set up a bean curd plant in Madagascar and the Chinese medicine drinks plant set up in Canada in 1990 by a Hanzhou provincial enterprise (Tseng, 1993, p. 100). Other cases, of which there are many examples, involve Chinese firms establishing overseas subsidiaries to overcome protection in the foreign market. Some examples of this form of foreign direct investment include: Hanzhou provincial enterprise's joint venture with a rubber plantation in Malaysia to produce 'student shoes' for the protected (62 per cent duty) Malaysian market (Tseng, 1994); Shanghai Bicycle Corporation's plant in Ghana and two plants in Brazil which together produce 800 000 bicycles for the local markets; the small (US$260 000) investment by China Globe Electronics Joint Corporation in a joint venture with Treatlink Co. Ltd of the UK to produce 300 colour TV sets a day using Chinese SKD (semi-knocked-down) parts; and the even smaller reported US$12 000 investment by the Long March Shoes Making Factory of Shijiazhuang City in a wholly-owned Tennis Shoes Co. Ltd in Nairobi which by 1994 had a registered capital of US$1 million and sales of US$6 million.[15]

Protection-led investment to develop export markets can also occur in third party countries where the intention is to use those countries' quota rights or preferential treatment in other countries' markets. Most of the many enterprises established in Mauritius by Chinese firms are of this type, such as that owned by the Shanghai Knitting Corporation which employs 700 workers and exports T-shirts to the European Union. Similar garment factories have been established in other countries, such as Jamaica to exploit the USA market and Fiji, aimed at the Australian market.

Diversification

Foreign direct investment to diversify their activities and to develop overseas markets is engaged in by some of China's larger enterprises, with the encouragement of the government which is keen to see the development of Chinese conglomerate multinationals modelled on the example of the Japanese and Korean trading houses. For example, following the loss of its trade monopoly in 1987, and the crash in the oil market, China Chemical Products Import and Export Corporation – better known internationally as SINOCHEM – applied for and was given permission to diversify its activities. These included permission to engage in overseas investment. In six years it transformed itself into a diversified multinational conglomerate with 62 subsidiaries spread across Asia, North and South America, Europe and Africa. Its activities include its original trade in chemical products and transportation and storage, real estate development, tourism, consultancy, insurance and manufacturing (including a phosphate fertilizer plant and oil refinery in the USA). Its average annual turnover between 1988 and 1993 was US$12.14 billion, placing it in the 'Fortune 500'. In 1993 it announced an investment in an oil refinery and fertilizer plant in Indonesia, in a joint venture with a group of leading Indonesian businessmen, involving a total investment of around US$3 billion.[16] CITIC (under the State Council) has also emerged as a multinational conglomerate, as already noted.

China Resources (owned by MOFTEC) is another Chinese enterprise which has developed into a multinational diversified conglomerate over the last ten years. China Resources has used Hong Kong to internationalize its activities.[17] China Resources is one of the 'four heavenly kings', that is, the four major enterprises established in Hong Kong before the 1949 Communist Party takeover of China. The other three, each with a specialized (and monopolized) function in looking after China's economic interests in Hong Kong and through Hong Kong into the world economy, are the China Merchants Steam Navigation Co., the Bank of China and China Travel Services. Other mainland companies established subsidiaries in Hong Kong before the reforms of 1978, but the monopoly of China

Resources on trade flows between Hong Kong and China was not broken until Fujian Province and Tianjin Municipality established trading enterprises in Hong Kong in 1975 and 1976 respectively. In the face of the loss of its monopoly and with the encouragement of the Government of China, China Resources began to use its Hong Kong base to internationalize its operations. It now has several, mainly trade, subsidiaries abroad, especially in the USA, Singapore and Thailand. It has also formed joint ventures with Indonesian firms to develop forestry projects and by 1992 had subsidiaries in various countries (including Austria, Australia, the USA, Canada, Japan, and South Korea) with involvement in international trade, retail trade and real estate development.

Apart from the national level state-owned enterprises the provincial and municipal level state-owned enterprises have also used their Hong Kong bases to venture out into world markets, with involvement in both non-trade and trade activities. For example, the Fujian Enterprise (Holdings) Ltd owns companies in Australia, Canada, the USA, Japan, Thailand, Argentina and Peru where it is involved in a joint venture fishing and fish products company. Sales of fish meat and powder processed in Peru and exported back to China amounted to US$9 million. Similarly, Guangdong Investment, the second largest mainland company listed on the Hong Kong stock exchange and controlled by Guangdong Enterprises (Holdings) Ltd. – owned by the Guangdong government – has also expanded beyond Hong Kong onto the world stage.[18] In addition to the usual sites for Chinese overseas investment, Australia, Canada, the USA and Thailand, Guangdong Investment also has a strong presence in Europe with subsidiaries in Britain, Germany and France – where it has built a Chinatown in the eastern suburbs of Paris.[19]

Another new Chinese multinational conglomerate is China National Export Bases Development Corporation (CHINASBASE). In 1994 CHINASBASE exported goods valued at US$721 million and imported goods worth US$306 million. It operated internationally though a network of overseas subsidiaries, with a total of 49 branches abroad, including wholly-owned subsidiaries in Australia, the USA, Spain, Russia, Malaysia and Hong Kong.

Although this paper is primarily concerned with China's foreign direct investment in non-trade activities, the extensive growth of overseas trade and service subsidiaries should also be noted as a major, and rapidly growing, activity. The Bank of China, for example, had 460 subsidiaries in 18 countries and regions by the end of 1993 – and more have been added since then. According to the most recent accounting data, that for mid-1992, the Bank of China's overseas branches had assets of US$113.37 billion, deposits of US$51.66 billion and a loan book of US$27.35 billion – and all three have seen substantial expansion since then. Apart from involvement in financing China's trade flows, the Bank of China's overseas network, including that of its subsidiary the

Bank of China Group in Hong Kong, has played a major role in raising capital on international capital markets for investment in China.[20] In 1996 the Bank announced the establishment of a merchant bank subsidiary in the City of London. Other Chinese banks have now established overseas branches. In other areas, China Merchants bought a British insurance company and an insurance brokerage company in 1988. Note should also be made of the rapidly growing foreign exchange earnings from overseas engineering, labour supply and turnkey construction projects, often managed through companies established overseas. In 1979 there were 36 such contracts involving 8 countries and earning China US$51 million. In 1993 there were 11 605 contracts in 158 countries which earned a total of US$6.8 billion.

In sum, once Chinese enterprises were allowed to invest abroad they took advantage of the opportunity to do so with alacrity. They have rapidly increased their foreign direct investment in preference to expanded investment in the home market. They have had a wide range of motives for doing so, all consistent with the objectives of the Government of China. The investments have been made globally, although there are, as already noted, some countries in which there is a strong concentration.

CONCLUSION

Since China reopened its economy in 1978, observers have been mesmerized by the rapid growth in its foreign trade and in the inflows of foreign direct investment. China has become one of the world's largest trading nations and one of the leading absorbers of foreign direct investment. What has gone largely unnoticed is that China has also become a major player on world capital markets. As was noted in the Introduction, the International Monetary Fund recognizes China to be the eighth largest supplier of capital on world markets. Despite the difficulties with statistics of outflows of capital, the numbers are impressive whichever measure is used. Gross long-term outflows of capital totalled US$120 billion over the seven year period 1989–95, amounting to almost half of the US$241 billion long term capital inflows over the same period. Outflows of foreign direct investment over that period totalled US$15 billion, outward portfolio investment US$2 billion, and errors and omissions, usually considered to reflect long-term capital flight, a massive US$55 billion. And it is generally recognized that the inflows are overestimates and the outflows underestimates.

Analysis of the outflows of capital from China is difficult, due to the paucity of reliable disaggregate data. This is obviously true of the illegal flows, captured to some extent in gross terms in the errors and omissions item in the balance of payments. It is also true of the foreign direct investment and portfolio investment as well, as neither the source country, China, or any of the 135 host countries track the data by end use. Apart from piecemeal and anecdotal data gleaned from company reports and newspapers the only source of data on end use is that published by MOFTEC in its annual *Almanac of China's Foreign Economic Relations and Trade*. Any official data based analysis of the motivations and social desirability of capital outflows is, therefore, restricted to using data for government approved outflows, which are obviously likely to reflect government imposed criteria for such flows, as most of the outflows are being determined by the decision making of managers of individual, publicly owned, enterprises within a framework of policies which encourage such flows. This limitation has to be kept in mind when evaluating analysis, such as that in this paper, which seeks explanations for the legal, government supported, flows.

The arguments used by the Government of China to explain its introductions of policies to encourage outflows of capital – securing access to raw materials and other essential inputs, securing access to proprietary technology, increasing foreign exchange earnings and diversifying and globalizing the activities of China's larger enterprises – are fully consistent with the economic logic of the western theories of foreign direct investment, and are reflected in the reported outflows.[21]

MOFTEC data indicate a pattern of global dispersion of investment by Chinese enterprises, but with a strong concentration in a limited number of countries – Hong Kong, Australia, Canada and the USA. The investments in these countries are diversified, but there is something of a concentration in Hong Kong on trade and service sector activities, on the securing of raw materials in Australia and Canada and on securing proprietary technology in the case of the USA. Investments in the last three of these countries tend to be larger than average in scale while the average investment in most other countries was quite small in international terms at well under half a million US dollars. Globally there is no sectoral concentration, with Chinese enterprises investing in all sectors of the economies in which they take an interest. For the most part, Chinese enterprises invest through joint ventures, except for the many smaller 'Mom and Pop' enterprises.

Turning to the firm level data, garnered from newspapers, magazines and company reports, examples were found of most of the theoretical cases which would be predicted by western economic theory. Examples were found of Chinese overseas investment motivated by the desire to secure access to raw materials, to secure access to proprietary technology and to develop new markets and to develop markets behind protective trade barriers. Several examples were also found of large central, provincial and municipal level state owned enterprises turning themselves into multinational conglomerates, with the encouragement of the Government of China, through overseas investments aimed at horizontal and vertical integration. Some of these companies are using their new multinational status to raise capital on world markets to invest in China – although the net flow is still substantially negative. This was true, for example, in the case of CITIC Australia. Chinese investment in Australia has been growing rapidly and stretches into every sector of the economy.

China is determined to catch up for lost time in its efforts to develop its economy. It sees itself as an emerging world economic power. One of the ways it plans to expand this power is by encouraging the flow of foreign direct investment into China, partly by encouraging the establishment of giant multinational corporations with global reach. But it is also seeking to expand on the role it plays in the world economy and to enhance its development prospects through investment in the acquisition of productive assets in other countries. China has a lot of catching up to do and as it does so the outflows of capital from China for investment in other countries will grow rapidly to levels which reflect its economic size and its ambition to be a substantial player in the world economy. Although we cannot put accurate figures on it, we can conclude with confidence that China has become a major overseas investor and that the size of the role it is playing on this stage is growing. We can also conclude that many Chinese enterprises are now major multinational companies and that many more will be joining their ranks in the near future.

NOTES

1. Many people have helped in the preparation of this chapter and my thanks are due to them. In particular, thanks are due to Deborah Wall who undertook tedious newspaper library work in Sydney and London, unearthing much interesting and useful information. The paper also draws on background papers prepared in China by Gong Borong, Liu Huimin and Wang Lina and on the MA dissertation written by Bai Huamao at the University of Sussex. Frances Perkins of the East Asia Analytic Unit of the Australian government in Canberra and Guy Sandstrom of the Australian Embassy in London helped with data on Australia. Ki Fukasaku, Helen Hughes, Nancy Wall and Adrian Wood provided very helpful critical comments on the first draft.
2. Figures for *China Daily Business Weekly*, March 10–16, 1996.
3. 'World Economic Outlook', International Monetary Fund, Washington DC, May 1995, Chart 32, p. 83.
4. Ibid., p. 78.
5. Peter Norman, 'The few and the many', *Financial Times*, 28 April, 1995, p. 16.
6. As explained by Michael Mussa, Director of Research of the IMF, in a letter to the author.
7. That is net of registered outflows of capital and of capital flight.
8. There are no reliable data on any aspect of China's outward foreign investment. Authors have to choose which set of heroic assumptions they will make in order to say anything at all. This paper takes the conservative position. This is based on relying for the most part on Ministry of Foreign Trade and Economic Co-operation (MOFTEC) data. This data is made up from approved applications from enterprises for permission to undertake overseas foreign investment.
9. As reported in the *Hong Kong Economic Journal*, 16 February, 1995. Quoted in Yun-Wing Sung (op cit.).
10. Trade enterprises, for which much less data are available, include all service activities such as banking, trading houses, transport facilities, hotels and restaurants.

11. *Hong Kong Economic Times*, 4 January, 1992 and *Far Eastern Economic Review*, 16 January, 1992.
12. See below for more details of China's investments in Australia.
13. 'China forges Peruvian links with $312 steel accord', Sally Bowen, *Financial Times*, 14 January, 1993.
14. 'China's overseas investment', Huang Wei, *Beijing Review*, 21–27 March, 1994.
15. The last three examples are taken from Wang (1995).
16. 'Indonesia: China plans investment', *Far Eastern Economic Review*, 13 May, 1993, p. 75.
17. See Tseng (1993) and Sung (1995) for a fuller discussion of the activities of Chinese multinationals in Hong Kong.
18. See 'Child prodigy: Guangdong investment can't help but grow', Luoise do Rosario, *Far Eastern Economic Review*, 15 September, 1994 for an account of the company's activities in Hong Kong.
19. The range of countries in which China is investing is constantly being expanded – it is now investing in South Africa, having obtained approval for investment in 11 textile and light industry companies. See 'China keen on S Africa links', *Financial Times*, 13 February, 1995.
20. 'BOC expands overseas business', *China's Foreign Trade*, February 1994, p. 21.
21. See for example the work of John Dunning (1988, 1990, 1991 and 1993).

REFERENCES

Dunning, John H. (1988a), *Explaining International Production*, London: Unwin Hyman.

Dunning, John H. (1988b), *Multinationals. Technology and Competitiveness*, London: Unwin Hyman.

Dunning, John H. (1990), 'Explaining outward investment of developing countries', in K. Kumar and M. McLeod (eds), *Multinationals from Developing Countries*,

Dunning, John H. (1991), 'Governments on multinational corporations: from confrontation to cooperation', *Millenium*, **20**.

Dunning, John H. (1993), *Multinational Enterprises and the Global Economy*, New York: Addison Wesley.

Lardy, Nicholas R. (1995), 'The role of foreign trade and investment in China's economic transformation', *The China Quarterly*, **144**, December.

Ni, Nick (1994), 'Mainland investment surges into HK', *China Business Review: South China Morning Post*, 3 March.

On, Kit Tam (1996), 'Chinese outward foreign direct investment and Australia', Canberra, School of Economics Management, The University of New South Wales, Mimeo.

Sung, Yun-Wing (1991), *The China–Hong Kong Connection*, Cambridge: Cambridge University Press.

Sung, Yun-Wing (1995), 'Chinese outward investment in Hong Kong: trends, prospects, and policy implications', A paper prepared for the OECD Development Centre, Department of Economics, Chinese University of Hong Kong, 16 May 1995, Mimeo.

Tseng, Choo Sin (1993), 'Foreign direct investment from the People's Republic of China, in *Proceedings of the 1994 Louis Vuitton Moet Hennessy Conference*, INSEAD Euro Asia Centre, Fountainbleu.

Tseng, Choo Sin (1994), 'The process of internationalisation of PRC multinationals', in Hellmut Schutte (ed.), *The Global Competitiveness of Asian Firms*, London: Macmillan Press.

Wang, Lina (1995), 'Chinese firms' investment abroad', Paper prepared for the OECD Development Centre.

Table 10.4A Long-term capital balance (US$100,000,000)

Item	1989	1990	1991	1992	1993	1994	1995
Long-term capital balance	49.50	64.54	76.70	6.56	274.11	357.56	382.49
Long-term capital Inflow	119.93	116.11	128.58	276.42	503.54	606.89	660.67
Long-term capital outflow	–70.33	–51.57	–51.88	–269.86	–229.43	–250.33	–278.18
Foreign direct investments in China	33.92	34.87	43.66	111.56	275.15	337.87	377.36
Direct investment outside China	–7.80	–8.30	–9.13	–40.00	–44.00	–20.00	–20.00
Foreign purchases of Chinese stocks and bonds	1.40		5.65	3.93	36.47	44.93	17.24
Chinese purchases of foreign bonds and stocks	–3.20	–2.41	–3.30	–4.50	–5.97	–3.80	–0.79
Foreign government loans to China	9.54	14.41	10.26	15.01	26.50	33.75	34.65
Payments on foreign government loans	–1.48	–5.78	–3.42	–6.29	–9.22	–7.79	–8.60
International organizations loans to China	12.46	13.11	13.41	15.83	21.37	32.98	19.91
Payments on international organizations loans to China	–2.17	–2.12	–2.74	–2.02	–2.12	–10.00	–2.75
Bank loans from abroad	11.42	13.46	27.43	27.68	3.80	–	33.40
Payments on bank loans from abroad	–32.21	–8.99	–16.46	–59.96	–2.49	–48.08	–61.66
Deferred payable balance	0.11	2.42	1.19	0.80	0.45	4.47	7.12
Deferred receivable balance	–0.15	–0.51	0.22	0.84	–3.74	–0.53	–7.14
Local government and central departments loans from abroad	38.85	21.36	9.70	6.59	13.21	33.22	37.97
Payments on local government and central departments loans from abroad	–10.22	–9.69	–4.37	–29.30	–34.10	–30.38	–20.97
Equipment offered by foreign investors through compensation trade	3.17	2.37	2.93	2.76	0.55	0.19	0.48
Rents for equipment offered by foreign investors through compensation trade	–2.57	–2.10	–2.35	–8.14	–0.53	–0.33	–0.54
Payable rents for equipment in international rentals	6.19	6.19	6.87	7.97	16.19	8.12	14.09
China's loans to foreigners	–1.93	–1.95	–1.30	–1.47	–2.06	–1.78	–1.75
Receipt of principal on China's loans to foreigners	0.37	0.48	0.63	0.07	0.35	0.97	0.94
Other capital balance	0.35	0.31	0.19	–32.11	–15.70	–10.55	–2.86
Memo item: Errors and omissions	3.25	–31.31	–67.92	–82.74	–98.04	–97.74	–178.10

Note: The category 'Long-term capital outflow' does not appear to be the sum of its parts in the table. Similarly the figure for 'Long-term capital inflow' in the 1996 volume is 607.89 while it was 606.89 in the 1995 volume (the figure used in this table) although none of its constituent elements is shown as having changed.

Source: State Statistical Bureau, *Chinese Statistical Yearbook 1993, 1994, 1995* and *1996*, Beijing: State Statistical Publishing House 1993, 1994, 1995 and 1996. The 1995 volume inadvertently substitutes the 1990 data for that of 1992.

Table 10.5A Geographic distribution of China's overseas non-trade enterprises (US$ million)

	Totals to 1993				1994				Totals to 1994		
	No. of enterprises	Total investment	Of which Chinese	Chinese share (%)	No. of firms	Total investment	Of which Chinese	Chinese share (%)	Total investment	Of which Chinese	Chinese share (%)
Canada	72	696.57	368.51	52.9	3	1.85	1.02	55.1	698.42	369.53	52.9
USA	204	430.50	320.91	74.5	14	13.96	6.37	45.6	444.45	327.28	73.6
Australia	82	1228.87	324.41	26.4	4	2.65	1.59	60.0	1,231.52	326.00	26.5
Hong Kong	138	202.75	135.14	66.7	1	0.12	0.12	100.0	202.87	135.26	66.7
Russian Fed.	220	191.08	95.19	49.8	5	1.29	0.57	44.2	192.37	95.76	49.8
Thailand	108	116.72	48.5	41.6	14	16.07	6.19	38.5	132.79	54.69	41.2
Chile	5	21.85	21.5	98.4					21.85	21.50	98.4
Malaysia	47	40.49	19.58	48.4	2	5.02	1.18	23.5	45.51	20.76	45.6
Mexico	25	19.00	15.98	84.1	2	0.56	0.20	35.7	19.56	16.18	82.7
Macao	24	34.35	15.88	46.2					34.35	15.88	46.2
Singapore	44	44.14	13.44	30.4	4	2.74	1.93	70.4	46.88	15.36	32.8
Japan	75	39.90	13.27	33.3					39.90	13.27	33.3
Brazil	13	20.98	12.27	58.5	3	1.12	0.51	45.5	22.11	12.79	57.8
Nigeria	17	31.66	11.02	34.8	2	2.55	1.14	44.8	34.21	12.44	36.4
Philippines	23	17.82	7.25	40.7	2	2.22	1.97	88.7	20.04	9.22	46.0
France	11	26.98	8.86	32.8	1	0.30	0.10	33.3	27.28	8.96	32.8
Germany	25	12.82	7.81	60.9	3	1.46	0.98	67.1	14.28	8.80	61.6
Turkey	5	11.85	6.28	53.0	2	4.32	2.22	51.4	16.17	8.51	52.6
Bangladesh	24	23.59	7.64	32.4	1	0.90	0.35	38.9	24.29	7.99	32.9
South Korea	4	22.24	4.86	21.9	5	5.25	2.22	42.3	27.49	7.08	25.8
Mauritius	16	15.78	6.78	43.0					15.78	6.78	43.0
UK	7	11.15	5.07	45.5	1	0.98	0.98	100.0	12.13	6.05	49.9
Bermuda	2	10.02	5.01	50.0					10.02	5.01	50.0
Yemen	7	10.34	3.19	30.9	1	0.99	0.99	100.0	11.33	4.18	36.9
Italy	6	15.69	2.99	19.1					15.69	2.99	19.1
Total of above	1204	3297.14	1481.34	44.9	70	64.35	30.63	47.6	3,361.29	1,512.27	45.0
China Total	1657	3692.30	1687.05	45.7	106	124.49	70.62	56.7	3,816.79	1,757.67	46.1

Note: Data is ranked by total amount of Chinese investment in 1994.

Source: *Almanac of China's Foreign Economic Relations and Trade, 1995/96*, pp. 948–51.

Table 10.6A Industrial distribution of China's overseas enterprises at the end of 1993

	Hong Kong and Macao	Africa	Asia	North America	South America	South Pacific	Western Europe	Eastern Europe and CIS	Total
Total no. of enterprises	1789	213	752	535	162	194	301	533	4479
Trade enterprises	1648	57	301	265	48	64	188	89	2660
Non-trade enterprises	141	156	451	270	114	130	113	444	1819
China's investment (US$million)	3201	80	260	771	88	400	99	254	5153
Share of investment (%)	62	2	5	15	2	8	2	5	100

Source: *Reform of the Four Major Economic Systems and Enterprise*, China Economic Publishing House, 1994. The data in this table are not consistent with those in Table 10.7A, which come from a different source. The inconsistency is assumed to be of a similar nature for both trade and non-trade investments.

Table 10.7A Industrial distribution of China's overseas enterprises at the end of 1993

	Hong Kong and Macao	Africa	Asia	Americas	South Pacific	Western Europe	Eastern Europe and CIS	Total
Non-trade enterprises								
Production	38 (2%)	78 (37%)	209 (28%)	201 (29%)	77 (40%)	69 (23%)	184 (35%)	856 (19%)
Contract projects	85 (5%)	60 (28%)	183 (24%)	114 (16%)	43 (22%)	31 (10%)	202 (38%)	718 (16%)
Resources development	18 (1%)	18 (8%)	59 (8%)	69 (10%)	30 (15%)	13 (4%)	38 (7%)	245 (5%)
Trade enterprises								
Technology and trade	796 (48%)	28 (13%)	851 (11%)	103 (15%)	6 (3%)	31 (10%)	19 (4%)	1068 (24%)
Transport and communications	23 (1%)	7 (3%)	7 (1%)	19 (3%)	3 (2%)	3 (1%)	13 (2%)	75 (2%)
Finance and insurance	157 (9%)	11 (5%)	102 (14%)	96 (14%)	34 (18%)	72 (24%)	59 (11%)	531 (12%)
Catering and tourism	547 (31%)	3 (1%)	84 (11%)	73 (10%)	1 (1%)	69 (22%)	17 (3%)	794 (18%)
Consultancy	98 (5%)	2 (1%)	7 (1%)	13 (2%)	–	7 (2%)	1 (0%)	128 (3%)
Medical	9 (1%)	6 (1%)	12 (2%)	4 (1%)	–	6 (2%)	–	37 (1%)
Other	18 (1%)	–	4 (1%)	5 (1%)	–	–	–	27 (1%)
Total	1789	213	752	697	194	301	533	4479

Note: Percentages do not total to 100 due to rounding.

Source: *Reform of the Four Major Economic Systems and Enterprise*, China Economic Publishing House, Beijing, 1994, and University of International Business and Economics, *Journal of International Business*, Beijing, June 1994.

11. Pension reform in central and eastern Europe: the good, the bad and the unsustainable[1]

Nicholas Barr*

It may seem tactless to celebrate such eminent retirements with a chapter on fiscally problematic pension systems. As will become clear, however, the Universities Superannuation Scheme suffers from few, if any, of the problems discussed below, so that the honorands can at least sleep comfortable in the knowledge that promises about their pensions will be kept.

The same, alas, cannot be said for large numbers of pensioners in central and eastern Europe (CEE) and the former Soviet Union (FSU). This chapter is organized (as Bernard taught me) as follows. The first part discusses why the inherited system of pensions was relatively well adapted to the pre-reform system but badly adapted to a market economy. The second section sets out the resulting problems which pension systems face throughout the former communist world. The third section discusses a range of reform for state pensions and the fourth policy directions for private pensions.

SYSTEMIC CHANGE

Pensions in their Pre-reform Context

Income transfers historically made up a much smaller share of GDP in CEE and the FSU than in the West, with a larger role for price subsidies.[2] The welfare impact of the cancellation of most of the subsidies is an important part of the context.

Prior to the reforms, the structure of wages and income transfers was relatively well-adapted to the needs of the old system. Wages were low and fairly undifferentiated; and income transfers were awarded to broad groups of people, such as families with children (through family allowance) and the elderly

* Both Bernard and Maurice taught me during my LSE undergraduate days. In addition, Bernard was my tutor during my third year. He was the person who made me go through my essays on the blackboard in his study, forcing me to explain to him (and hence to myself) what the theory said. Thus it was Bernard who made me realize what it was like *really* to understand what I was studying. He was also a great drinking companion.

(through pensions). Pensions were generous: they were a high fraction of workers' previous earnings; they were awarded at a relatively young age; and, for the most part, they were not withdrawn if the recipient continued to work. This, it can be argued, was appropriate in a system where wages were below their market-clearing level. Pensions, therefore, had to be a high fraction of wages to provide an adequate standard of living in old age; and, because low wages led to a continuing excess demand for labour, it made sense to allow pensioners to continue to work with little or no loss of pension.

Pensions in the Context of a Market Economy

The structure just described is poorly-adapted to the needs of a market economy, which requires wages to be differentiated because of the resulting incentives to efficiency. But if the variation in wages and incomes across people grows larger, income transfers can no longer be aimed at *groups*, but need to be targeted in more sophisticated ways which take account of differences in *individual* circumstances through social insurance (that is, benefits conditioned on a contributions record) and social assistance (that is, poverty relief awarded on the basis of an income test or some other indicator of poverty).

A key part of the strategy for reform, therefore, is improved targeting. This has two aspects:

- to ensure effective poverty relief, benefits should go to *all* who need them, that is, there should be no significant gaps in coverage (this is known as horizontal efficiency);
- to contain costs, benefits should go *only* (or mainly) to those who need them, that is, there should not be excessive 'leakage' of benefits (known as vertical efficiency).

Most political discussion focuses on vertical efficiency, in that it relates to the cost of benefits; but horizontal efficiency is equally important, since it has a direct bearing on the effectiveness of poverty relief.

Alongside better targeting, it is necessary to ensure that income transfers, to the extent possible, assist the operation of the labour market; improving incentives is therefore essential. Finally, more sophisticated targeting requires an administrative structure capable of putting it into effect.

PROBLEMS WITH THE INHERITED SYSTEM

As indicated in the preceding paragraphs, problems are of four sorts: many pensioners are poor; nevertheless, the cost of pensions is high; the pension system, particularly the contributions regime, creates adverse incentives; and administration is weak.

Inadequate Poverty Relief

There is a mistaken view that accurate targeting is possible only by awarding benefits on the basis of an income test, that is, where the amount of benefit is exactly related to individual or family income. Income tests, however, have major costs: they are administratively demanding, can be intrusive and hence stigmatizing and can create major disincentives to work effort and to saving. Accurate targeting, moreover, does not always require an income test. There are two ways in which the poor can be identified: through an income test, or via *indicators* of poverty, that is, possession by the individual/family of one or more easily observable characteristics which are highly correlated with poverty, for example ill-health, the presence of children in the family or, of particular relevance to this paper, old age. Pensions, being based on old age, thus use indicator targeting.[3]

The inherited system of pensions faced two strategic problems. First, on top of the well-known problems of defining and measuring poverty, there were few data on people's incomes. Since communism, officially, had no poverty, there was no need to collect poverty data (indeed, the system discouraged such enquiry). This is an area in which real progress has been made, in that most countries now have a household survey of some sort.

Second, the adequacy of the minimum pension could be questionable. The problem arose because the minimum level of the major benefits was often not tied to a poverty line but either to the average wage or to the minimum wage. The problem if the minimum benefit is tied to the average wage is that it falls if average wages fall – which is exactly what happened during the early transition.[4] Alternatively, if the minimum benefit is tied instead to the minimum wage, the problem is that the minimum wage is highly political, especially when subsidies on basic commodities are being reduced.

Though poverty has increased substantially in all the transition countries, attempts at quantification must be heavily qualified. For well-known reasons (Atkinson, 1987, 1989 ch. 1, 1991; Barr, 1998 ch. 6), income is a highly imperfect yardstick of individual welfare even in the West. In the transition economies the problem is even worse.

- Pre-transition figures on income took no account of the non-availability of goods, nor of the fact that access to goods was easier for some groups than others. The problem then is how to interpret changes in people's incomes.[5]

- The transition led to sharp changes in relative prices, making it difficult to estimate inflation and hence difficult to assess what happened to people's real incomes.[6]
- With increasing informalization, significant amounts of income, particularly in the private sector, are not captured in official statistics. There is growing evidence (Cox et al., 1995; Garner, 1995; Torrey et al., 1995) that households adopt a range of informal coping strategies, including transfers within the extended family, own production (that is, growing food on a family plot), and employment in the informal sector, which parallel formal sector activities. Official statistics may understate GDP by as much as 20 per cent, and in some countries even more (see Gomulka, 1998).

Despite these measurement problems, a number of stylized facts emerge. First, in almost all the reforming countries there has been an increase in poverty, often a sharp increase (Milanovic, 1995, table 2; Cornia, 1994, table 10) and in inequality (Milanovic, 1995, table 2; Torrey et al., 1995, table 4). As examples, the poverty headcount rose from low levels under the old system to an estimated 20 per cent in Poland in 1993–94, 17 per cent in Bulgaria, 32 per cent in Romania, an average of 36 per cent in the Baltics, and to 43 per cent in Russia (Milanovic, 1995, table 2).

The losers are disproportionately the unemployed and children (Fajth, 1994). The winners are people who are better-educated and/or those with jobs in the private sector (Milanovic, 1995; Rutkowski, 1996).

Pensioners, by and large, have held their ground (Milanovic, 1995) relative to wage earners. This does *not* mean that pensioners have done well. It merely means that their losses have not been significantly greater than those of wage earners. Virtually all the reforming countries have experienced falls in output exceeding 15 per cent, and frequently of between a quarter and a third. Even allowing for the fact that some output was valueless and that official figures overstate the drop, the scale of the output decline dwarfs anything the West has experienced since the Great Depression of the 1930s. Old-age poverty, in short, is a major and continuing problem.

Inadequate Cost Containment

Though many pensioners are poor, pension expenditure is high, mainly because of the very large numbers of beneficiaries. The core of the problem is that the normal retirement age in CEE and the FSU is 60 for men and 55 for women; and large groups such as miners and teachers were able to retire even earlier.

The problem is exacerbated by the ease with which receipt of benefit can be combined with work. Old age pensioners can generally work full time, or nearly full time, with no loss of benefit. Similarly, people can qualify for invalidity pension even if they have suffered no loss of earning capacity. An individual who loses a limb, but whose long-run health and working capacity are unaffected, will generally receive a *continuing* partial invalidity pension whilst performing his or her old job and receiving a full wage.

The resulting problems are substantial. As Table 11.1 shows, the typical woman pensioner in the Czech Republic enjoys over four more years of retirement than her American counterpart, and five years more than her German counterpart. For men the difference is closer to one year. The comparison for Hungary, Poland, and Russia is broadly similar. Thus people draw pensions for longer in CEE and the FSU than in the much richer countries of the West.

Table 11.1 Duration of retirement: selected OECD and transition countries

	Average age at which pension is first paid		Life expectancy at average age at which pension is first paid	
	Men	Women	Men	Women
Canada (1990)	63.3	63.1	17.1	21.3
Germany (1990)				
blue collar	62.7	63.8	15.9	19.4
white collar	63.0	63.1	15.7	19.9
UK (1990)	65.5	61.0	13.4	17.1
USA (1990)	63.7	63.5	15.9	20.0
Czech Republic (1994)	59	55	16.7	24.4
Hungary (1993)	59	54	15.9	23.8
Poland (1994)	59	55	16 3	23 8
Russia (1994)	58.5	53.5	13.9	23.3
Slovak Republic (1994)	59	54	16.4	24.6
Average:				
OECD countries			15.6	19.5
Transition countries			15.8	24.0

Note: Life expectancies are estimated from official period life tables and official mortality rates. They are suitable to compare countries, since they take into account different age structures and mortality patterns. But they are not necessarily accurate projections of the duration of retirement, since no allowance is made for improvement in mortality rates. In most developed countries, there have been substantial decreases in mortality rates over age 55 in the past 20 years. To calculate the life expectancies of a cohort reaching retirement would require assumptions about future mortality rates. For the purpose, for example, of assessing the soundness of a social security system, it would be essential to do such calculations.

Sources: Average age at which pension is first paid: Canada, Germany, UK, USA: OECD: *New Orientations for Social Policy*, Social Policy Studies No. 12, OECD, 1994, Table 7. Transition economies: World Bank data.
Life expectancy at average age at which pension is first paid: Official sources.

The multitude of pensioners can create a vicious circle in which high pension spending (16 per cent of GDP in Poland in 1995) leads to high payroll contributions, to incentives not to declare employment, and thus to still higher contribution rates. Yet pensions in most countries remain low because there are so many pensioners. The combined effects of unemployment, widespread informal activity, low pensionable age, and, in some countries, lack of rural coverage have led to low ratios of contributors to pensioners (Table 11.2). Poland, for example, has 4.6 people of working age for each person aged 60 or more, but only 1.9 of them pay social insurance contributions. Bulgaria has little more than one contributor per pensioner. Medium-term projections in many countries show that present arrangements are not sustainable.

Table 11.2 Population structure and contributors per pensioner in selected transition economies

Country	Persons of working age per person over 60	Contributors per pensioner
Albania	7.9	1.0
Bulgaria	2.9	1.2
Czech Republic	3.5	2.0
Hungary	3.2	1.5
Poland	4.6	1.9
Romania	3.6	2.0
Russia	2.9	1.9

Source: Calculated from Andrews and Rashid (1996), data for figures 17 and 19.

Despite much debate, progress in addressing these problems has been very limited. The age at which pension is first paid has, if anything declined. By far the worst example is Poland, where half of all workers due to reach pensionable age within five years already receive a pension. Access to disability pension is also easier (though by a narrower margin) in Poland than elsewhere.

There is limited good news. Some countries are close to bringing in legislation to raise the retirement age, though the actual age of retirement has thus far continued to *fall* in all countries except the Baltics. The terms on which a person can receive a pension while continuing to work have been made less generous: the Baltics, Hungary, Poland and Russia have introduced a retirement test or have restricted access to pensions in other ways (for example paying a pension to someone who continues to work, but only if he or she is working in the private sector). In addition, many countries have partially or totally withdrawn pensions for special groups.

Adverse Incentives

Problems arise particularly through the way social insurance contributions are organized. The social insurance contribution is generally paid entirely by the employer, the absence of a worker contribution having been regarded as one of the victories of socialism. The problem if the entire contribution is paid by the employer (and even worse when employers faced a soft budget constraint) is that everyone thinks that contributions (and hence benefits) are paid by someone else. This is the classic third-party payment problem, in which there is no incentive for anyone to restrain spending (see Barr, 1994, ch. 2). There is an exact parallel with fee-for-service medical care financed by insurance.

A second problem with contributions is that they are large, typically 40–45 per cent of the gross wage, though in some countries they have been considerably higher. Such high contributions interfere with the competitiveness of enterprises and depress the demand for labour and in particular – given the high cost of benefits for mothers with young children – the demand for female labour. They also create incentives for labour to migrate to the informal sector and/or for underdeclaration of workers' incomes.

Progress has been very limited. Employers still pay the entire (or almost the entire) contribution. Contribution rates remain high, thus driving people into the informal sector, eroding the contributions base and thus further harming the finance of benefits.

Poorly-structured Administration

As discussed earlier, a widening income distribution necessitates more sophisticated targeting of benefits, which in turn requires greater administrative capacity. Yet benefit administration at the start of the reforms was lamentably underpowered in all the countries.

The first problem was the excessive complexity of benefit structures. Under the old system, most benefits were long-term (family allowance, pensions). Individuals receiving short-term benefit from the public authorities were few and could therefore receive 'Rolls Royce' treatment. In addition, little emphasis was put on administrative efficiency. For both reasons benefit structures tended to be highly complex, an unsustainable situation with large-scale unemployment.

A second set of problems arose out of the major role of enterprises in administering benefit. Enterprises provided information to employees about entitlement, assisted with pensions claims and were involved in the payment of short-term benefits as part of an individual's pay packet. This approach becomes increasingly unsustainable as job mobility increases, as enterprises face hard budget constraints, and as large numbers of people work for small-scale employers or become self-employed. What is needed is a major transfer of administration from the enterprise to the public benefit authorities. A further problem is the extent to which the social insurance authorities are ignorant of individual records. All but the smallest enterprises pay social insurance contributions *en bloc* on behalf of their employees. The social insurance authorities have no knowledge about individual contribution records. Individuals approaching retirement, with the aid of their employer, must put together a dossier of their entire work history to establish their contribution record. For the same reason, the social insurance authorities generally have no knowledge of individual recipients of short-term benefits and family allowance. Both problems impose major limitations on the range of reforms which are administratively feasible in the short run.

Finally, administrative capacity was, and remains, limited. Records are generally of the pencil-and-paper variety (as recently as May 1990 Gosplan's Moscow office was reputed not to have had a fax machine). The main method of getting short-term benefits to recipients was through the employer. For benefits such as pensions, the main vehicle of payment was (and is) cash through the postal system – a particular problem during times of rapid inflation.[7]

There has been little progress in moving benefit administration from the enterprise to the social insurance authorities. A number of countries (Hungary for example) have embarked on major projects to upgrade administrative capacity, including the development and installation of a computer system capable of maintaining individual social insurance records. Progress in a number of areas (for example, pensions paid electronically to the pensioner's bank account) must await progress in financial institutions and telecommunications.

SOLUTIONS 1: REFORMING THE STATE SYSTEM

Reforms are of three sorts: reducing payroll deductions to reduce distortionary incentives; reducing the number of beneficiaries to contain the fiscal burden; and strengthening administration to assist more effective targeting.

Reducing Payroll Deductions

The level of payroll contributions needs to be reduced and their structure simplified. It might be argued that since real wages are low, high contribution rates are not a major problem. That view is mistaken. High employer contributions give incentives against new employment; encourage worker and employer to collude in fraud, for example, by declaring a lower wage than the worker actually receives; create incentives to unofficial employment; distort the relative price of labour and capital; and take from enterprises resources needed for investment in new plant and equipment. There are three ways of reducing the employer's contribution: through improved targeting of benefits; by paying non-insurance benefits through general taxation; and by sharing the contribution between worker and employer.

Targeting benefits more efficiently

The aim should be to set the level of all the main social insurance benefits such as pensions at or above an *individual* poverty line. Social assistance (that is, income-tested, often locally-organized, poverty relief) should be defined relative to a *family* poverty line. To the extent possible, the minimum benefit should be fully protected against inflation.

Better targeted uprating is another potential source of savings. As discussed earlier, benefits tied to earnings are problematic. If real earnings fall they fail to relieve poverty, and if real earnings rise they conflict with cost containment. A policy which combines cost containment with effective poverty relief has two legs:

- the minimum level of all the major benefits and of social assistance is fully protected against price increases;
- while the need for fiscal stringency persists, benefits above the minimum should be increased only to the extent that the budgetary situation permits.

The first part ensures effective poverty relief, the second that it is achieved at minimum cost. As the economic situation improves, real benefits above the minimum can be partly or wholly restored. Though the strategy is clear, the administrative and political difficulties of uprating benefits during times of high inflation should not be overlooked.

Paying non-insurance benefits through general taxation

This change requires clarification of the distinction between insurance and non-insurance benefits, on which a start has been made in several countries. Though policy in the short term may have to concentrate scarce resources on protecting the minimum benefit, the relation between contributions and benefits could usefully be strengthened as soon as economic conditions permit. The move to a stronger relation between contributions and benefits increasingly rules out the use of social insurance for non-contributors, and thereby removes from social insurance much of the social assistance function. The narrower scope of social insurance has already excluded many people who were previously covered, for example, disabled people with no contribution records, or part of the agricultural population who, after the dissolution of cooperatives, are unable or unwilling to pay contributions.

Though there is general agreement that the relationship between contributions and benefits should be strengthened, the extent to which it is *strictly* actuarial is a policy option. Social insurance has two distinct roles: (a) as a device to address failures in private insurance markets (Barr, 1998, ch. 8); and (b) as a device which allows redistribution from rich to poor within a generation and/or between generations. The extent to which social insurance embodies redistribution is a value judgement: the lower the weight given to redistribution, the stricter the relationship between contributions and benefits. Where there are no redistributive goals, the relationship will be strictly actuarial. Where social insurance does incorporate redistribution (as typically in the West) it is, nevertheless, desirable that benefits should be related *at the margin* to individual contributions, and contributors and beneficiaries should perceive this to be so. The argument is important. It is open to policy makers to have a pension formula which is redistributive in the sense that worker A, who has twice the earnings of worker B over her working life, gets a pension which is higher than B's, but less than twice as high. However, if either A or B retires early, her pension should be actuarially reduced relative to the pension she would have received at age 65.

There are at least three reasons for strengthening the relationship: on equity grounds (for example, the early retirement provisions for miners discriminate against other groups in the workforce); to minimize distortions to individual retirement decisions; and because of the strong incentive to evade contributions if workers do not see a clear relationship between contributions and benefits. It is important that some of the impetus to enforce contributions comes from incentives rather than administrative activity, not least because enforcing contributions, particularly in the growing private sector, will be a continuing problem. In the medium term, therefore, a closer relationship between contributions and benefits is a key component of the social insurance strategy. Poverty relief should increasingly be based on social assistance and other tax-funded benefits such as family allowance.

Sharing social insurance contributions between worker and employer

Sharing the contribution would follow the typical pattern in the advanced industrialized countries. The social insurance contribution should be divided between the employer and the individual worker, with the worker's contribution appearing as a deduction on his or her payslip. The theoretical importance of the division can, of course, be debated. The incidence of the contribution depends on the relative factor and product demand and supply elasticities and is independent of where the contribution is legally imposed. In theory, therefore, it does not matter how the contribution is shared between worker and employer. This result does not, however, necessarily hold in the short run, nor in situations where markets are not competitive. Moreover, worker contributions have important implications for the political economy of reform. They give a political signal about responsibility which is particularly important during the transition: that the state is responsible for establishing the general framework of social protection, but that the individual, through earnings and contributions, is substantially responsible for him/herself. Where contributions are paid wholly by the enterprise, and even more if the enterprise faces a soft budget constraint, neither workers nor employers face any incentive to moderate their claims. With a worker contribution, any increase in benefits results instantly in increased contributions. The resulting economic signal is that it is the *worker* who pays, at least in part, for social insurance benefits.

Reducing the Number of Beneficiaries

Equalizing pension age

The first step is to start to raise women's retirement age towards that of men. This is not just a matter of fiscal prudence but also of horizontal equity (Britain remains an outlier among the advanced industrial countries in having a lower retirement age for women than for men[8]).

Raising the age of retirement

The ratio of pensioners to workers is high both because the official pensionable age is low by western standards and because for significant numbers of people the effective age of first receipt of pension is even younger than this. Early retirement in Poland in 1991 absorbed one third of all expenditure on old age pensions. Similar problems exist in all the CEE countries. The facts are clear. Policy, however, is a difficult balance between different objectives. In the medium term, pensionable age should be increased, with early retirement only on the basis of an actuarially reduced pension or actuarially higher contributions. This would remove artificial incentives to early retirement, improve the equity of the system as between different groups of workers, and ease administration. Short-term policy is more difficult. The argument for raising the effective pensionable age is the resulting substantial saving in public expenditure. There are two arguments for caution. First, increasing the pension age might not be politically feasible in the short run. Second, western experience shows the demotivating and debilitating effects of long-run unemployment, especially for the young. A case can therefore be made for encouraging older workers to retire; this would assist restructuring and/or open up jobs for younger people.

It is important to be clear what is being criticized and what is not. The problem is not the outcome, early retirement, but the process leading to that outcome, in particular the absence of any clear connection between the contributions paid by an individual and the benefits he or she receives. The problem can be resolved in the medium term through a closer relationship between contributions and benefits. In the short term, however, there is an acute conflict between restructuring and employment for the young on the one hand, and cost containment on the other.

Other measures to reduce the number of pensioners

Reducing access to pensions would yield large savings whilst still offering effective poverty relief to the old and disabled. First, the award of invalidity pension to anyone whose earning capacity has not been reduced could be discontinued, with compensation for permanent loss of a faculty which does not reduce earning capacity taking the form of a lump-sum payment. Though the policy is clear, implementation is problematic because of the difficulty of assessing 'earning capacity'. However, it is not administratively difficult to stop paying invalidity pension to people who continue in their old job at their old rate of pay. As discussed earlier, this is a common occurrence in CEE.

Combining work with receipt of pension is another problem area. Again, there is a conflict of objectives. On the one hand, the ability to combine continuing work with a more or less full pension is costly. This suggests that there should be a retirement test, at least for people below normal retirement age (for example, by withdrawing pension from anyone who earns more than a fairly small amount, or at least paying such individuals a lower pension). Note that an effective retirement test creates savings in two ways. If a person does not retire, there is a saving in pension payment; if he or she does retire, a job is released which can be filled by an unemployed person, thereby reducing expenditure on unemployment benefit. The argument against this approach is that early retirement makes it easier to make older workers redundant, and thus assists restructuring. This suggests that during the early transition, rather than impose a *retirement test*, it is worth considering a *change-of-job* test, whereby individuals who retire but find another job are allowed to keep at least part of their pension. Once more, though the policy is clear, implementation is problematic; Soviet enterprises were adept at organizing fictitious job changes. This sort of problem can be sidestepped for people who become self-employed, where there is a strong case for allowing them to keep some or all of their pension.

Strengthening Administration

A final set of reforms relates to the need to strengthen administration – for income transfers generally and for pensions in particular.

First, and critical, the reform process will necessitate a move from enterprise-based to individual-based benefits and contributions. At present, enterprises administer most short-term benefits; and the social insurance/pension authorities generally know nothing about individual recipients. This creates confusion about the respective roles of wages and benefits; workers need to be clear that wages are determined mainly by productivity, not by distributional goals. In addition, administration imposes a substantial compliance cost on enterprises, which will harm their competitiveness, especially in an international context. In western Europe the great bulk of benefit payment is organized by the social insurance/pension authorities.

On the contributions side, if the social insurance/pension authorities are to administer benefits, they need to know about *individual* contributions. This is not at present generally the case. Automating contributions and benefits would lead to two sorts of saving: (i) administration *per se* would be cheaper; (ii) automation would open up policy options particularly for cost containment through better targeting which are not possible with manual systems, for instance a capacity to raise the basic pension fully in line with inflation, but pensions above the minimum by a smaller amount.

SOLUTIONS 2: INTRODUCING PRIVATE PENSIONS

Though many of the less advanced reformers should probably concentrate on getting their state systems in order, some countries are developing private pensions or considering their introduction. Most state pensions operate on a pay-as-you-go basis (current pensions are paid out of current contributions); most private schemes (whether compulsory or voluntary) are funded by the savings people accumulate during their working lives. Recommendations for reform can usefully be divided into two sorts: those which are essential to any pension reform, which can therefore be asserted fairly forcefully; and those where policy makers face a range of options.

Essential Components of Reform

A central part of pension reform is to ensure that public pension spending is compatible with economic growth. Problems with public spending must be addressed directly; private pensions are no solution to excessive spending on state pensions, especially when the public schemes are as overextended as in most transition countries. Second, any pension reform needs to be financed in some way. Adding a funded scheme to an existing scheme means building up capital to pay future pensions while continuing to service current pensions. This is a bit like people making loan repayments for two houses, their own and their parents', at the same time. If the parents' home is small and the children's income rising (as, for example, in China), payment is not a major problem. But if the parents' home is large and the children's income low or shrinking (as in CEE and the FSU), the pensions of their parents will have to be financed in some other way, such as taxation, asset sales, or borrowing.[9] Introducing private pensions therefore needs to be part of a strategy which also embraces public pension spending.

A third essential element is regulation and enforcement to protect contributors and pensioners which, in turn, require effective government. In many of the reforming countries the necessary financial market regulation, including agreed and enforced accounting standards, does not yet exist. Putting such regulation into place, though a large task, is an essential first step in building private pensions. Especially where there are large pension funds, safeguards are needed also to prevent government from trying to politicize the allocation of investment.

Finally, funded pensions need time to mature. It takes up to 40 years for workers to accumulate enough to support themselves in old age, though this might, in some cases, be speeded up by endowing pension funds with privatized assets.

Policy Options

Eventually, the transition countries are likely to end up with a pension system which combines three elements: a state component, normally pay-as-you-go; a funded component, normally private; and, where the funded component is compulsory, a third component to which individuals can make voluntary additional contributions to funded schemes. Within this framework, each country has strategic choices about the relative size of the three components and precisely how each of them is designed.

How large and how redistributive should the state pension be? Poor countries cannot afford to spend much. The cheapest way to maximize poverty relief in such cases is through flat-rate pensions. As fiscal constraints relax, other policy options become possible, including a larger flat-rate pension (as in the Netherlands) or a pension at least partly related to previous contributions (as in the United Kingdom and the United States).

How should private, funded pensions be designed? Should they be organized through individual accounts (Argentina, Chile, Denmark), or should it also be possible for employers to organize schemes, as in many European countries? The choice between the two approaches depends in part on how broadly policy makers want risks to be shared. As a separate issue, how far should pensioners be protected against loss and high inflation – risks which are particularly salient in an economy undergoing major reform – and through what mechanism? The state might underwrite at least some of the inflation risk: pensioners should not face substantially more risk than wage earners; in addition, the collapse of private pension schemes could undermine the political consensus underpinning economic reform.

Should membership be compulsory? Pay-as-you-go schemes are, by their nature, compulsory. Some experts argue for small public pensions and compulsory membership in private pension schemes, as in Chile. But compulsion raises difficult issues. The Czech Republic has a larger-than-subsistence public pension and is bringing state pension spending under control by using a partially funded scheme, with tax advantages to encourage contributions. But the Czech authorities did not consider it politically feasible to take the further step of mandating contributions to the new private schemes. Many other transition countries will also find this difficult, given that private savings in the past have been all but wiped out by inflation.

Pension Packages

A typical system in Europe and North America has a state pay-as-you-go pension with a wider role than subsistence, complemented by a variety of regulated, privately managed, funded pensions. Individuals may also make voluntary additional contributions to funded schemes. The three components address different purposes: the state scheme is concerned mainly with poverty relief and (often imperfectly) with redistribution, the second tier helps people to redistribute their income across their lifetime, and the third allows for differences in individual preferences. This approach accords a significant role to social solidarity and shares risks fairly broadly; but it can also come under severe financial pressure when faced with the twin threat of a slowly growing economy and a rapidly ageing population. An alternative approach used in Chile and Singapore has a small public component. In Chile the state pension is a minimum guarantee for private pensions; people above the minimum receive no state pension. For most, pensions are provided by one or more funded, regulated, individual schemes. Individuals can also make voluntary additional contributions. In this approach there is no redistribution from rich to poor or between generations other than that provided by the minimum pension guarantee. Recent reforms in Latin America (Argentina, Colombia, and Peru) adopt something of a middle ground between the two approaches (see Queisser, 1995; Vittas, 1995).

The precise choice depends on a country's objectives and its constraints. Chile and several of the high-performing Asian economies gave priority to economic growth and therefore adopted more individualistic systems which encourage high savings. Some transition economies face tighter constraints – economic, political, and social—than these countries, which have long-established market systems, relatively sophisticated banking systems and capital markets, and relatively stable prices – and Chile introduced reform at a time of budgetary surplus. Moreover, government capacity in those countries is high. Social constraints also differ. While the extended family continues to be important in the high-performing Asian economies and strong family support structures also exist in the Central Asian republics of the FSU, they are weaker in CEE and the other countries of the FSU.

CONCLUSION

The pervasive theme is that the inherited pension system threatens the economic sustainability of the reforms. From a fiscal perspective the solution is (perhaps) to reduce pension levels and (certainly) to reduce the number of beneficiaries. To do so too precipitately, however, puts at risk the political sustainability of reform. Reform here, as in so many other areas, is a matter of balancing competing objectives.

Notwithstanding these difficulties, the successes of reform, at least in some countries, should not be overlooked. By 1995, output in Poland had returned to its 1989 level; and in 1995, in sharpest contrast with 1989, Poland had one of the fastest growth rates in Europe. Notwithstanding uncertainty and privation during the early transition, infant mortality in Poland fell between 1989 and 1995; and over the same period life expectancy rose by one year for men and six months for women. Alongside economic benefits are the political benefits from a return to democracy. Though it will be a long haul, there are grounds for optimism, particularly for the countries of central Europe.

NOTES

1. This paper draws heavily on work during two stints at the World Bank, and particularly on Barr (1994, ch. 9) and World Bank (1996).
2. Kopits (1991) found that in CEE subsidies were up to 22 per cent of GDP, whilst cash benefits were only 10 per cent. In the European Union, the comparable figures were 6 and 16 per cent.
3. For detailed discussion of targeting, see Atkinson (1995) and Barr (1998, chs 10 and 11).
4. Indeed, the whole purpose of the incomes policies which normally accompanied the early transition was to ensure that wages were *not* fully protected against inflation.
5. Suppose that before the transition, a pint of milk, when available, cost 1, and individual X had an income of 1000. After the transition, milk is always available, and costs 5, and individual X still has an income of 1000. On the face of it, individual X is poorer; but if he/she could rarely get milk under the old system, matters are much less clear.
6. There are at least two sets of problems. With non-market clearing prices (that is, under the old system), both Paasche and Laspeyres indices may overestimate inflation, and hence also overstate the fall in real wages and living standards. Second, in the face of sharply changing relative prices, the pattern of people's consumption changes, thus sharply changing the weights which are used to calculate a consumer price index. The use of a consumer price index to measure inflation in these circumstances is, to say the least, problematic.
7. I first learned that pensions were paid through the postal system in Poland in January 1990, at a time when inflation was 80 per cent per month.
8. Though reform has been announced, raising women's retirement age over time to that of men.
9. The analogy is taken from Fox (1995).

REFERENCES

Andrews, E. and M. Rashid (1996), 'The financing of pension systems in central and eastern Europe: an overview of major trends and their determinants', World Bank, *Social Challenges of Transition* Series, World Bank Technical Paper No. 339.

Atkinson, A. (1987), 'On the measurement of poverty', *Econometrica*, **55**, July, 749–64, reprinted in Atkinson, A., 1989, ch. 2.

Atkinson, A. (1989), *Poverty and Social Security*, London: Harvester Wheatsheaf.

Atkinson, A. (1991), 'Poverty, economic performance and income transfer policy in OECD countries,' *World Bank Economic Review*, **5**, January, 3–21.

Atkinson, A. (1995), 'On targeting social security: theory and Western evidence with family benefits', in D. van de Walle and K. Nead (eds), *Public Spending and the Poor: Theory and Evidence*, Baltimore and London: The Johns Hopkins University Press, 25–68.

Barr, N (1998), *The Economics of the Welfare State*, 3rd edition, Oxford: Oxford University Press, and California: Stanford University Press.

Barr, N. (ed.) (1994), *Labor Markets and Social Policy: The Transition and Beyond*, New York: Oxford University Press.

Cornia, G. (1994), 'Income distribution, poverty and welfare in transitional economies: a comparison between eastern Europe and China', UNICEF, ICDC, Innocenti Occasional Papers, Economic Policy Series No 44, Table 10, p. 38.

Cox, D., Z. Eser and E. Jimenez (1995), 'Family safety nets during economic transition: a study of inter-household transfers in Russia', paper presented at the National Academy of Science Workshop on Economic Transformation and Households, Washington, DC, 7–8 September, 1995.

Fajth, G (1994), 'Family support policies in transitional economies: challenges and constraints', UNICEF, ICDC, Innocenti Occasional Papers, Economic Policy Series No. 43.

Fox, Louise (1995), 'Can eastern Europe's old-age crisis be fixed?', *Finance and Development*, **32** (4), December, 34–7.

Gamer, T (1995), 'Moving to a better world? Coping and Behaviors during economic uncertainty: a view from eastern Europe', paper presented at the National Academy of Science Workshop on Economic Transformation and Households, Washington, DC, 7–8 September, 1995.

Gomulka, S. (1998), 'Output: Cause of the Decline and the Recovery', in P. Boone, S. Gomulka and R. Layard (eds), *Emerging from Communism: Lessons from Russia, China and Eastern Europe*, London and Cambridge, Mass: MIT Press, 13–41.

Kopits, G. (1991), 'Fiscal reform in European economies in transition', IMF Working Paper WP 91/43, Washington, DC: International Monetary Fund.

Milanovic, B. (1995), 'Poverty, inequality and social policy in transition economies', Research Paper Series, Paper No. 9, April, Table 2, p. 14.

Queisser, Monika (1995), 'Chile and beyond: the second-generation pension reforms in Latin America', *International Social Security Review*, **38** (3–4), 23–39.

Rutkowski, Jan (1996), 'High skills pay off: the changing wage structure during economic transition in Poland', *Economics of Transition*, **4** (4), May, 89–111.

Torrey, B., T. Smeeding and D. Bailey (1995), 'Rowing between Scylla and Charybdis: income transitions in central European households', paper presented at the National

Academy of Science Workshop on Economic Transformation and Households, Washington, DC, 7–8 September, 1995.

Vittas, Dimitri (1995), 'Argentina's new integrated pension system: first year assessment', mimeo, Washington, DC: The World Bank.

World Bank (1996), *World Development Report 1996: From Plan to Market*, New York: Oxford University Press.

12. A government role in training markets in developing countries: theory and policy

Eliakim Katz and Adrian Ziderman

In virtually all countries, the government has assumed an active role in skills development. This chapter discusses the rationales for this central role, with a particular emphasis on training for the formal sector in developing countries. The appropriate role for government in the finance and delivery of training is expected to vary from country to country and within countries over time. The government role should be an adaptive one, reflecting a country's changing training needs, which in turn will differ with its level of economic and institutional development.[1]

1 PRIVATE MARKETS FOR TRAINING

Historically (and this remains largely true today for the traditional sector in many developing countries), the government's role in training provision has been a very limited one. It was the small enterprise that assumed the dominant role in skill creation, particularly in general training in transferable skills. Informal apprenticeships in craft trades were the primary training venue, but small enterprises also offered training at other skill levels, including internship in accountancy and law.

In the financing of training, the role of the firm was minimal. Typically, trainees paid for their training, usually by receiving a lowered wage during training (the difference between the wage of skilled worker and the trainee wage represents the implicit fee for training); alternatively, or in combination, a lump sum fee was paid at the outset. In return for their investment in training, trainees expected enhanced earnings reflecting their augmented productivity. The small enterprise, be it the master craftsman or a legal practice, assumed a dual role; in addition to serving its customers, it also sold training services to its employees.

This is a far cry from the situation today. In most countries, traditional private training markets have proved too limited to meet the broader skill needs associated with industrial development and technological change. Government has now entered as a leading actor in the market for training in most countries in the world. Government has become a major provider of training courses (in vocational schools and specialized training institutions). Moreover, it now finances a significant share of training programmes.

2 THREE ROLES FOR GOVERNMENT

Government's active role in vocational training and manpower skills development for the formal sector is displayed in three broad, but fairly distinct, activities: providing supportive services, providing training itself and providing financing for training.[2]

The umbrella role of providing supportive services is relevant at all stages of development though its coverage may vary. Among the wide range of supportive services the government may offer are measures to create a climate of opinion conducive to training, encouraging tripartite collaboration among employers, workers and government, and enhancing the appeal of industrial careers and training (Castley and Alfthan, 1986). The state (or a specialized agency) may also play a regulatory function through services that enhance the quality of training, such as testing and certification, research and curriculum development; it may promote enterprise training by providing training assistance, knowhow and advisory services.

Yet the main thrust of government intervention in pre-employment training has been in training provision and finance. The government may provide training directly through public sector training institutions and state vocational schools. Or it may finance, wholly or in part, a wide range of training activities, either by providing its own training courses at little or no cost or by heavily subsidizing training courses provided by nongovernment institutions, such as private vocational schools, proprietary training institutions or enterprise-based training.

3 RATIONALE FOR GOVERNMENT INTERVENTION

Can the active role that most governments assume in providing and financing training be justified in efficiency terms? Why cannot we rely upon the interplay of coordinating market forces, in the form of the private training choices of workers (or parents) as consumers, and the profit-maximizing activities of private training suppliers, to ensure the socially optimal amount of training? In short does the state have to provide training? Must it finance training'? In this section, a range of arguments are adduced to support a significant role for government in training markets. These are discussed under four main headings: externalities, property rights in training, market imperfections and weak private training capacity.

3.1 Externalities

Individuals deciding to invest in training are motivated by expected higher earnings and other, mainly job-related, benefits; they will not capture, and therefore do not take into account, any broader benefits that may accrue to society as a whole from a better trained workforce. From a societal point of view, individuals may not invest enough in training; too few resources would flow into training and skills acquisition. These positive externality benefits from ensuring an adequate supply of skills are frequently cited to justify public financing of training. Indeed, the traditional justification for a government financing role in education in general is couched in terms of externalities. Positive externalities derived from general education include lower fertility, the facilitation of political and economic transactions and intangible benefits stemming from more enlightened parents and citizens. In the absence of government subsidy, too little education would be demanded – and supplied. The education system would under provide.

Although relevant for training, this type of externality argument is likely to be less strong than it is for general education. Vocational education and training is much more narrowly focused on providing skills that are relevant to a specific occupation or a job and therefore unlikely to provide the full range of externality benefits that are associated with general education. The more narrowly vocational that training becomes, the fewer the wider societal benefits will it provide and the weaker the case for public subsidy, as the training investor (usually the worker) captures a greater proportion of the total benefits of training.

3.1.1 Macroeconomic arguments

Nonetheless, there are certain externality benefits of training that are less strongly associated with general education. The availability of a skilled labour force may make a contribution to the attainment of macroeconomic goals of society: these will be over and above the direct output benefits stemming from (and mainly captured by) the trained workers themselves. Vocational training develops a broad skilled and technical labour base that is able to meet the needs of rapidly changing industrial organization and technology, as well as to engineer this process of growth and industrial change. Yet firms as a whole may not always be willing or far-sighted enough to ensure a sufficient intake of trainees in transferable skills vital to the economy, that is, to meet broader national long-term needs rather than their own particular requirements over the medium term.

It has been argued that it is desirable to subsidize training to improve the general infrastructure for investment. One version of this argument lies in terms of bottleneck skills, the avoidance of a shortage of workers with key, strategic skills in new or growing industries, which may act as a break on economic development. An additional macroeconomic argument relates to the provision of skilled manpower to strengthen export-related industries, thus contributing towards the mitigation of balance of payments problems, scarce foreign exchange and self-sufficiency objectives.

Workers are often employed in teams; their output, and wages, are dependent on their interaction with other team members. (Indeed, even individuals working separately are almost invariably dependent on the efficiency of other workers.) Such interactions are likely to result in externalities, in which the level of training of an individual worker will affect the output produced by the whole team (or by other, individual workers). In addition, the outputs of non-team members are likely to be affected by the team's productivity and, hence, by the individual training level of each team member. Moreover, in a team where members receive a wage equal to average team output, free rider problems arise. Individual workers will not in general take such externality effects into account when making their training decisions, thus resulting in a level of training investment that is socially suboptimal. We shall consider two simple models of this type of externality problem in training investment.

3.1.2 Production function externalities

Let the output of worker i be given by the strictly concave function,

$$X_i = F(T_i, T) \tag{12.1}$$

where T_i is the level of training belonging to person i and T is an average (for example, geometric mean) of training owned by the other workers. Individual i chooses T_i to maximize his net income, π_i, by solving

$$\underset{T_i}{\text{Max}}\, \pi_i = pX_i - cT_i \tag{12.2}$$

where p is the price of a unit of output and c is the price of a unit of training. Hence, assuming a regular, interior solution, this yields

$$\frac{\partial \pi_i}{\partial T_i} = pF_1 - c = 0 \tag{12.3}$$

so that the Cournot–Nash equilibrium training condition is $F_1\ (T, T) = (c/p)$.

The social optimum is, in contrast, given by solving

$$\operatorname*{Max}_{T}\ npF(T,T) - ncT \tag{12.4}$$

yielding the condition

$$pF_1\ (T, T) + pF_2(T, T) - c = 0 \tag{12.5}$$

so that

$$F_1 + F_2 = c/p. \tag{12.6}$$

Hence, since $F(T, T)$ is strictly concave, the socially optimal amount of training for an individual worker exceeds the amount of training workers will buy on the basis of their private calculations.

Firms, being the ultimate employers of teams of trained workers, might well be interested in providing the socially-correct amount of training; this outcome may be thwarted in a number of ways. First, to the extent that workers finance this training in one way or another, they may be unwilling to undertake it. This could follow if the training that workers receive is optimal for them in the training firm (in which other workers have appropriate amounts of training), but excessive in terms of the training levels of workers in other firms. In other words, if the training firm can offer the worker a guarantee that other workers in the firm will not be free riders upon his training, he might buy this training if he intends to stay in the firm for a long period. However, such a guarantee is only of limited use to a worker who intends to quit or for whom there is a probability that he will have to leave the firm early on.

An individual's decision to buy training within the firm will thus depend on his probability of leaving the firm, and on the probability of being able to find other employment with appropriately trained co-workers. Clearly, this latter probability will increase with the number of trained workers of a given specialization in the industry/economy, and the social problem may be mitigated if a critical mass of trained workers is achieved.

3.1.3 Sharing output: training as a public good

A similar kind of problem, which might be very pertinent to the training issue, is the joint product problem. Let there be n workers in a team of workers, and their joint output, Q, be given by

$$Q = F(T_1 + T_2 + T_3 \dots + T_n) \tag{12.7}$$

when F is a strictly concave function and $T_i(\mathrm{i} = 1, \dots, n)$ is the amount of training acquired by worker i. Each worker receives Q/n in wages, so that, assuming a Cournot–Nash equilibrium, worker i solves

$$\underset{T_i}{\mathrm{Max}} \frac{Q}{n} - cT_i. \tag{12.8}$$

Hence, assuming a regular and interior solution yields

$$F_i(T, T, \dots, T) = nc. \tag{12.9}$$

The social optimum is found by solving

$$\underset{T}{\mathrm{Max}}\, Q - ncT \tag{12.10}$$

which yields

$$F_1(T,\dots,T) + F_2(T,\dots,T) + \dots F_n(T,\dots,T) = nc \tag{12.11}$$

so that the socially optimal T obviously exceeds the privately determined value of T. Note the similarity between this public good type of problem and the previously discussed case of externalities in production.

The presence of externalities constitutes the classic form of market failure, justifying government intervention in such markets. An additional though related form of market failure, that is particularly relevent to training markets, stems from the lack of property rights of firms in the training vested in their workers. We turn to such property rights issues in the next section.

3.2 Property Rights over Training

A major form of market failure in training markets stems from a firm's lack of property rights in training, an issue first given prominence in the training model of Becker (1975). In general, firms that train do not have property rights over this training, which is vested in their workers. If firms paid trained workers less than their enhanced marginal product, in order to recoup the costs of training, then trained workers would find it advantageous to move to new firms where they would be paid their full marginal product, and where no deduction for the cost of their training would be made. Contracts, that tie the trained worker to the firm over the period in which the firm recoups training costs, have not proved to be viable or easily enforceable in most instances in practice, particularly where training is informal, and on-the-job. Thus, firms are unwilling to finance the training of their workers in general skills – those that are transferable to other firms; these costs are then passed onto workers.

But workers too may be unable to pay for general training, if they lack savings and cannot borrow to finance the training (see next section) or if the deduction of training costs from wages during training would lead to an unacceptably low net training wage. Again, difficulties of enforcing contracts may rule out workers making delayed payments to the firm for training, via eductions from trained workers' wages over a period of time. Hence, the interaction of poverty, inadequate capital markets and the inability of firms to obtain property rights over the human capital sold (on credit) to their workers, all interact to bring about a further market failure in training.

The forms of training that firms will offer workers will, therefore, tend to be narrow and untransferable, that is, firm specific; but such specific training is unlikely to be of the type that yields significant externalities and thus carries a high social return.

Some solutions to this problem may be available, that improve the prognosis. First, a monopsonist for a particular type of human capital may well be willing to finance the training of its workers, knowing that they have little potential employment elsewhere. The oil industry, for example, is often monopolized and acts as a monopsonist for certain types of skill. Of course, workers can always migrate to other countries so that even a domestic monopsony may be at some risk in losing its investment in its labour force.

Second, as we have argued elsewhere, there may be asymmetric information between training and recruiting firms concerning the skill levels, and potential outputs, of trained workers (Katz and Ziderman, 1990). If workers move to new firms, the new employers are unlikely to be sure of their skills, whereas current (training) employers are. Workers will initially receive less than their full value in new firms, a factor that will curb their wish to move. In turn, their current employers will be prepared to provide, and share in the finance of, worker training in general skills. However, this applies to cases where a worker's output cannot be readily measured. If the trained worker's output is quickly and easily discovered by new firms, then his skill level (including training) will reveal itself quickly in any new firm, once again making it worthwhile for the worker to move and making non-specific training investments by firms unlikely. But we have argued that general training will not be easily and costlessly transferable to other firms; hence, firms will share in the finance training in industry-related or economy-wide, general skills.

A third solution to the property rights problem in training is for the firm to lend the training costs to the worker rather than form a partnership with him. If the firm adopts this strategy, it may have a claim on the worker's assets and earnings, even if he leaves the firm. This solution will be available only in a country where individuals are easy to trace and where a trainee may have some assets. In the absence of these factors, a loan by the firm will not provide the firm with much of the required security to facilitate investments in general training.

Related to the property rights problem is the issue of poaching: the tendency for firms to recruit (or 'poach') trained workers from other firms. The poaching argument runs along these lines. To meet their skilled labour needs, firms can choose to train directly, to recruit trained workers from outside, or opt for a combination of these. Firms that poach inflict costs on firms that train because of the greater wastage of newly trained workers to the poaching firms. Training firms will react by cutting down on their training effort, resulting in a general under provision of trained workers. Such considerations underscored the design of the UK Industrial Training Act of 1967; its levy-grant system was largely directed towards offering substantial incentives to firms to prefer the training of workers over poaching them from other firms.

However, a critical literature, initiated by Lees and Chiplin (1970), argued against this approach, and particularly against offering subsidies or grants to firms to encourage them to train. Based on Becker's distinction between general and firm-specific training, they gave prominence to the concept of a 'poaching illusion' that was leading to unjustified interventions in training markets. Since firms have no interest in recruiting workers with skills specific to other firms, the poaching phenomenon is confined, by definition, to generally trained workers. But the poaching of generally trained workers does not impose costs on training firms; because of the problem of establishing property rights in training, it is the trainee and not the firm who finances training in general skills. Thus, they argued, grants made for training in transferable skills constitute an unjustified reimbursement of training costs, since they are not in fact incurred by the firm.

A newer literature that argues that firms do in fact finance general training (at least in part) has tended to restore the relevence of the poaching argument and the issue of property rights; references are provided in Katz and Ziderman (1990).

In view of the above discussion, it may be concluded that the option that firms train their employees in transferable skills is only partially viable. The property rights problem is a major problem in the training of workers in developing countries.

3.3 Market Imperfections

If markets for training work imperfectly, underinvestment in human capital will ensue and the training system will fail to provide the economy with the supplies of skilled manpower necessary for development.

3.3.1 Capital market imperfections

Capital market imperfections and the deleterious effect of risk and uncertainty on worker-financed training can constitute a case for remedial action by the government. Worker finance of enterprise training typically takes the form of reduced wages during the training period. Yet the larger the training costs, and the shorter the period of training, the greater will be the required fall in wages during training. Workers may not find it possible to sustain this loss in wage income during training, particularly if they are lacking in financial assets; moreover, poorly functioning capital markets in developing economies deny to many workers the possibility of financing training through loans. Indeed, even in economies with better developed financial markets, loans to finance human capital investments may not be forthcoming. Unlike other investments that can constitute the collateral for the loans that finance them, human capital investments, embodied as they are in the trained workers themselves, are not readily accepted as security by financial institutions. Workers will be forced to forgo training investments, even though intrinsically profitable.

Even where funding is available, workers are likely to underinvest in general training. The worker pays for training in anticipation of enhanced earnings that accrue over time. He must face the risk that these returns will not be forthcoming. These risks will be considerably greater for the individual than for society, which can pool and diversify these risks. Workers are likely to display greater risk averse attitudes than does society as a whole. Uncertainty as to the outcome of training will raise the private rate of time preference above that of society. Worker-financed training, therefore, is likely to fall short of the societal optimum.

3.3.2 Capital market imperfections: risk aversion and diversification

Capital markets play a major role in enabling investors to diversify their portfolio of assets, thereby reducing risk. A weak or imperfectly functioning capital market is likely to involve an investor in higher levels of risk; this, in turn, will affect investment in general, and training investment by individuals in particular, both the quantity and the type of training undertaken.

A well-functioning capital market will lead to individuals investing in fewer training skills. The phrase 'Jack of all trades and master of none' carries the idea that training in a given, well-defined field offers, at least up to a point, increasing returns to scale, be it because of fixed cost elements in training or because of a convex production function (with respect to training). Therefore, if diversification in ways other than by diversifying skills were possible (such as through the capital market), individuals would be able to take advantage of the increasing returns to specialized training by investing in narrower, specialized fields.

Thus, where a well-functioning capital market is present, an individual could dilute his investment in training and diversify in the following way. He could buy assets in the market that are weakly or negatively correlated with his own acquired skills. For example, an individual trained as a gas worker might invest in a competing industry such as the electrical industry, and in other industries whose fortunes are likely to move independently or in the opposite direction to the gas industry. This would create a better risk portfolio for the individual, and the knowledge that he will be able to diversify after he has trained will give him an incentive to both specialize more and train for a longer period.

In the absence of a capital market, it is possible to diversify also by holding assets other than human capital. However, the indivisibilities involved in such assets as well as their lack of easy tradability render them relatively unattractive. Even with well-functioning capital markets, sizeable amounts of wealth are needed in order to invest both in training and other assets, so the poor may be unable to widely diversify anyway.[3]

It is clear that the absence of a well-functioning capital market is likely to reduce the amount of training undertaken as well as to make for less training specialization, since less specialization allows more diversification. Thus, there will be a demand for general rather than specialized forms of training. Also, the demand for training as such is likely to be relatively low, since the mean return to general training is likely to be low,[4] as compared with the mean return to specialized training. To the extent that the excessive risk in specialized training could have been (at least partially) removed in a well-functioning capital market, it may well be socially superior for more specialized and lengthier training to take place; the number of electronic engineers may be too few from a societal point of view, whilst there may be too many machine operators and drivers. The lack of a well-functioning capital market may result in superficial, short and non-specialized training that is socially suboptimal.

A possible solution to this problem is for large (extended) families to diversify the risks inherent in specialized training by the pooling of risks, with each family member undertaking a different specialization. In this case, the large family would be acting as a surrogate for the capital market. Unfortunately, this is unlikely to be an effective solution to the problem. Economic growth and the act of training itself are both likely to loosen family ties and reduce cooperation within the family. Hence, in the absence of a legally enforceable risk-pooling contract, *ex post* default towards their family by trainees is likely, a fact which will impede the *ex ante* pooling of risks.

Can firms, by providing on-the-job specialized training, solve the diversification problem? To answer this question, two issues must be addressed. First, if firms do offer such training, will workers be interested in acquiring it? Second, given the lack of a capital market and its diversification possibilities, will firms be able to offer efficient, specialized training?

We consider these issues in turn. As discussed above, given their inability to diversify, workers will be interested in non-specialized rather than specialized training. Now, it is possible that they will be prepared to acquire specialized human capital at a subsidized price, but since they will in general pay the firm in full for training (in terms of lower wages during apprenticeship and early working years), they will effectively be buying this risky human capital at full cost. Therefore, an offer of specialized training by firms (paid for by workers) is likely to be rejected by workers. Non-competitive firms which make supernormal profits may be prepared to reduce or eliminate the price of specialized training to their workers. Thus, one situation leading to a positive outcome on this issue is the existence of non-competitive firms interested in specialized workers. However, it is a second-best solution.

Secondly, modern finance theory teaches us that firms need not diversify their activities to reduce risk, if a well-functioning capital market exists. This is because shareholders of firms can diversify their portfolio of shares in the capital market, obviating the need for individual firms to diversify. Now, it seems likely that such specialized training as is offered by a firm will be subject to economies of scale, in the sense that the training of more workers in a given specialization will be less costly per worker. In the absence of a reasonably effective capital market, however, the firms themselves will need to diversify to reduce risk and will thus employ less workers per specialization. Thus a non-utilization of economies of scale in specialized training will result. Firms, to the extent that they do train workers, will therefore provide this training inefficiently.

In sum, capital market imperfections and the implicit problems for both firms and individuals in diversifying investments in developing countries may be seen as constituting a valid justification for government intervention in this market.

3.3.3 Capital market imperfections: ineffective financial intermediation

In this section we consider how a failure of financial intermediaries to provide a bridge between savers and investors can constitute a potential cause of training underinvestment in developing countries. The absence of capital markets in many developing countries, or poorly functioning ones, prevents funds from being channelled readily from savers to investors. This hinders the undertaking of investment generally and of training in particular. We argue that, because of some of its inherent features, training investments will be especially hard hit by this problem.

First, if self-generated funds to finance investment in general, and investment in training in particular, are not readily available, individuals will need loans to finance investments. However, given the lack of financial intermediation, such loans will not be forthcoming. Indeed, even if the burden of the cost of training could be shifted from workers to their employers, the latter similarly will find it difficult to obtain funds. Second, to the extent that for most individuals, training may be a sizeable, once-and-for-all investment, an individual may have to accumulate savings over a period of time to finance it. The absence of an adequate capital market may make such savings unattractive by providing little in the way of secure, liquid, medium-term saving instruments with a reasonable return. Thus, self-finance for training also will be affected adversely, even if the individual or his family could, in principle, finance it out of savings.

The absence of a capital market in which to finance training investments will tend to be particularly detrimental to the poor in developing countries. This is because the poor are least likely to possess, or have access to, the initial wealth with which to invest in training. Hence, the absence of a well-functioning capital market will deter training in a biased way, particularly affecting the poorer members of society. In this case, poverty combined with capital market imperfections will beget poverty.

The existence of a secondary or informal capital market will not be of help. This is because, given the lack of information regarding both the vector of characteristics of individuals seeking to borrow to train and uncertainty regarding the rate of return to particular forms of training, the risks facing potential lenders will be sizeable. Combining this with the fact that small-scale money lending institutions or individuals cannot, in general, be well diversified between borrowers and/or types of borrowers, it follows that they will act in a more risk-averse manner than is socially warranted. Small moneylenders may be reluctant to lend in cases where large financial institutions, such that exist in the West, would be willing to lend.

Two further issues make the problem particularly acute for the issue of training. First, the time horizon for training and the return on training investment tends to be very long, probably being considerably longer than for most physical investment. This makes it an unattractive and risky avenue for loans.[5] Second, training is embodied in individuals and has no counterpart in physical assets. Given the absence of slavery and/or enforceable labour contracts, lenders do not have a recourse to any collateral in the event of a default nor, indeed, can they do much if the individual absconds or shirks.

3.3.4 Negative effects of government policies

Government policies relating to aggregate economic activity and the operation of individual markets shape a country's economic environment, that in turn affects the incentives to produce and acquire skills. Certain policies may be adopted with important or overriding social objectives in view. Yet they may lead to unintended side-effects, in the form of distortions in training markets, by altering the benefits and costs of training for individuals and enterprises, and influencing incentives for skills development.

These arguments are particularly relevant to government labour market policies which impinge negatively on the efficiency of enterprise-based training. Minimum wage legislation may thwart trainee-financed general training, by preventing the training wage from falling sufficiently to pay for general training.

This leads to a shortfall of generally trained workers. A parallel argument applies when strong union pressures prevent the wages of trainees falling to cover training costs.

Administered wage systems, and unduly narrow skilled wage differentials, will discourage worker investment in general training, as the worker-borne training costs will be insufficiently offset by higher earnings after training: private returns will fall short of social returns and the system will under train. In both cases, corrective training grants to workers (which may be administered by firms), may be justified.

We have noted that the amount of general training will be suboptimal where workers are more risk averse, and have greater uncertainty about training outcomes, than society as a whole. Yet, frequent and sizeable changes in government economic policy, such as often take place in developing countries, are likely to introduce a greater variability into the return from different types of training, thus adding to the problems of uncertainty. Probable effects of a variable government policy include the following:

- Via the increased return rate uncertainty, he will incur increased consumption at the cost of investment/saving in general (though, under certain circumstances, it has been shown that increased uncertainty may increase saving/investment);
- This uncertainty may result in a bias towards physical investment which has a scrap value, as compared to training;
- The uncertainty will introduce a bias towards training with an early return;
- It will lead to a bias towards training, where the return is less prone to variability in response to economic changes. The training for those industries which are responsive to change will tend to be shunned;[6]
- It will bring about introduction of socially wasteful rural-to-urban migration as families attempt to build portfolio protection against this uncertainty;
- On the other hand, the increased uncertainty may introduce a bias towards general as opposed to specific type investments, an outcome that may be desirable.

To this economic instability must be added political instability, as a force that will both reduce total training and cause biases in training, in potentially suboptimal ways. In addition, physical investments may flow abroad in the presence of political instability, thus reducing the need for and return to trained personnel.

Income taxation constitutes a further government-induced problem affecting training, given that the private return to an activity will, due to taxation, fall short of the social return. While this problem is universal and not specific to developing countries, certain aspects of the problem may be particularly acute in developing countries. The formal urban sector of the economy will tend to be taxed more heavily than the rural and informal sectors because a less-monetized, rural sector is difficult to fully tax and the evasion of taxes is greater in an informal cash-basis sector. Taxation will impose a bias against training for the formal sector, which may be important for developmental needs.

The maintenance of high interest rates, in an attempt to use the capital account to balance trade deficits (due to excessively high exchange rates), may cause training investment with an early return to be undertaken, in preference to training with a long-run horizon.

3.4 Weak Enterprise Training Capacity

Enterprises may be unable or reluctant to discharge their training role adequately. In those countries where the modern sector is as yet underdeveloped – enterprises are small and trade associations poorly developed – the enterprise base may be too narrow to provide the capacity for structured on-the-job training, particularly apprenticeship training, to meet the needs of that sector. Small firms may lack the managerial competencies and foresight to organize in-house training; they may lack also relevant personnel management capacity and costs may be high as they are unable to benefit from any scale economies in training.

This lacuna would seem to provide a clear opening for the development of specialized training institutions by the private sector or for joint off-the-job training schemes by industry; yet such initiatives may not be forthcoming, particularly in lower income countries due to a lack of knowhow, enterprise, a suitable organizational framework, or capital. There are exceptions, notably in middle-income level countries: in Brazil, SENAI, the national central training institution, was set up on the initiative of industry and financed by a levy on enterprise payrolls. Apart from training provision in public sector institutions, other intervention measures may include the establishment of group or industry training schemes and the provision of technical assistance to promote company training.

Government intervention, then, may be justified. But the case here is one for provision of services (in the absence of private sector initiatives) not for finance. While courses at state training centres are usually free or highly subsidized, the justification for government financing and subsidy (as opposed to provision) does not lie in the weak training capacity of enterprises.

Finally, in countries at all income levels, there are apparent indications that non profit-maximizing behaviour by firms may lead them to undertrain. However, evidence of low levels of company training is not necessarily indicative of underprovision of training by firms. In practice, small firms with simple technologies and low worker mobility may have minimal needs for formal training. Even in larger firms, the lack of extensive formal training courses may be veiling an extensive network of non-structured training activities (for some evidence see Ziderman and Horn, 1995, on training maps in Colombia). Training subsidies and incentives (perhaps in combination with such activities as training promotion and exhortation) may be employed where there is underprovision of training by firms: however, where the underlying cause is weak or inefficient management, the positive response to these measures may be small.

4 DESIGNING APPROPRIATE INTERVENTIONS

While a case has been made for government intervention in training markets, it is less clear whether this should take the form of financial intervention or training provision. Indeed, type and extent of required government intervention will differ from country case to case, depending on a wide range of factors such as those relating to a given country's economic development, the quality of existing training institutions (on and off the job), and distortions in the economic environment that may militate against training development. The case for government intervention may indicate a need for government provision but not the finance of training (and vice versa).

Nevertheless, we can reach some general conclusions regarding the role of government in training. These are set out in schematic form in Table 12.1, relating to some of the underlying causes of undersupply of training discussed in Section 3.

Table 12.1 Policy options

Reason for state intervention	Policy options: Training finance	Training provision	Complementary policies*	
Externalities	P	N	–	–
Property rights	A	N	P	Levy-grant schemes; tax exemptions for training
Market imperfections	A	N	P	Deal with source of market imperfections
Weak private training capacity	N	A/P	P	Build firm training capacity

Notes
P = Preferred policy approach.
A = Acceptable (second best) approach.
N = Policy is not justified.
* = Policies may not be feasible.

Of the arguments for a public role in the training market, the appropriate government response is clearest in the case of externalities. In situations where private training markets underprovide in the sense that the benefits from training accruing to society exceed private benefits, government subsidies can bring about a movement towards an optimal situation. The cost of the subsidy may be met out of general taxation legitimately on the grounds that society as a whole benefits (via its externality effects) from the extra training thus generated. Yet, while justifying subsidies, externalities do not justify government provision.

A major practical problem with the traditional externality argument concerns the appropriate *size* of the required subsidy, given the elusive nature of many of these externality benefits and the notorious difficulties associated with their measurement. The danger of costly oversubsidization, and overprovision, of training is ever present.

In many countries governments have taken steps to encourage firms to train in general skills, given the threat of poaching. Apart from direct subsidies to training firms, such measures have included company tax exemptions for training firms (a notably successful scheme is in place in Chile[7]) and the introduction of levy grant systems, based on company payroll levies, and therefore not requiring government finance. The rationale of the latter type of schemes is the cross-subsidy of training firms, financed by a levy on non-training firms (potential poachers); a review of international experience of such schemes in developing countries is given in Whalley and Ziderman (1990).

Government economic and social policies may lead to distortions in incentives for individual and employer investment in training. To the extent that distortions cannot be eased by modifying the policies in question, government finance may be justified as a second-best solution.

For example, minimum wages legislation is widely seen as an essential measure for protecting low-paid workers. While the deleterious effects on self-investment in general training (even if recognized) will not be regarded as constituting a sufficient case for its repeal, some legislative compromises may be possible. The granting of a special legal status to apprentices, with the exemption of a trainee's wage from the effects of minimum wages legislation would constitute one possibility. In the absence of such arrangements, then the subsidizing of apprenticeship wages may be in order.

If wages are uncoupled from productivity and the wage–skill profile compressed for equity reasons, individuals will underinvest in skills development. A second-best solution involves compensating for the distortion of economic benefits to individuals by reducing their costs for skills development. This can be achieved by the use of individual training grants or by subsidizing enterprise training.

While the development of government-backed training loans schemes would be the appropriate response to imperfectly functioning financial markets, they may not be feasible because of the lack of a sufficiently developed administrative framework in many economies, and the unwillingness of trainees to risk borrowing against uncertain future earnings. Again, in these circumstances, trainee wage subsidization may be appropriate.

While finance intervention (though not provision) in the training market may be justified in terms of both externalities and market imperfections, the two cases differ in one important regard. Subsidies constitute the correct treatment for externalities whether in training or other markets; in the case of market imperfections it is only where more direct measures to deal with the sources of market imperfections are ruled out (usually on administrative or political grounds) that government finance is justified, as a next-best solution.

Where training underprovision is due to weak training capacity of enterprises or private training providers, it is preferable to deal with the source of the problem than to offer palliatives. However, the appropriate policy response is not clear cut. If the cause of institutional failure is non-profit-maximizing behaviour of firms, stemming from inefficient or weak management, the appropriate response is a corrective, educative one. Training advisory services would have a role to play here, though firms may not react positively to such policies, precisely because management is ineffective. In this case, public sector provision of training is indicated, supported by the complementary promotional policies which may achieve some degree of success over the longer term.

In practice, many countries have chosen to use financial incentives to encourage enterprises to train, employing a wide range of measures including training subsidies, grants, and writing off training expenses against tax obligations. While the available evidence is not extensive, many of these measures have not been very effective: they subsidize needlessly well-run firms that already train, while weakly managed firms either do not respond or may do so by establishing training programmes designed more to maximize financial entitlement under the scheme than to contribute to relevant skill creation in the firm.

The economic environment shapes the incentives for employers and individuals to invest in skills development. Conditions for government intervention are present in virtually all countries, developed and industrialized. However, because economic environments differ, and are subject to change, there can be no single prescription for training policy. Instead, the role of the government in training markets has to be based on local conditions and informed by careful economic analysis. The policy matrix in Table 12.1 constitutes a checklist that may be useful for probing the justification for training interventionalist policies in a given country situation.

NOTES

1. The interested reader should consult Dougherty and Tan (1991), which represents the best available survey of issues and options for the finance of training in developing countries.
2. This chapter focuses on training for the formal sector in developing countries. We do not discuss issues related to government intervention in training for the informal urban and rural sectors in developing countries; nor does it deal with special government training programmes in industrialized countries directed to the adult unemployed.
3. Theoretically, an alternative way of diversifying an investment in training is to sell short an asset related to the individual's training. However, even in the developed markets of the West, the facility of selling short is fraught with problems and legal restrictions as well as not being available for more than a year. Since training is long-term investment, diversifying by selling short is not relevant in this case.
4. Providing the substitution effect relating to the low mean return of investment in training outweighs the income effect of compensating for this low return by greater investment in training.
5. To the extent that the risks and uncertainty are the lowest that the economy might face, the individual response to them might not be suboptimal.
6. Such industries may be identified by the variability of unemployment in them and comparisons with the industrialized countries may be made by looking at the beta coefficients, used in the Capital Asset Pricing Model, for different industries.
7. Broadly similar schemes in South Africa, Brazil and Malaysia proved to be less successful and have since been withdrawn.

REFERENCES

Becker, Gary (1975), *Human Capital: A Theoretical and Empirical Analysis with Special Relevance to Education*, New York: National Bureau of Economic Research, 2nd edition.

Dougherty, Christopher and Jee-Peng Tan (1991), 'Financing training: issues and options', PRE Working Paper Series No. WPS 716, Washington: The World Bank, July.

Castley, Robert and Torkel Alfthan (1986), 'Training for industrial development: how governments can help', *International Labour Review*, **125** September/October, 545–60.

Katz, Eliakim and Adrian Ziderman (1990), 'Investment in general training: the role of information and mobility', *Economic Journal*, **180** December, 1147–58.

Lees, Dennis and Brian Chiplin (1970), 'The economics of industrial training', *Lloyds Bank Review*, **96**, 29–41.

Whalley, John and Adrian Ziderman (1990), 'Financing training in developing countries: the role of payroll taxes', *Economics of Education Review*, **9** (4), 377–88.

Ziderman, Adrian and Robin Horn (1995), 'Many paths to skilled employment: a reverse tracer study of seven occupations in Colombia', *Education Economics*, **3** (1), 61–79.

Index